# CHRISTIAN MISSION-JEWISH MISSION

# CHRISTIAN MISSION-JEWISH MISSION

*Edited by*

**Martin A. Cohen**
and
**Helga Croner**





A Stimulus Book

Paulist Press ■ New York ■ Ramsey

Library of Congress
Catalog Card Number: 82-60856

ISBN: 0-8091-2475-0

Published by Paulist Press
545 Island Road, Ramsey, N.J. 07446

Printed and bound in the
United States of America

# Contents

# Foreword: The Many Meanings of Mission

*Helga Croner*

Mission—as perceived by missionaries and those missionized, in former centuries and in our own time, in the eyes of Christians and Jews—that is the topic of this volume. It is indeed a multifaceted picture.

Jewish mission, according to Martin Cohen, embodies the drive for survival. Without a purpose or mission, Judaism is "incomprehensible." Indeed, how could a people endure persecution for so long a time unless it was for a mission that transcends individual life? The traditional mission of Jews is to glorify Yahweh's name, to give an "example of holiness" to the world. Cohen cites a modern reform prayer book that reformulates this mission, a mission implicitly or explicitly acknowledged by Jews of all persuasions. It speaks of the revelation at Sinai as an event that "released a torrent of spiritual energy . . . inspires and guides us still, and it will redeem the world."

Kwesi Dickson describes Christian mission in Africa where, to the distinct uneasiness of Western missionaries, people took much more readily to the Hebrew Scriptures than to the New Testament. The Hebrew Scriptures have a "demonstrable cultural continuity" with African life and thought, Dickson says. The Exodus motif in particular appeals to nations struggling for recognition and cultural and economic independence. Dickson, however, relates that even today many African churches strictly conform to Western models, thereby alienating their members from African life. Yet there also exist so-called "independent" churches, where indigenous languages are used and traditional African values are incorporated into Christian thought. Dickson suggests that African Christians must now go beyond mission to develop their own theology which, in turn, may influence Western thought.

C.S. Song writes about Asian countries and notes that many of the Third World theologians tend to pluck out certain Old Testament themes and interpret them for their own purposes without ever acknowledging an intellectual or spiritual debt to the Jewish people. Liberation theologians in general do not trouble themselves about the historical meaning of, for instance, the Exodus motif in Jewish thought or liturgy. It is worth mentioning that John Pawlikowski, in an earlier volume of this series, *Christ in the Light of the Christian-Jewish Dialogue,* treats this aspect of liberation theology extensively.

Song, in particular, speaks of a change from "resignation to determination" in Asian countries. Although these nations are crying out for help in their political and spiritual struggles, Christians in Asia are beginning to see that God's mission in the world cannot be monopolized by Christians. They have to recognize and work with the adherents of the other great religions in Asia. Song conceives of the mission of human restoration in Asia as a "parable of the suffering God."

Eugene Fisher describes the evolution of Christian mission throughout the centuries, especially in reference to the Church's attitude toward the Jews. It is a somber history which reveals that only in most recent times has the Church begun to struggle with the problem of witnessing to Christ vis-à-vis other faiths without assuming a position of superiority. Fisher cites Pope John Paul II, declaring that Christians and Jews must work jointly for peace and justice among men—a vision, that is, of a joint mission. That is a far cry from, say, the days of Innocent III who asked that Jews not be slain, "lest the Christian people forget divine law."

Michael McGarry delves into Catholic mission theology today. He shows how the concepts of salvation, Christ, and the Church are main points of departure for various theological views of mission. Those who wish to minimize the mission task stress the "universal salvific efficacy of Christ," an attitude that Hans Küng considers a syncretistic trend. McGarry treats the thought of Karl Rahner extensively, for the German theologian has frequently proposed that mission be based on the notion of universal grace and salvation. Rahner's opinion has not gone unchallenged, and Vatican II documents do not quite support him. Yet many contemporary Roman Catholic theologians tend to stress the commitment to social change; they are less intent on convert-making than on liberating individuals and peoples from the "social sins" visited upon them.

McGarry emphasizes that "as believers of both testaments know and proclaim," God does not call only to people as individuals but to communities as well. And the Jewish people stands as a sign par excellence for a community called by God. Abstaining, therefore, from an attempt to convert Jews does not bespeak theological timidity but a faith in revelation.

David Stowe views mission in other countries as well as in the United States as partnership in social and theological education. To him, too, mission is clearly conjoined to politics. It assists the poor on a level "between large-scale government efforts and the rural family." Stowe also recognizes a mutuality of mission between rich nations and poor, between developed and developing countries.

The reverse influence of the Third World on Western culture and theology is discussed by Richard DeRidder. As an Evangelical Christian, he grapples with the tension between *diakonia* and *kerygma* in mission—an aspect that is also considered by Eugene Fisher as a Catholic. DeRidder frankly admits the necessity of a mission to the Jews, although no longer in such crude ways as have obtained in previous centuries. But the New Testament clearly demands, DeRidder says, that Jesus Christ be witnessed before all peoples.

Daniel Polish argues that monotheism ought to be the renewed rallying point for the three faiths of Judaism, Christianity, and Islam. He contends that drawing believers away from their faith's particular interpretation of monotheism may not only be undesirable but unnecessary. The mission of Jews, for example, is to witness the "glorification of Yahweh's name" and thereby call others to the highest aspirations in their own monotheistic faiths.

Polish discusses the most recent trend within Reform Judaism—vigorously opposed by other segments of Jewry—that Jews ought to actively approach both non-committed or non-affiliated members of other faiths as well as nominal Jews who may be reclaimed for Judaism.

This short overview indicates the wide spectrum of mission and missiology reflected in this volume. The unifying thought underlying all the views expressed here seems to be that mission is no longer a static concept. Many of the basic problems of our time find a distinct echo in the idea of mission. The theory and practice of mission has challenged the theologians to redefine their basic theological positions.

# Historical Developments in the Theology of Christian Mission

*Eugene J. Fisher*

## I. THE CONCEPT OF MISSION IN THE BIBLE

### A. The Hebrew Scriptures

#### *1. Attitudes Toward Other Peoples*

Viewed as a whole, the Hebrew Bible is remarkably innocent of anything approximating our modern concept of "mission,"[1] which is to say a more or less organized effort to "proclaim" one's religious insights to other people for the purpose of influencing them to become members of one's own religious community.[2]

In the Hebrew Scriptures, of course, there is no concept of a particular "mission to the Jews" at all, since the Jewish people are already constituted as a people because of God's initiative. But curiously, at least from a Christian point of view, there also seems to be little or no sense of a "mission to the Gentiles" in the Hebrew Bible's vision either. Jonah goes out to preach to the Ninevites, but he calls on them only to repent, not to join the Jewish covenant. They are "saved," not as converts to Judaism but precisely as Ninevites.[3]

While there is no sense of missionary outreach in the Hebrew Scriptures, there is clearly a sense of universal witness. Israel is to be a light to the nations (Is 49:6) as well as a blessing to them (Gn 12:2; 17:6; Sir 44:21). In Isaiah, as in Genesis, this mandate of witness[4] is specifically linked to the covenant and is constitutive of the very notion of Jewish peoplehood.

> I the Lord have called you in righteousness . . . and set you for a covenant of the people, for a light to the nations, to open blind eyes to bring out prisoners from the dungeon and those that sit in darkness from the prison house (Is 42:6).[5]

Along with this ethical witness of social commitment, there is also an educative and eschatological aspect to Jewish witness:

> In the end of days, the mountain of the Lord's house will be established as the top of the mountains . . . and all the nations shall flow into it, and many peoples shall go and say, come let us go up to the mountain of the Lord, to the house of the God of Jacob, and he will teach us his ways and we will walk in his paths. For out of Zion shall go forth the teaching and the word of God from Jerusalem (Is 2:2–3; cf. 56:7).

But even in this end time the peoples, although they will praise the Lord "with one voice," do not seem to be envisioned as any the less "peoples."

Nor does it seem that the peoples are intended to become Jews and take on themselves the sweet obligations of Torah. All humanity, as Genesis puts it, is created "in the image of God" and given the mandate to "fill the earth and subdue it" (Gn 1:27–28), thus standing in a special relationship of responsibility to God for creation. This relationship is covenantal (Gn 9:7–9) and does not seem to be in any way threatened or superseded by God's more particular election of Israel (Gn 12:1–3). Indeed, God can choose other particular peoples for particular tasks and blessings:

> Are you not like the Ethiopians to me, O men of Israel? says the Lord. Did I not bring the Israelites from the land of Egypt as I brought the Philistines from Caphtor and the Arameans from Kir? (Am 9:7, NAB).

Thus other nations and rulers can validly be seen as fulfilling the divine will in judgment of Israel itself (e.g., Is 10:5–6). The history of salvation is universal without being universalist, particular without being particularist. This tension dominates the Hebrew biblical vision.

### *2. Attitudes Toward Other Religions*

Another tension dominates the Hebrew biblical attitudes toward the "pagan nations"[6] and their religions, attitudes that will deeply influence later Christian attitudes toward other religions and hence all subsequent Christian understandings of "mission."[7] Despite the universal statements such as those cited above, from which a relatively positive attitude may be drawn, the bulk of the descriptions of other religions in the Hebrew Scriptures can only be described as negative.[8]

The harsh judgments of other religions in Scripture, of course, must be seen in the context of the equally harsh judgments upon Israel and the hints, here and there, that even pagan religion can be a proper response to God (e.g., Mal 1:11). Pietro Rossano, of the Vatican's Secretariat for Non-Christians, speaks of a "sapiential economy" in the Hebrew Scriptures which views God's Wisdom as available to and manifesting itself through all human striving for divine truth.[9] Taking the negative attitudes into account, Rossano concludes:

> Thus the religions as such do not appear in antithesis to God's self-communication. . . . The Bible appears to be hostile toward the religions only when they represent a threat to the covenant, or assume forms of a cosmic and vitalistic monism, or draw people to worship idols and thus substitute the creature for the Creator. But when the Bible encounters forms of pure religion or forms that are reconcilable with faith in the God of the Covenant, it welcomes them and takes them up. One need only refer to the cases of Melchizedek, or Jethro, or Job; these are non-Jewish religious personalities who are nevertheless recognized and praised for their faith.[10]

Jesus, of course, continues this biblical tradition of holding up the faith of non-Jews as a model for the chosen people when he praises the centurion: "I tell you I have not found so much faith among the Israelites" (Lk 7:9).[11]

From different portions of the Hebrew Scriptures, then, one could validly derive any number of "theologies" of other religions and consequent theologies of mission. Clear only is the fact that, with a few significant exceptions, the negative attitudes prevailed in Christian interpretation of both Testaments, and that these negative judgments of other religions formed the foundations on which were built the major understandings of the Church's "mission" to them. Schlette comments:

> If the total position regarding exegesis and the use made of Holy Scripture by the Fathers and in the Middle Ages and indeed down to our own times is taken into account, with the neglect of the perspectives of sacred history that prevailed, it can scarcely be expected that an attempt would

> have been made to scrutinize more precisely the mostly negative statements [about the religions] of Scripture from the point of view of their context and in the perspective of the economy of redemption, and to bring into higher relief the few positive statements contained in Scripture.[12]

## B. The New Testament

### *1. Mission to the Gentiles*

The comments made above concerning the plurality of attitudes in the Hebrew Scriptures, and the ignoring of that plurality in subsequent Christian tradition, can only be repeated and, if anything, emphasized when we turn to the New Testament and its interpretation. Here, new questions and dimensions are added to the ancient ones.

In the immediate wake of the paschal event and the first Christian Pentecost, the followers of Jesus continued to consider themselves Jews and to address their message to their fellow Jews (Acts 2:14, 22, 29, 36, 42–47). And so, in this early period, it remained until Paul came with his astounding new question: What about the Gentiles? Do they have a place as Gentiles, or must they become Jews first? (Acts 15).

The time-frame of these events needs to be carefully considered. Even the Ethiopian eunuch (Acts 8) is brought to Christ, not directly but through interpretation of the Hebrew Scriptures, which he had been studying. Since the eunuch was "on a pilgrimage to Jerusalem" (v. 27), it is likely that he had already converted to Judaism, or was in the process of doing so when Philip saw him on the road. And even after the baptism of Cornelius (to the astonishment of "the circumcised believers": Acts 10:45), Stephen travels about "making the message known to none but Jews" (11:19).

Paul's defense of his practice of baptizing Gentiles without circumcision or instruction in the Law undergirds and occasions his whole treatment of the Law[13] in his Epistles: "Does God belong to the Jews alone? Is he not also the God of the Gentiles? . . . Are we then abolishing the Law by means of faith? Not at all. On the contrary, we are confirming the Law" (Rom 3:31). In Acts, his defensive reaction to criticism tends to reflect more pique than theology: "The word of God has to be declared first of all to you; but since you reject it and thus convict yourselves as unworthy of everlasting life, we now turn to the Gentiles" (Acts 13:46).[14]

Krister Stendahl has rightly pointed out that the context of Acts 4:12 is all important for determining its scope and limitations.[15] The statement "There is no salvation in anyone else, for there is no other name in the whole world given to men by which we are to be saved" has long been considered a mandate for the necessity of the conversion of all persons from their own religion to Christianity if they are to be "saved" (a term which itself has a wide range of interpretations, as we shall see). Acts 4, however, takes place *before* the question of inclusion of Gentiles is posed. Peter is engaged in Acts 4 in an inner-Jewish, not a Gentile-Christian or even a Jewish-Christian exchange. He is called to account for his wonder-working, not his faith: "By what power or in whose name have men of your stripe done this?" It is not in relation to the *Shema* (Dt 6:4) that Peter's response is given, but in view of the relationship of the people to the leaders of the Jewish community (4:21), a dominant pattern in Luke. "Thus we note that Peter here speaks within Judaism, fully identifying with Israel. . . . Here is a confession, not a proposition. . . . The foregoing observations," Stendahl concludes, "suggest to me that Acts 4:12 is not a good basis for an absolute claim in an absolute sense."[16] It is a witness, but not a theological proposal.

The Gospels reflect the fact that the early Christian communities continued to wrangle over the question of inclusion of Gentiles, and over the extent and nature of the call to preach the good news, with varying results.

One of the great early questions, as we have seen, was whether the good news could be proclaimed to Gentiles at all. According to Acts, Paul seems to have resolved this by determining that the Jews, having in a sense a "right of first refusal," had exercised that right (Acts 13:46; 18:6; 28:28). Since the majority of Christians were still Jews at the time, it is obviously difficult to conclude that "the Jews" refused the message, though this is what the increasingly gentilized Church seems to have later concluded.[17]

In Mark, the question is posed dramatically. Jesus responds to the Hellenic woman's plea with: "Let the sons of the household satisfy themselves at the table first. It is not right to take the food of the children and throw it to the dogs" (Mk 7:27). Though Jesus ultimately relents, praising not so much her faith (as Luke would have emphasized) as her humility or cleverness, the saying itself has to go down as one of Scripture's harshest attitudes toward other nations.

Luke's version of the commissioning of the twelve (9:1–6) and of the seventy-two (10:1–15) does not explicitly raise the question. From the use of the traditionally prophetic "It will go easier on the day of judgment for Tyre and Sidon than for you" and Luke's deep interest in the question (e.g., his depiction of the faith of centurions: Lk 7:9; 24:47), the omission of reference to the question may be significant.

It is also of interest that the commissioning of the seventy-two in

Luke is sandwiched between the description of Samaritan inhospitality to Jesus' messengers (9:51–56) and the parable of the good Samaritan (10:25–37).

Though much has been said of the "universalism" of this parable, it is important to note that the Samaritans represent a special case and may not be very relevant to the question of New Testament attitudes toward other religions for the purposes of this discussion. The Samaritans were not "idolators" but practiced their own (they believed, and still do, "true") form of biblical Judaism. For Jews, the Samaritans were in a unique category. They were not "goyim" and the very closeness of the two communities accounts for the bitterness of the relationship.[18] John's narrative of the meeting with the Samaritan woman at the well (Jn 4) thus may reflect Jesus' attempt to heal a particularly painful division of Jews from people who were already for all practical purposes co-religionists rather than any sort of universalist model.[19]

Matthew's version of the commissioning of the twelve does record a tradition in which the proclamation of the kingdom (which, after all, was *Jesus'* message; the proclamation of Jesus as the Christ is, in the light of the resurrection, the *Church's* message)[20] does specify going to Jews alone: "Do not visit pagan territory and do not enter a Samaritan town. Go instead after the lost sheep of the house of Israel" (Mt 10:6; cf. Mt 15:24).

While it is unclear as to what subgroup of Jews would constitute the "lost sheep," this tradition of exclusion, meticulously preserved by Matthew, sets into higher relief Matthew's own resounding conclusion to both his Gospel and the early Christian controversy over the nature of Christian mission.

> Full authority has been given to me both in heaven and on earth; go therefore and make disciples of all the nations. Baptize them in the name of the Father and of the Son and of the Holy Spirit. Teach them to carry out everything I have commanded you. And know that I am with you always, until the end of the world (Mt 28:18–20; NAB translation).

The conclusion of Acts likewise reflects its author's view that Christians not only may but ought to reach out to the Gentiles: "Now you must realize that this salvation of God has been transmitted to the Gentiles—who will heed it" (28:28). Luke wisely concludes his narrative before the martyrdom of Paul in Rome.

While the apostolic Church after the debate reflected in the pages of the New Testament comes to a clear consensus on the permissibility and even necessity of proclaiming the post-resurrection message of Jesus to the world at large, it does not seem to do so on the basis of a conscious theology of the religions or their possible role in God's plan of salvation. St. Paul's speech in Lystra (Acts 14:8–18) contains a hint both of the Jewish notion of the universal availability of divine wisdom (14:17) and the notion that in the new age for humanity, choices will have to be made: "In past ages he let the Gentiles go their way" (14:16). The speech in Athens (Acts 17:16–32), which likewise contains only indirect Christological reference, contains the same two elements of openness to divine truth reaching the nations in and through their own religions ("they were to seek God, to grope for him and perhaps eventually to find him": v. 27) and a call to repent in view of the imminence of the eschaton ("God may well have overlooked bygone periods when men did not know him; but now he calls on all men everywhere to reform their lives. He has set the day . . .": vv. 30–31). Neither of these speeches was particularly successful but then "the day" proved to be not so imminent either, which is another tension within New Testament theology pertinent to the present discussion. As many scholars have pointed out, if the end which justifies is "not yet," the Church has no right to arrogate to itself all the universal characteristics of that period.[21]

The resolution of the debate in the Council of Jerusalem by James is strikingly rabbinic. He interprets Peter and Paul to speak of God's concern "with taking from among the Gentiles a people to bear his name" (Acts 15:14) and concludes that this can be done on the basis of the Noahide covenant alone: "We should merely write to them to abstain from anything contaminated by idols, from illicit sexual union, from the meat of strangled animals, and from eating blood" (v. 20), going on to acknowledge the role of the synagogue in proclaiming Torah "in every town" throughout the known world (v. 21). The Gentiles, while maintaining only the universal covenant obligation of Gentiles as determined in Jewish *halakhah,* could take their part in rebuilding the eschatological "hut of David" (v. 16). Gamaliel couldn't have said it better!

With regard to the nature and function of other religions in God's scheme, then, the New Testament has relatively little to say to the systematic theologian. Its questions are not ours: How do we view other religions? Can people be "saved" in and through them or must they become Christians? What is God's will for them in this interim time in between Jesus' first coming and his awaited second coming in glory as the Messiah? The New Testament's question, in the first instance, was limited to whether or not one could go to the Gentiles at all, and if so on what basis to accept them into the growing community. As we shall see, the Church in the first few centuries had to, and did, come to some clear opinions on these matters out of the exigencies of their time. Impressed and imbued with the overwhelming reality of what God had done for all humanity in Jesus, the conclusion was eventually reached that all should join in the mystery. And influenced by the negative views of the Hebrew Scriptures toward idolatry (without much reflection on the positive side of it all), the patristic Church reached the further consensus that *without* formal inclusion in the Church, other people would have a hard time "groping" and "finding" God.

### 2. *Mission to the Jews*

With the exception of Romans 9—11, there is no real discussion in the New Testament over whether or not to go "to the Jews" with the message of Christ. This seems to have been presumed. Again, most of our modern questions are unasked, and therefore unanswered.

While the universal significance of the Christ-event for all humanity is quite clear, especially in the Epistles and John (and will become a major theme in later missionary theory), how the Jews relate to this universal vision is susceptible of a variety of interpretations, depending on how one reads which texts.

1 Timothy 2:4, for example, asserts the principle of God's universal salvific will: "He wants all men to be saved and come to know the truth." The author of the Epistle then goes on to specify the latter portion of his assertion: "And the truth is this: God is one. One also is the mediator between God and man, the man Jesus Christ, who gave himself as a ransom for all" (v. 5; cf. Heb 8:6; Mt 20:28; Gal 1:4).

Questions here abound, as they do with most scriptural passages which one age or another of Christian history has wished to use in a particular (or particularist way): Are "being saved" and "knowing the truth" coterminous concepts? Must one formally join the Christian Church to participate substantially in either? Does God's universal salvific will mean a will to "save" all humanity through joining the Church, or can God "save" in and through the various world religions?

These are the general questions of all evangelizing, and texts can be adduced on various sides of any argument. For example, the American Lutheran theologian, Carl E. Braaten, uses many of the same texts utilized by the authors of the 1974 Lausanne Covenant of world Evangelicals[22] to show that the universal significance of the Christ-event can be held without construing membership in the Church as causally related to salvation.[23] Contemporary views of such questions will be dealt with in another contribution to this volume.

But even if the most particularist interpretation of the universalist New Testament texts is taken, one would still have to ask how and in what way these can be said to apply to the very particular, indeed unique reality of the Jewish people who already "know the Father" in and through the Sinai covenant.

Biblically, salvation is "from the Jews," even for John (4:22), whose Gospel is arguably the most polemically anti-Jewish writing of the New Testament. It is not something the Church has to offer *to* the Jews as a people. Jews simply do not "fit" into any conceivable scheme that one can derive out of New Testament attitudes toward humanity in general. They are certainly not "goyim." Nor is there anything in the New Testament to suggest that God's covenant with them has been "abrogated" by God's will.

Certainly, one can find in the New Testament strong reflections of the bitterness of the split which occurred between Judaism and nascent Christianity between the death of Jesus and the setting-down of the Gospels. One can even find, as Rosemary Ruether and others have done,[24] seeds of the "teaching of contempt" toward Jews and of the *verus Israel* notion that so deeply scarred Christian attitudes toward Jews in the patristic period and which perdured up to the present day.[25] But whether or not "the Jews" rejected or even killed Jesus, and whether or not the God of love turned vindictive toward them as a result, is not really relevant to the point at hand: Was God's self-revelation to the Jews on Sinai (Torah) insufficient, flawed, in some way inadequate for salvific purposes? Do the Jews need the mediation of Christ to come to the Father, or are they already there?

Such are our basic questions today, I would suspect, with relation to developing a theory of the need for a Christian mission to the Jews. In the New Testament, however, they are not asked. Most of the New Testament simply presupposes that the Jews are God's people, just as its authors presume that *the Bible* is the Hebrew Bible. Numerous texts, as we have seen, can be cited to show how the New Testament authors coped with the, for them, startling notion that Gentiles too could be included in some way through Christ among the chosen. These range from the polemical ("the stone that the builders rejected," etc.) to the universal, as we have seen.

John Koenig has observed that although Jesus' death opens up God's ancient election to Gentiles (Mk 15:37–39), "it challenges in no way the permanent validity of that election for the Jewish people."[26]

Similarly, Paul's invectives against "the Law," in Galatians and elsewhere, do not lead to the conclusion that Torah is invalid *for Jews,* but simply that Jesus replaces Torah *for Gentiles,* who can thereby become "sons of Abraham" (Gal 3:7–9). "Does this mean that the law is opposed to the promises (of God)? Again, unthinkable!" (Gal 3:7–9).

Paul comes close to the questions we would ask only in his ultimately enigmatic discussion of Jewish-Christian relations in Romans 9—11. While elsewhere, his argument is with Jewish-Christians who would question his evangelization of the Gentiles, or attempt to convince the Gentile converts to observe Torah, here the question is not so much the Law as the promises.

In Romans, Paul seems to take a somewhat more moderate stance toward the Law, calling it "holy and just and good" (7:12) and even of the spirit in origin (7:14). It is human weakness, not the Law as such, that is the basic problem (7:7—8:4; 10:3). Romans is hardly complimentary to Jews. Though "zealous for God, their zeal is unenlightened" (10:1–2), and Israel's unbelief is judged to be willful and persistent (10:16–21).

Yet just when Paul reaches the bottom line where one might expect an unequivocally negative judgment and a consigning of the Jews to the scrap-heap of salvation history, Paul begins to back off. The unbelief of all but a remnant of the Jewish people is discerned as *God's will* (9:18: 11:7–10) and part of God's plan to make room for inclusion of the Gentiles (11:11–16, 25). It is a mission "of mercy" entrusted by God to Israel in view of the imminent end of days (11:30–32). The Jews will play their role in God's plan precisely by remaining Jewish, *not* by converting to Christianity.[27]

God has not rejected the Jews (11:1–2) but continues to preserve and hold them "most dear" as always. "God's gifts and his call are irrevocable" (11:28–29). Ironically, Israel is called by God in the present age to fulfill its ancient calling to enlighten the Gentiles precisely by refusing the Gospel. "What the Gentiles receive through their righteousness by faith, namely, the fulfillment of God's promised mercy, Israel gains through its original election."[28]

Krister Stendahl has noted that Paul writes this key section (10:18—11:36), including his final doxology, without mentioning the name of Jesus Christ. Significantly, Paul predicts only that in the end time "all Israel will be saved" without mentioning anything about their being saved "in Christ" or by way of conversion to the Church. All that, Paul feels, is better left to the "inscrutable" judgments of God. Stendahl comments:

> Before (Paul) is through he will lecture the Gentile Christians (11:13) that they have no business in trying to convert the Jews. Paul seems to have discerned two things: (a) an attitude of superiority and conceit in the Gentile Christians (11:25), which makes them unsuited for such a mission, and (b) that the Jesus movement is to be a Gentile movement—apart from the significant remnant, the link by grace (11:5).[29]

Subsequent Christian history has more than confirmed the aptness of both of these Pauline insights.

Stendahl derives more out of Romans 9—11 with reference to conversion of Jews than many other commentators. And it is clear that the text does not supply an adequate basis for a fully satisfactory theology of the mystery of the sacred relationship that perdures between the Church and the Jewish people. But his studies do point to one scripturally valid option that *could* have been taken by the Church in its approach to the Jewish people over the centuries.

To summarize this all too brief survey of biblical testimony on the question of mission, one can discern the following points:

1. The Hebrew Scriptures, which proclaim the oneness and universality of God above all, and God's Lordship over all time and all nations, does not translate this universal vision into a strong mandate for conversion of the Gentiles, leaving God free to act when and where he wills. On the other hand, the Hebrew Bible says little that would preclude such a development either, so that the Jews in certain periods have themselves been active proselytizers.

2. The New Testament proclaims the uniqueness of the Christ-event in human history and the universality of Christ's Lordship, insights which *are* translated by the evangelists into a mandate for a mission to the Gentiles. This notion may be yet another debt of the early Church to Pharisaic Judaism, which was actively reaching out, with a good deal of success, for converts during this period (Mt 23:15). Paul seems to have had his greatest initial success among the "God-fearers" already attracted to Judaism (Acts 13:43), while his early direct appeals at Lystra (14:18) and Athens (18:32–34) were not noticeably productive of converts.

3. The New Testament authors take a variety of stances on Jews and Judaism, many negative and polemic in the inflated rhetoric that was the

style of the day. But this was *as* Jews speaking to fellow Jews, not as "outsiders" condemning Israel in absolute fashion as the Gentile Church would soon learn to do over the course of the next few centuries. The major question facing the early Church was whether or not Gentiles could be included in the Christian community. That Jesus' message was for the Jews was (rightly) presumed; the Christian message about Jesus seems also, but on less secure grounds, to have been presumed without a question. Paul's provocative challenge in reversing the accepted pattern of "to the Jews alone" and "to the Jews first," with his implication that it may be against God's will to try to convert the Jews at all, was not picked up in later New Testament writings, nor in the subsequent history of the Church, which went off on another theoretical track altogether, developing the negative strata of New Testament teaching on the Jews into an absolutely-formulated systematic "teaching of contempt." Paul's questions thus still remain unanswered, as do ours as Christians seeking to renew our understanding of Jews and Judaism today.

4. Whatever the disposition of such questions, two things are clear from the biblical record concerning the Jews. First, God's relationship to the Jewish people has been and remains a unique one, not reducible to any general or "universal" formulae derived from biblical attitudes toward "the nations." Second, God's election of the Jewish people as a covenant community was, and remains, permanent (Gn 17:13, *et al.*) and eternal, with lasting significance on its own terms for salvation history.

## II. MISSION IN THE PATRISTIC PERIOD

### A. Mission to the Pagans

Influenced by the vigorous opposition of the Hebrew Bible to idolatry, and faced with intermittent persecution, the early Fathers of the Church tended to be generally harsh in their attitudes toward non-Christian religions. This negative attitude was not entirely motivated by triumphalism, for they were convinced of the absolute necessity of the individual pagan's conversion to Christ if he or she was to be saved. While one might find a ray of light here or there among the great philosophers of the [illegible]
world (reflecting the universal availability of the "e[illegible]
all humanity), pagan *religions* were as such corrupt[illegible]

In the preface to *De Principiis,* for example, [illegible]
that "we ceased to seek for truth among all who cl[illegible]
opinions (Greeks and barbarians alike), after we ha[illegible]

Christ was the Son of God and were persuaded that we must learn it from Himself." In *Contra Celsum,* Origen resoundingly rejected the contention of Celsus that "there is nothing wrong in each nation observing its established method of worship, that it is an obligation on all men to live according to their country's customs, and that it matters nothing what different nations call God."[30]

Origen argued that religious differences do matter. Jesus, he said, is unique. He cannot be equated with other great religious figures nor with the moral qualities expounded by the philosophers. He shares in the absolute reason and righteousness of God. No teacher can add anything to Jesus. While Origen saw a certain nobility in "great Plato's" doctrine of the soul, Plato's philosophy, he felt, could not lead others successfully any more than it led Plato himself to a worthy worship of God. Nor did Plato's philosophy save him from "polluting his worship with idolatry." The aim of those who follow Jesus, for Origen, could only be "to win over to righteousness, truth and the other virtues those who, until they receive the doctrine of Jesus Christ, live in darkness about God and in ignorance of their Creator."[31]

In the Fathers, we find the two major theories of mission which would dominate Christian thought through the ages: either other religions are wholly false, even demonic in origin, or they exist by way of divine condescension, having a certain educative value as *praeparatio Christi* which the plenitude of the revelation of the Gospel fulfills.[32]

Clement of Alexandria sought to take a positive view of Greek philosophy without condoning the "immoralities" of Greek religious beliefs:

> Accordingly, before the advent of the Lord, philosophy was necessary to the Greeks for righteousness. . . . For this was a schoolmaster to bring the Hellenic mind, as the law to the Hebrews, to Christ. Philosophy, therefore, was a preparation, paving the way for him who is perfected in Christ.[33]

Clement thus projects unto Greek philosophy that part of Paul's notion of the Law which saw it as a necessary preparation for Christ within a staged vision of salvation history. Thus, the philosophy of the pagans, if not their religions, could be seen to fall within God's plan of salvation.

Justin Martyr, in his *Apologies,* exemplifies both the positive and the egative poles of the ambiguous patristic attitude toward non-Christian reus thought. On the one hand, Justin denounces the polytheistic cults work of demons who had rebelled against God and were now attempting to lead humanity astray into immorality and idolatrous worship of themselves.[34] The many evident similarities between pagan cults and Christian worship, he believed, were merely the result of demonic cunning designed to confound the unwary.[35] This negative or "dialectical" view of other religions became a standard one, for centuries influencing Christian appreciation of all the great world religions it was successively to encounter. It largely determined practical mission methods, if not express mission theory.[36] According to this view, even as articulated today in certain mission circles, the "pagans" are in a calamitous state. Of themselves they can do nothing salvifically meritorious, living as they do "in darkness and the shadow of death" (Lk 1:79). What is Christian stands in unique relation to God, wholly other and wholly opposed to the corruption outside the saved community, as light stands to darkness.[37] The 1974 Lausanne Covenant would seem to affirm quite strongly this dichotomous view of the relationship between Christianity and the other world religions (most of them wholly unknown to the Church Fathers, of course):

> We also reject as derogatory to Christ and the Gospel every kind of syncretism and dialogue which implies that Christ speaks equally through all religions. Jesus Christ . . . is the only mediator between God and man. . . . All men are perishing because of sin, but God loves all men, not wishing that any should perish but that all should repent. Yet those who reject Christ repudiate the joy of salvation and condemn themselves to eternal separation from God.[38]

Justin, however, was also quite capable of a more positive approach at least to certain "higher" elements of paganism. Like Philo before him,[39] Justin was deeply impressed with the Logos-concept of Greek philosophy, identifying it with the creative aspect of divine Wisdom. Since humanity, created in the image of God, participates in the Logos through the capacity for reason, the words of human reason, though to some extent distorted by sin, can be understood to be informed in part by the Logos, which is made perfectly manifest in Christ. It is the Logos, then, who spoke through the great pagan philosophers to lead humanity away from demonic darkness to its ultimate perfection in the light of Christ. As with Clement, the philosophers have an ordained role in God's plan:

> We have been taught that Christ is the first-born of God, and we have declared above that He is the Word of whom every race of humanity were partakers. Those who lived reasonably (according to the Logos)

> are Christians, even though they have been thought atheists, as, among the Greeks, Socrates and Heraclitus and the like. . . . For whatever either lawgivers or philosophers uttered well, they elaborated by finding and contemplating some part of the Word. But since they did not know the whole of the Word, which is Christ, they often contradicted themselves.[40]

This fulfillment style of approach, which would see the individual soul to be by nature "Christian" and ever in search of the plenitude Christianity alone can provide, also runs like a thread through Christian missionary history. It is touched in the optimistic conception of nature and reason that characterizes Scholastic thought, as well as the positive attitudes of Christian humanism and the tolerance of the Enlightenment.[41] Karl Rahner, finally, will make the move to applying it to other religions as such in his "anonymous Christian" approach, since faith is of necessity social and must be communally embodied.[42]

The patristic authors, it should be remembered, wrote during a time of tremendous expansion on the part of the Church. From its first outreach into Samaria (Acts 8), the Christian community as a whole, soldiers and sailors, merchants and travelers, all strove to spread the Gospel by personal propaganda. The *Didache* and the *Shepherd of Hermas* both mention a special group called "apostles" or vocational missionaries, and an organized catechumenate soon became part of every Christian community. By the time of the Edict of Milan (313), it has been estimated, almost one-eighth of the population of the empire were Christian. With the Edict, Christianity became a mass movement, enjoying state support and becoming convinced that its destiny was to convert "all the peoples," joining humanity together into the one Church, not just a new people taken "from among the nations," as the New Testament had envisioned, but a new people who would *include* all the nations. Conversionary zeal and success had given a radical new turn to the biblical ideal of being a "light *to* the nations." Universalistic particularism, better known as triumphalism, had become an essential element of the Christian ethos.

### B. The Place of the Jews

In the midst of this great success story, however, one nagging "failure" stood out in ever sharper relief. Why was it that the Jews refused to come aboard? Paul and the apostolic Church had faced this same question, ascribing it, on biblical precedent, to Jewish "blindness" as a "stiff-necked" people. It was on this image that the patristic apologists came more and more to rely, ignoring the more positive biblical testimony to Jewish faithfulness (the Deuteronomic cycle always has the Jews turning back to God in repentance, but those passages were conveniently omitted from their citations) and Paul's hint in Romans 9—11 that perhaps God's will was involved.

Rather quickly, an intricate "teaching of contempt" was developed concerning the Jews, transforming the polemical rhetoric of the New Testament into the absolute, metaphysical categories of Greek philosophy. Jews did not simply *do* evil things, they did them because they were inherently evil. Texts such as Nehemiah 9:26 and 1 Kings 19:10 (cf. Rom 11:3) were cited (on the model of the speeches of Acts) as proofs that Jewish apostasy from God and murderousness toward the prophets, leading up to the ultimate murder of Christ, had always characterized Jewish history.[43] Lactantius, and other apologists, delighted in embellishing the scriptural accounts with details about how the Jews killed the prophets with "exquisite tortures."

Compounding the embarrassment, of course, was the fact that pagan apologists could and did use Jewish unbelief and Christian rejection of Torah observance as polemical devices. Origen thus cites Celsus as arguing: "If the prophets of the God of the Jews foretold that Jesus would be his Son, why did he give them laws by Moses. . . . Yet his Son, the man of Nazareth, gives contradictory laws. . . . Who is wrong? Moses or Jesus?"[44] And Julian the Apostate asks, not so innocently:

> Now since the Galileans say that, though they are different from the Jews, they are still, precisely speaking, Israelites in accordance with their prophets, and that they obey Moses above all and the prophets . . . why is it that (they) do not abide even by the traditions of the Hebrews or accept the law which God has given to them? . . . But point out to me where there is any statement by Moses of what was later rashly uttered by Paul. . . . Where does God announce to the Hebrews a second law besides that which was established? Nowhere does it occur.[45]

Gradually, though the two communities seem to have gotten along quite well during the early centuries,[46] many Christian leaders seem to have talked themselves more and more into an absolute "either/or" approach. Bishops wrote pastoral letters complaining that their people continued to go to Jewish rabbis for blessings. And John Chrysostom's justly infamous diatribes against the Jews seem to have been occasioned by the fact that so many of his flock preferred rabbinic sermons to his own:

> But since there are some who consider the synagogue to be a holy place, we must say a few things to them as well. Why do you reverence this place when you should disdain it, despise it and avoid it. "The law and the books of the prophets can be found there," you say. What of it? You say, "Is it not the case that the books make the place holy?" Certainly not! This is the reason I especially hate the synagogue and avoid it, that they have the prophets but do not believe in them, that they read these books but do not accept their testimonies. . . . If the Jewish rites are holy and venerable, our way of life must be false. But if our way is true, as indeed it is, theirs is fradulent.[47]

Not only was the continued existence of the Jews, then, a potential embarrassment in Christian missionary efforts among the pagans, but Judaism was also perceived by at least some Church leaders to be potentially attractive to those already Christian. Chrysostom's emphasis on the uniqueness of Christianity from Judaism, while often crudely put, represented an important and essential insight in the development of the Church's self-awareness. Blurring the distinctions between the two traditions (as done today, for example, by movements such as "Jews for Jesus" and the "Messianic Jews") can only result in a syncretism which, despite its appeal as a proselytizing tactic, does justice to the essential claims of neither tradition.

After its establishment as a state religion of the Empire, Christianity soon learned how to influence Roman law to its own advantage, particularly on the question of conversion.[48] While the law of the co-emperors Honorius and Theodosius in 409 exempted Jews from the general legal obligation of pagans (*coelicoli,* "sky-worshipers") to present themselves for baptism within the year, it made Jewish proselytism of Christians a capital offense. Jews who became Christians, on the other hand, were legally protected. Their families could not disinherit, or even reduce their inheritances. For the same reason of fear of conversion, the marriage of a Jewish man to a Christian woman was forbidden (though not the obverse) and Jews could not hold Christian slaves. Jews were also blocked from military careers and any civil offices that might include the power to judge or pass sentence on Christians.[49] Christianity was learning to use law as a missionary tool regarding the Jews, a practice that would characterize Christian "mission" to the Jews throughout the Middle Ages.[49a]

The differing fates of Jews and pagans under Church rule backed by the power of the state in the waning days of the Empire illustrate the curious ambivalence of Christianity toward Judaism. The Church's position vis-à-vis pagan religions was entirely clear-cut: paganism had to be destroyed and all pagans converted to Christianity for the sake of their salvation. The Church's "mission" to the Jews, however, remained ambiguous. On the one hand, legal incentives and limitations were enacted to embody the increasingly vitriolic rhetoric of the Christian "teaching of contempt" toward Judaism. On the other hand a lingering respect, seldom vocalized but clearly framed in the distinctive legislation concerning Jews, continued to maintain the tradition of the unique character of the "spiritual bond" that links Judaism and Christianity in uneasy covenant one to the other and both with the same God of Abraham, Isaac and Jacob. Conversion of Jews might be a much desired goal, but not at the expense of that essential respect which flows from the very heart of the Christian mystery itself.[50]

A fifth-century illustration of this ambiguous Christian posture is found in the Code of Justinian:

> Let no one who has done no harm be molested on the ground that he is a Jew, nor let any aspect of his religion result in his exposure to contumely; in no place are their synagogues or dwellings to be wantonly damaged. . . . But so too do we judge it opportune to warn the Jews that, elated as they may be by their security, they must not become insolent and admit anything which is opposed to the reverence due to Christian worship.[51]

## III. THE MEDIEVAL MISSION

### A. General: Barbarians and Muslims

The first distinctive feature of this epoch was the dissolution of the Greco-Roman world and the migration of nations. With the barbarians, there was no *preparatio evangelica* of classical philosophy or universal culture. Monasticism replaced both the bishop and the laity as the main missionary agents. Conversion took place on a tribe-by-tribe basis rather than individually or as a mass movement supported by state power. The "imperial mission," which saw the evangelization process become part of the expansion of medieval kingdoms, originated with t
received its typical expression under the Holy Roma
a form of missionary endeavor not without its ill si
ued through the age of exploration and colonizatio
teenth century, for example in the royal patronage

Portugal which "became more a political instrument of colonial and imperial policy than a missionary instrument."[52]

The appearance of Islam in the seventh century and its unprecedented success did not produce any entirely new Christian mission theories, but intensified existing ones. Christianity reacted initially to Islam essentially as it had to paganism: as a menace that had to be overwhelmed before it overwhelmed the Church. Hence the Crusades. Their failure (the Crusaders' states were finished by the end of the thirteenth century) and the almost total lack of results of the Franciscan Order's dedicated and generally positive apostolate among the Muslims tended to promote the popularity of the negative side of the Church Fathers' attitudes toward pagans.

Equally consistent with patristic thought, however, Thomas Aquinas was able to construct a somewhat more positive attitude based on the bridge of Arabic philosophy (to which medieval Scholasticism owed its existence in the first place, of course). In *Summa Contra Gentiles* (the very title of which testifies to the dawning awareness that the time of the earlier complacent assumption that Christianity had already "won over" the world to Christ was over), Aquinas notes that since Muslims do not share any Scriptures with Christians, religious discussion must be based on natural reason alone, which can bring one to a knowledge of the existence and essential attributes of God.[53] This knowledge would constitute a "natural theology," in mission terms a *preparatio evangelica,* which could be perfected by the revealed truths of the Bible.

In the late thirteenth and fourteenth centuries, the proliferation of Italian merchant communities in the East to an extent offset the loss of the mission bases in the Crusaders' states. While the Eastern Churches were blocked by the threatening power of Islam, Western religious orders such as the Franciscans traveled with the traders to establish missions as far away as China. The carnage of the Black Death, however, diminished the numbers of potential missionaries, and the advance of the Ottoman Turks and the progress of Islam in central Asia severed communication and led to the gradual dissolution of many of these missionary outposts. Christianity was once more thrown back into Europe. One of the few areas of expansion lay with Russian Orthodoxy which, as in the Western Church, saw colonization and evangelization as two aspects of the same drive to the Pacific. Following the fall of Constantinople in 1453, Islam was seen by Russia as a serious threat, and evangelization became virtually co-terminous with "Russification."

In such a period of embattled retrenchment, when Christianity was faced with the reality that it was not likely to convert the world in the near future (a dilemma analogous in impact, one may say, to the first century realization that the eschaton may not be so "imminent" after all), it is little wonder that as M. W. Baldwin puts it, "although Crusade projects failed, the Crusade mentality persisted."[54] Attempts to understand Islam, such as those by William of Tripoli and Ricoldus, were without sequel. After the end of the thirteenth century, with the exception of some scattered Franciscan efforts in inner Asia and the continuing Christian push down the Iberian peninsula, organized missions to Muslims ended.

Boniface VIII's *Unam Sanctam,* with its reiteration of Cyprian's phrase, *extra Ecclesiam nulla salus,* is typical of the mood: "We believe that there is one, holy, catholic and apostolic Church . . . outside of which there is no salvation. . . . We declare that it is necessary for salvation for every human creature to be subject to the Roman Pontiff."[55] Yet the Church would a bit later reject the Jansenist attempt to absolutize this phrase, condemning Quesnel's *extra Ecclesiam nulla conceditur gratia* ("outside the Church grace is not conceded": D. 1379). As Schlette remarks, "The question is, what is meant by *extra* and *Ecclesia* and *gratia* and *salus* in these two antithetical statements of the doctrine of faith?"[56] While the former, interpreted rather literally, became the functional principle behind missionary zeal, the latter notion, even if only expressed in caveats such as "baptism by desire" or salvation *ex moralitate,* preserved the core of an important option to the wholly negative portrait of the salvific potential in non-Christian religions. One way of posing the question, on which there is still no consensus, is whether the ancient principle, *Deus vult omnes homines salvos fieri,* means a mandate for universal conversion of all peoples to the Christian religion or is rather an expansion of God's freedom to act to save all persons in the context of their own historical and cultural traditions. Fortunately, this essay has not been charged with answering that question, only framing it.[57]

## B. Christian Legislation on the Jews in the Middle Ages

### *1. The Conversionary Motive*

While Muslims were met only on the field of battle as faceless, deeply-feared hordes of "infidels" (this despite their firm belief in the one God and numerous other beliefs they shared with Christians), Jews had the dubious distinction of being the only representatives of a "non-Christian" religion with which most Chrisians were likely to come into personal contact. It must be noted at the outset that Jews survived in Europe in such large numbers in the Middle Ages because they were officially tolerated there, owing, one can only presume, to the biblical aura that surrounded them as heirs of Abraham "in the flesh" and fellow believers at least in the first part of what Christians by this time considered "their" Scripture.

At times the distinctiveness of the Jewish people in Christian eyes worked to their detriment, as for example in the widespread presumption that Jews were responsible for spreading the Black Plague by poisoning the wells. At other times the uniqueness of the Jews was lost sight of, as in the easy transference of Crusader animosity from the Muslims to the far more reachable Jews as the Crusaders ran into stiff opposition in the Middle East. Already in the first Crusades, in 1096 and 1146, large-scale massacres of Jews took place throughout Europe. The Crusaders, despite the strenuous efforts of Bernard of Clairvaux, found it easier to force-convert and slaughter the "infidels" in their midst than to undertake the arduous journey to Palestine.[58]

Medieval attitudes toward the Jews are seen most clearly in the large and specific body of canonical legislation concerning them. No other group outside the Church received such extensive and detailed treatment in papal legislation. This body of law well illustrates both the ambiguity of Christian attitudes toward Jews—a true love-hate relationship with emphasis often on the latter—and the uniqueness of Judaism in the Christian vision when compared to all other religious groups. Jews, for good or ill, are simply irreducible to any general or universal category in any adequate theological system of evaluating the relationship of the Church to other world religions, historically or today. Owen C. Thomas rightly comments on the history of Jewish-Christian relations in the light of Christian relations with other religions in general:

> By the second century the Church confronted Judaism as another religion, but its relation to Judaism was so unique that it can hardly be taken as a type of its relation to any other religion. . . . Moreover, the terrible and shameful history of Christian treatment of the Jews has rendered it useless as a model (for Christian interpretation of other religions) in the moral sense.[59]

Early and medieval Christian legislation concerning the Jews, as Edward A. Synan has shown, was essentially concerned with the question of conversion, whether this involved on the one hand legislation prohibiting Jews from holding Christian slaves,[60] or on the other placing Jews under the official protection of the papacy, with the sanction of excommunication for those Christians who would do violence to Jews in any way or attempt to bring about their conversion by force.[61] Addressing Pascasius, the bishop of Naples, at the end of the sixth century, for example, Pope Gregory I wrote in a letter that was to become basic to all subsequent papal legislation:

> The Jews of Naples have registered a complaint with us, asserting that certain people are attempting in an unreasonable fashion to restrain them from some of the solemnities connected with their own feast days. . . . If this is the truth, they seem to be expending their energy on an extraordinarily empty project; for of what use is this when, even though they have been put under this prohibition . . . it avails nothing toward their faith and conversion? . . . One must act, therefore, in such a way that, owing to our reasoning and meekness, they might desire to follow us rather than to fly from us, in such a way that, showing them what we say out of their own books, we might be able to convert them with the help of God to the bosom of mother Church.[62]

Gregory, in a letter to the patriarch of Constantinople that found its way into Gratian's *Decretum* and thus into the effective magisterium of the medieval Church, sought to ban all forced baptism. Again the reasoning lay in the Pope's judgment on the most fruitful strategy for attracting converts to the Church.

> Your fraternity knows well what the canons say concerning bishops who wish to be feared for their blows: We have been constituted shepherds, not persecutors, and that outstanding preacher says: Argue, instruct, admonish with all patience and doctrine (2 Tim 4:2). A novelty, indeed a thing unheard of, is that doctrine that extorts faith through blows![63]

Sadly, forced conversion and conversion by governmental "persuasion" (taxation, laws limiting the building and repair of houses of worship, etc.) were all too commonplace in the medieval world.[64] Thus, while forced baptism was vigorously opposed by the Popes throughout the Middle Ages, once it was done to a particular person, the same Popes viewed it as an irrevocable act. The Fourth Council of Toledo, for example, ruled in a canon (which also came to be included in Gratian's *Decretum*) that "henceforth no one (may) bring force to bear in order that (the Jews) must believe." Yet, based on a letter of Pope Gregory IV (827–844), the same canon continued: "These (Jews), however, who long ago were forced to Christianity . . . it is necessary that they be obliged to hold the faith which they received by violence or necessity, lest the Name of the Lord be blasphemed . . . since now it is obvious that they have been associated in the divine mysteries."[65]

*2. The Providential Role of the Jews*

The basic motivation for papal legislation protecting the Jews from forced conversion lay then in the nature of faith itself as a free act. This was, as such, a general doctrine applicable in principle to all non-Christians, then as now. A second major motivation for the protective legislation also surfaces in Synan's survey, one which is pertinent to the Jews alone. "There is no moment," Synan concludes, "when Christian legislation on the Jews is silent on their providential role, especially as guardians of Scripture and as destined for final salvation. That Jews are the people first chosen by God and never abandoned, is less a fall than a 'stumbling' (Rom 9:1–11, 32), remains Catholic teaching."[66]

This second theological motive, which reflects the unique spiritual bonds linking the Church and the Jewish people, was traditionally phrased in papal documents in as negative a manner as possible. For example, addressing the Count of Nevers, Pope Innocent III (1198–1217) argued that

> . . . although (the Jews) ought not to be slain, lest the Christian people forget divine Law, (they) ought nevertheless to be dispersed over the earth as wanderers, as that their countenance might be full of ignominy and they might seek for the Name of the Lord Jesus Christ.[67]

Here, the stick joins the carrot as a social goad to conversion. Yet, such an approach, I would suggest, also implies a startling admission. Grudgingly framed as it is, the notion of a continuing providential role for the Jews as Jews clearly implies the necessity, from the Church's point of view, of preserving the Jewish people—albeit in "ignominy." While its framework promotes the conversionary ideal, the notion of Jews functioning to remind Christians of the Law presumes their existence, not as potential converts, but precisely as Jews. Logically, if one does not want all Jews slain, one would not want the Jews as a people to disappear by way of conversion either. For in both cases the effect is the same: the loss of a crucial element of God's overall plan of salvation. In brief, the Church's essential mission in and to the world would be crippled without a living Jewish witness to the truth of God's Torah.[68]

Christianity has thus, I would argue, always had a curiously ambiguous, even bifurcated attitude toward the conversion of the Jews. On the one hand, it was a goal to be sought above all others, since Jewish "refusal" to accept Jesus as the awaited Messiah has classically been the most serious embarrassment to Christian theological claims. Even today, Jewish converts are paraded on television as a special sort of Christian triumph. On the other hand, as Paul worked it out (however incompletely) in Romans 9—11, the Church has always had a sneaking suspicion in the back of its mind that perhaps the reason for the Jewish refusal is due to God's will, in which case conversion of the Jews as a people would, if successful, be a calamity for the Church. Paul thus puts off the question until the end time. Only *after* "the full number of Gentiles enter in" will "*all* Israel be saved." In the meantime, there is paradox and mystery.

## IV. FROM THE RENAISSANCE TO THE POST-COLONIAL AGE

### A. The Age of Discovery and Western Expansion

In the late medieval period the two principal mendicant orders, perhaps best typified by Raymond of Penafort and Raymond Lull, had begun to lay the groundwork for the theory and style of missionary activity that was to characterize the work up to the present, post-colonial period. Under the impact of Scholasticism and Renaissance humanism, a greater respect for the integrity and dignity of the human person began to emerge. Forceful conversion was eschewed, in theory, as improper, with stress laid more on the appeal of the "moral and intellectual superiority of Christianity."[69] Schools were founded to enable missionaries to study Arabic and the other languages and cultures to which they might be sent. The underlying theory, in short, shifted from the entirely negative "demonic" attitude of the Crusaders to the less rhetorically violent but only slightly less theoretically negative language of the "fulfillment" theory. (Who, after all, wants to be considered nothing more than an outdated, somewhat skewed "preparation" for someone else's "real truth"?)

#### *1. Expansion of Mission Territory*

The age of discovery opened a new missionary era, one no longer narrowly European but transoceanic (and thereby able to bypass on sea Islam's barring of the land routes to the Far East). Mission became a potentially worldwide endeavor. Whole new peoples were discovered who had existed for millennia without access to the Gospel. It came to be felt by many that God's universal salvific will meant that these peoples must have had some access to divine grace, *extra Ecclesiam* if not "outside" the impact of the Christ-event for all of human history. The mission question thus raised new questions for other doctrinal areas of Church teaching, especially ecclesiology. As we have seen, the ancient doctrine of *extra Ecclesiam nulla salus* had to be reinterpreted in the light of the opening of such vast new vistas.

New methods with implicit new theories of mission began to develop as missionaries gradually gained respect for the ancient cultures in which they found themselves. These ranged from the *doctrina-encomienda* to various forms of accommodation (bitterly debated back in Europe) introduced by the Jesuits in the "Paraguay Reductions" and in Japan, China, India and Indo-China. Evangelization of the Indians marched along with (and at times paved the way for) French and Spanish colonial expansion in the Americas. Hitherto unknown peoples were being added to the one Body of the Church, adding new dimensions to the concepts of "one, holy, and catholic." Along with the reunification of certain Eastern rite Churches to Rome, these developments spurred thinking toward a "diversity within community" understanding of the nature of the Church quite unforseeable when the Church existed only within the confines of the culturally uniform limits of European "Christendom."

*2. Protestant Missionary Efforts*

Until the end of the seventeenth century, Roman Catholicism virtually dominated the missionary field, as Catholic countries dominated the age of discovery and the opening of ocean trade routes West and East. This began to shift with the destruction of the Spanish Armada in the seventeenth century and the suppression of the Jesuits by Clement XIV in the eighteenth century. As W. C. Coleman comments:

> No greater blow could have been delivered to the (Catholic) missions than the removal from them of more than 3,000 Jesuits. The French Revolution marked the culmination of a century of mission decline which had begun with the missions' passing from Spanish and Portuguese dominance to the imperial and Protestant power of the Dutch and the English.[70]

By the beginning of the nineteenth century, Protestant mission agencies had proliferated. The Anglican Society for the Propagation of the Gospel in Foreign Parts, organized in 1701, sent missionaries to the Indians in the American colonies. German pietists had missions in India. William Carey, of the Baptist Missionary Society (founded 1792), translated the Bible into the languages of India and China and founded a college at Serampore for the training of Indian clergy. In 1886 the Student Volunteer Movement for Foreign Missions was founded with the optimistic watchword: "The evangelization of the world in this generation."

Protestant and Catholic theologians of this period offered few essentially new reinterpretations of traditional Christian models. Both Calvin and Luther depended heavily on the Epistle to the Romans for their interpretation of other religions: God has planted in humanity a sense or urging for the divine. For Calvin, this seed of religion is corrupted by sin into a "profusion" of falsehood and superstition.[71] For Luther, all religion reveals humanity's attempt to justify itself before God by its own achievement, whether morally or cultically. Such "works righteousness" is set over against salvation by the grace of God in Christ (note the dichotomous approach, again).

### *3. Developments in Mission Theory*

Nicholas of Cusa in the fifteenth century personified the spirit of the Renaissance that was to influence deeply the Enlightenment view. In *De Pace Fidei* (still a great title for a book on the subject!), Nicholas wrote that behind all the differences of religious practice there is a harmony of all religions, one universal religion on which all can agree. Nicholas' study, of course, was limited to the three historically-linked monotheistic traditions of Judaism, Christianity and Islam. And Jews and Muslims might well dissent from his view that the one true religion necessarily involves the doctrines of the Incarnation, the Trinity and the Mass.[72] But his search for a universal religion became a dominant theme of English Deism and Continental Rationalism (the Enlightenment), as exemplified in the seventeenth century writings of Herbert of Cherbury.[73] These notions would play a crucial role in the development of the concept of religious pluralism and separation of Church and state, attitudes unknown in the ancient and medieval worlds. And they would, in turn, influence deeply the twentieth century missionary approaches of many "mainline" Protestant denominations and also, through the mediation of John Courtney Murray, the framers of the Second Vatican Council's documents on religious liberty, non-Christians, and the Church's missionary activity (*Ad Gentes*).[74]

In the twentieth century, with the emergence of anti-colonialism in the so-called "third world," Protestant and Catholic missionaries began to re-evaluate the extent to which Western cultural traditions had been intermingled with the presentation of the Gospel. Leadership of local churches was increasingly handed over to an indigenous clergy, and a new look was taken of the positive religious as well as cultural values of non-Christian traditions. The search for a "universal" base-religion was progressively abandoned in favor of an appreciation for the entrenched and seeming permanent diversity of human religiosity. Christian missionaries continue to proclaim the good news as devoutly as before, but now with a new sense of dialogical understanding and a capacity to listen.[75] Mission theory today is beginning to take seriously the fact that Christianity has much *to learn* from other faith-traditions as well as to share with them, matters that are of significant religious (perhaps even salvific) value.

While Christianity in the last few decades has seen a resurgence of interest in evangelism and missionary outreach, this activity is taking place in the context of a different set of theological questions and options concerning other religions. These newer models have not yet coalesced into the emergence of a consenus on how to relate to other religions such as characterized previous ages. But the direction of greater openness and respect is clear, and the possibilities virtually limitless.[76]

## B. Contemporary Understanding of Mission

### *1. The Second Vatican Council*

In the light of the historically diverse experience of Christians sketched above, and of the relative newness of many of the fundamental questions being raised, it is perhaps natural that mission theology today has become such a highly controversial field of inquiry.

The teaching of the Second Vatican Council, as Gregory Baum has shown, can serve as a paradigm for this situation, since its various documents tend to presuppose quite distinct approaches to the theory of the Church's mission. While these are not necessarily incompatible, and while the documents take each other into account, at least by way of reference, there is little attempt to reconcile the underlying theories.[77]

Drawing on the universality of God's call in Christ to all humanity, the Decree on the Missionary Activity of the Church (*Ad Gentes*) sees the Church as "missionary by its very nature" (n. 2), and as "the universal sacrament of salvation" (n. 1; cf. *Lumen Gentium,* n. 48). Taking a decidedly scriptural approach, the decree posits "the essential reason for missionary activity" on God's "loving design, centered in Christ to give history its fulfillment by resuming everything in him (Eph 1:9–11)." Thus it asserts: "It is God's plan that the whole body of men which makes up the human race should form one people of God and be joined in one body of Christ."[78]

In this universal and eschatological perspective, all other religious claims became relative and temporary. In other religions there may be found "treasures (that) a bountiful God has distributed among the nations of the earth" (n. 11). "But whatever truth and grace are to be found among the nations, as a sort of secret presence of God, this (missionary) activity frees from all taint of evil and restores to Christ its maker. . . . And so, whatever good is found to be sown in the hearts and minds of men, or in the rites and cultures peculiar to various peoples, is not lost (but) healed, enabled and perfected for glory of God" (n. 9).

This vision, of course, draws its source in the fulfillment perspective of the Church Fathers. Since Christ's death and resurrection are universal in scope, divine grace is operative in the whole of humanity and salvation is offered to people wherever they are (nn. 2 and 5). But this same universal grace destines all peoples to the "full" enjoyment of God's presence, which is to be found only in the Christian Church.

Other documents of the Council project a different vision. The Declaration on Religious Freedom, *Dignitatis Humanae,* reflects the appreciation for religious pluralism in the world, not merely as a fact that must be tolerated, but as a divinely given reality.[79] Underlying (and in some tension with) even this, of course, is the significant modification made by the Council in the natural law theory.[80] Natural law theory, because of the dignity it accorded to human reason's capacity to discern universal truth (as in biblical wisdom literature), was itself on the more positive pole of attitudes toward non-Christian traditions as opposed to the demonic view of them. Though limited, reason (as in the case of the Greek philosophers) could attain to valuable religious insights. The Council, however, attempted to draw together the categories of "grace" and "nature" into a more unified vision. Charles Curran comments:

> The Pastoral Constitution on the Church marks a decisive turning point in the understanding of natural law and tries to integrate the natural law more fully into the whole schema of salvation history. Both in explicit words and in theory the document generally avoids understanding the natural as a relatively autonomous order unaffected by sin and grace. The first three chapters of Part One of the Constitution illustrate the newer methodological approach which tries to integrate the reality of the natural or the order of creation into the total Christian perspective.[81]

If such a perspective is applied to the question of religious pluralism, other religions can be seen as being dispensations of divine grace. Their existence can be viewed positively, not grudgingly, as a part of God's overall plan of salvation. Even Karl Rahner's theory of the "anonymous Christian" (itself an extension of the ancient fulfillment theory) is thus leading to question the notion of conversion of persons of other faith traditions to the Church.[82] For Rahner, as for *Dignitatis Humanae,*[83] faith is communal in its expression; the gift of grace is social as well as personal. Faith is mediated through the socio-cultural community of which the person is a part. For this reason, *Dignitatis Humanae* sees religious freedom as the right (as the search for religious truth is the duty) not just of individuals, but of religious communities as such:

> The freedom from coercion in matters religious which is the endowment of persons as individuals is also to be recognized as their right when they act in community. . . . Religious bodies have the right not to be hindered either by legal measures or by administrative action on the part of government . . . in their public teaching and witness to their faith (n. 4).

*Dignitatis Humanae*'s support of religious liberty is as absolute and universally applicable as the missionary call of *Ad Gentes*. While the two documents refer to and affirm each other, the question that is posed by their juxtaposition is not resolved: if Judaism and the world religions are valid dispensations of grace in any real sense, how can they be seen as provisional? Is religious pluralism something to be merely tolerated or is it, in itself, "a sign of God's manifold and inexhaustible richness?"[84]

Two other conciliar views, both more easily seen as compatible with *Dignitatis Humanae* than with *Ad Gentes,* also need mention here. The Declaration on Non-Christian Religions, *Nostra Aetate,* proposed that the Church's mission is to enter into dialogue with them,[85] for the sake of fostering spiritual values crucial to humanity as a whole (another universal vision, of course). The Constitution on the Church in the Modern World, on the other hand, seems to understand the mission of the Church as centrally a mission of service (*diakonia*), which is not merely a humanitarian effort but a preparation for the coming of God's kingdom on earth and thus a properly redemptive activity in response to God's call. Focusing on the kingdom of universal peace and justice raises the question of whether attempts to convert others will aid the development of harmony within humanity or lead to interreligious tensions that can harm the Church's basic mission to promote the establishment of God's kingdom of universal justice and peace on earth.

On the practical level, such questions seem to be working themselves out in more or less amicable fashion within bodies such as the Vatican Curia and the World Council of Churches, since both views have such solid biblical and traditional support behind them. The level of theory, however, is another question.[86]

*2. Evangelii Nuntiandi*

The *textus classicus* for contemporary Roman Catholic missionary activity is Pope Paul VI's moving Apostolic Exhortation, "On Evangelization in the Modern World."[87] (Cf., on this, the article by McGarry in this volume.) In it, Paul VI attempted to reconcile the service (*diakonia*) and proclamation (*kerygma*) models of the Church's mission. *Evangelii Nuntiandi* proclaims the primary importance of the "witness of life," to which "all Christians are called."[88] This is a witness of service in and to the world community. But without the *kerygma,* the proclamation of preaching and catechesis, this "wordless witness" given by all Christians "always remains insufficient" since "there is no true evangelization if the name, the teaching, the life, the promises, the kingdom and the mystery of Jesus of Nazareth, the Son of God are not proclaimed" (n. 22).

Yet, as in *Ad Gentes,* this latter and necessary form of Christian mission is not seen as co-terminous with the mission of the Church as such. The mission of proclamation is not something to which *all* Christians are called, as they are to witness, by the very fact of being Christian. Special training and commissioning are requisites for this second, "explicit" type of proclamation: "At every new phase of human history, the Church, constantly gripped by the desire to evangelize, has but one preoccupation: whom to send to proclaim the mystery of Jesus?" (n. 22).

In its treatment of non-Christian religions, *Evangelii Nuntiandi* adheres to the fulfillment theory. Citing from the Fathers, it acknowledges that the world religions "are all impregnated with innumerable 'seeds of the Word' and can constitute a true 'preparation for the Gospel.' "[89] One might, however, question the applicability of patristic insights to religions of which the Fathers were ignorant or which, like Islam, are certainly monotheistic and not at all "idolatrous" or "pagan" in any sense, developed *after* the patristic period. The same section clearly articulates the fulfillment approach:

> Even in the face of *natural religious expressions* most worthy of esteem, the Church finds support in the fact that the religion of Jesus . . . objectively places man in relation with the plan of God, with his action; it thus causes an encounter with the mystery of divine paternity that bends

> over toward humanity. In other words, our religion effectively establishes with God an authentic and living relationship which the other religions do not succeed in doing, even though they have, as it were, their arms stretched out toward heaven (n. 53; emphasis added).

Yet how can one interpret this notion of "natural religious expressions" when, as seen above, we are no longer so sure of where the boundary between "nature" and "grace" lies? This question becomes particularly acute with reference to the Jewish people. Judaism is (on indisputable and acknowledged biblical testimony) *not* a "natural religious expression," but a people of God called into being by God. The Jewish people is already (again, indisputably) "objectively" placed, as a people, "in relation with the plan of God, with his living presence and with his action." That relation may be a problematic one to us Christians (cf. the treatment of Romans 9—11, above) but it is definitely real and objective. *Evangelii Nuntiandi* does not resolve the question of mission to the Jews because it does not take up the mystery of the continuing existence of Judaism in faithful observance of the Sinai covenant.

### *3. The Challenge of Modern Christianity's Mission to the Jews*

How, then, does the question of Christian mission to the Jews fit in with the larger questions of the Church's overall relationship with other world religions? In one sense it fits quite well. To the extent that the Church, in practice and theory, stresses the *diakonia* side of its mission and adheres to the strict limitations on the *kerygma* implicit in the notion of religious liberty, specific "missions" to "evangelize" the Jews will be severely limited or ruled out. But Judaism, as the only religious community whose religious history Christianity must claim as its own, poses a unique set of dilemmas for the universalistic view not posed by other traditions. Jesus was, after all, a practicing Jew, not a Buddhist or even a Muslim. And, Christians affirm, he did not just "happen to be" Jewish. Jesus, in the Christian understanding of the divine plan, could *only* have been Jewish.

The concept of a Christian mission *to* the Jews is challenged today, then, by a growing Christian appreciation of the continuing role the Jewish people are called to play in God's plan. A recent statement of the American Conference of Catholic Bishops has posited this challenge as a basic element of contemporary Christian theological investigation.

> There is here a task incumbent on theologians, as yet hardly begun, to explore the continuing relationship of the Jewish people with God and

> their spiritual bonds with the New Covenant and the fulfillment of God's plan for both Church and Synagogue. To revere only the ancient Jewish patriarchs and prophets is not enough.[90]

The urgency of such theological inquiry, and the absolute necessity for dialogue with Jews as a necessary pre-condition to the re-evaluation of the Church's understanding of its unique relationship with the Jewish people, has been repeatedly stressed in the Catholic community by Pope John Paul II and local episcopal hierarchies.[91] Many of these official documents, Protestant as well as Catholic, are startling in the clarity they shed on the ancient ambiguities described in this chapter. They represent a clear and irreversible line of development that must be taken into account in any future discussion of the mission question.[92]

While many of the questions Christians ask in this area, such as how to relate the uniqueness of Christian-Jewish relations with the universal mandate to witness to the Gospels, remain unresolved, certain key factors are becoming more clear. In his address to the Jewish community of West Germany in November 1980, for example, Pope John Paul II unequivocally affirmed the continuing validity of the Jewish covenant, calling the Jews "the people of God of the old covenant never retracted by God" and "today's people of the covenant concluded with Moses." In his address, the Pope stressed dialogue as the proper Christian stance toward the Jews and proposed a *common* witness of the Church and the Jewish people to the world, a proclamation which, significantly, could include Islam as well.

> In all this it is not only a question of correcting a false religious view of the Jewish people which caused, in part, the misunderstandings and persecution in the course of history, but above all a question of the dialogue between the two religions which—with Islam—can give the world the belief in the one ineffable God who speaks to us and which, representing the entire world, wish to serve him.[93]

The Pope also joined the central mission of the Church to the continuing vocation of the Jewish people, referring to the "holy duty" to which Jews and Christians are called, as sons of Abraham, to "be a blessing for the world (Gn 12:2)." Mission, with relation to the Jews, is thus a joint venture in the light of the divine mandate to prepare the way for the kingdom of God. "They (Jews and Christians) engage themselves jointly to work for peace and justice among all men and people and in the fullness and profundity that God himself has disposed for us."[94] Again, it is not clear how the Pope would relate this teaching to the notion of a universal proclamation of the good news "to all the nations" (*goyim*), since he does not attempt to do so. But it is clear that the latter, general mandate cannot be understood without the biblical and theological particularities of the former with reference to the Jews. A recent resolution passed by the Synod of the Protestant Church of the Rhineland poses the issue even more strikingly:

> We believe in the permanent election of the Jewish people as the people of God and realize that through Jesus Christ the Church is taken into the covenant of God with his people. . . . We believe that in their calling Jews and Christians are always witnesses of God in the presence of the world and before each other. Therefore, we are convinced that the Church may not express its witness toward the Jewish people as it does its mission to the peoples of the world.[95]

Rolf Rendtorff of the University of Heidelberg comments:

> This declaration contains a quite clear and consistent argument. . . . It stresses the common basis of the Jewish and Christian faith. It speaks of the addition of the Gentiles to the people of God without annulling the election of the Jewish people and therefore shows the impossibility of a Christian mission to the Jews.[96]

Rendtorff's conclusion, of course, is not shared by all Protestants[97] or Catholics. A 1967 report of a study group of the World Council of Churches, the "Bristol Paper," noted that the group became divided "when the question was raised of the theological identity of Israel with the Jewish people of today" (an identity affirmed in all of the Roman Catholic documents cited above). Of great interest is the way in which the report drew out the consequences of differing ecclesiological models for witness toward Jews:

> If the main emphasis is put on the concept of the Church as the body of Christ, the Jewish people are seen as being outside. The Christian attitude to them is considered to be in principle the same as to men of other faiths, and the mission of the Church is to bring them, either individually or corporately, to the acceptance of Christ, so that they become members of this body. . . . If, on the other hand, the Church is primarily seen as the people of God, it is possible to regard the Church and the Jewish people together as forming the one people of God, separated from one

> another for the time being, yet with the promise that they will ultimately become one. Those who follow this line of thinking would say that the Church should consider her attitude toward the Jews theologically and in principle as being different from the attitude she has to all other men who do not believe in Christ. It should be thought of more in terms of ecumenical engagement in order to heal the breach than of missionary witness in which she hopes for conversion.[98]

The question of mission thus interrelates with a large number of other core theological questions facing the Church today and cannot finally be resolved without recourse to those areas. On the other hand, these other questions are equally in need of the perspectives and insights developed from the Christian-Jewish dialogue.[99]

Perhaps the best study of the question to date is given in Tommaso Federici's "Study Outline on the Mission and Witness of the Church."[100] In it, Federici follows the reasoning of *Dignitatis Humanae* concerning religious liberty to reject

> every form of unwarranted proselytism . . . every kind of testimony and teaching that in any way becomes a physical, moral, psychological or cultural constraint on the Jews, as individuals or as a community, that could in any way destroy or even diminish personal judgment, free will, full autonomy to decide. . . . The temptation to create organizations of any kind, especially for education or social assistance, to "convert" Jews, is to be rejected.[101]

The principles governing witness which Federici explicates in this section (II) pertain, of course, equally to all religious communities which Christians may encounter, as would the emphasis he places on the primacy of the witness of service in fulfilling "the biblical precept of mission to the peoples of the earth" (Section I) and "the will of the Church" to dialogue "with other Christian Churches, or the adorers of the God of Abraham (Jews and Muslims), or with the followers of other world religions and—with the necessary distinctions—even with atheists."[102]

Federici mentions, again on the general level only, the "knotty problem" raised by Paul VI in his discourse on the opening of the 1974 Synod of Bishops: "How can we reconcile respect of persons and civilizations and sincere dialogue with them . . . with the universalism of the mission Christ entrusted to the Church?"[103] Federici's own vision of mission *as* service and *as* dialogue, I believe, hints at certain ways of resolving the dilemma that can profitably be pursued today. And it is not irrelevent to note that the Church has always existed with fundamental, even paradoxical tensions at the core of its teachings (e.g., immanence and transcendence, the "already here" and the "not yet" of eschatology, or the mystery of the Incarnation itself). So Christians are not without ample precedent in facing such irreconcilables honestly, as Paul VI did.

All of the above principles and even dilemmas which Federici adduces in his paper, then, are equally pertinent (though perhaps to differing degrees) to the Church's encounter with world religions in general. But throughout his article, both in the biblical and the historical sections, Federici has also raised the uniqueness of the continuing Jewish faith witness from the Christian point of view in the light of salvation history. He returns to this theme in his conclusion, which can also serve as a conclusion for the present study:

> The central intuitions of other religious faiths may in their turn enrich the Christian, offering him fresh possibilities of expression, arousing in him valencies and potentialities that were formerly latent. But this can come about still more in contact with the Jewish tradition and its exegetical, liturgical and mystical treasures, its religious and philosophical thought. If this is true of other religions in relationship with Christians, how much more is it with the Jewish religion, to which Christians are and remain united by so many unbreakable ties.[104]

Federici's rabbinically poignant "how much more" is pregnant with possibilities for the future of Jewish-Christian relations. Frankly, neither he nor the historical survey offered in this chapter has adequately resolved all the many complexities that attend the superficially simple concept of Christian mission, whether to the nations or to the Jews. But perhaps some light has been shed here on why the Protestant Synod of the Rhineland felt compelled to proclaim "that the Church may not express its witness toward the Jewish people as it does its mission to the peoples of the world."

## NOTES

1. Many dictionaries of the Bible, for example, do not even have a listing for "mission" as such.

2. "This term has given rise to much discussion in recent years, because of its many analogous meanings. In the Scriptures 'mission' signifies the sending by God of a person for the purpose of communicating His will to other persons. . . . In

a generic sense, mission connotes a sending of persons with authority to preach in accordance with the text, 'But how shall they preach unless they are sent?' (Rom 10:15). In a more restricted sense, 'mission' has more frequently been limited to apostolic action in non-Christian regions. . . . This usage is principally juridical, and it occasions difficulties and misunderstanding today, due to the development of ecclesiastical organization in the mission regions" (*New Catholic Encyclopedia* IX, 1967, 904).

3. The point of the story is universalist: "Should I not be concerned over Nineveh, the great city, in which there are more than a hundred twenty thousand persons who cannot distinguish their right hand from their left?" (Jon 4:11).

4. On the development of the understanding of universal witness in Jewish tradition, see the relevant articles in this volume, and Helga Croner, Leon Klenicki eds., *Issues in the Jewish-Christian Dialogue: Jewish Perspectives on Covenant Mission and Witness,* Stimulus Book (New York: Paulist Press, 1979).

5. See also Ps 19:5; Jer 1:9–10; 2:3; 3:17; Zech 8:2–23; Zeph 3:19; Jl 4.

6. "Pagan" is here understood in a generic sense, as the equivalent of biblical (rather than the later, derogatory) *goyim.*

7. H. R. Schlette, *Towards a Theology of Religions* (New York: Herder & Herder, 1966) pp. 25f. Owen C. Thomas, ed., *Attitudes Toward Other Religions* (New York: Harper and Row, 1969) pp. 12f.

8. E.g., 1 Kgs 11:1–13; Jer 2:26–29; 10:1–16; Bar 6:7–72; Is 40:18–20; 44:9–20; 46:6–7; Wis 13:1—14:20; 15:6–19; 1 Mc 1:41–64; 2 Mc 4:1–11; Dn 14; and in various psalms.

9. P. Rossano, "A Roman Catholic Perspective," in G. Anderson, T. Stransky, eds., *Christ's Lordship and Religious Pluralism* (Maryknoll: Orbis, 1981) pp. 103–106. Orthodox theologian Georges Khodr takes a related approach in "The Economy of the Holy Spirit," in G. Anderson, T. Stransky, eds. *Mission Trends No. 5: Faith Meets Faith* (New York: Paulist Press, 1981) pp. 36–49.

10. P. Rossano, *op. cit.,* pp. 105f. One might also note that God can speak through non-Jewish prophets, such as Balaam.

11. Note the escalation and absolutization of the language in Matthew's more polemically-inspired version (Mt 8:10–12). Luke, of course, is attempting to justify here his argument for a mission to the Gentiles, as he does throughout his Gospel and Acts.

12. H. R. Schlette, *op. cit.,* p. 26. As examples, he gives Gn 6—9; Acts 4:8–17; 17:16–32.

13. On this, see Krister Stendahl, *Paul Among Jews and Gentiles* (Philadelphia: Fortress Press, 1976); E. P. Sanders, *Paul and Palestinian Judaism* (Philadelphia: Fortress, 1977); Gerald Sloyan, *Is Christ the End of the Law*? (Philadelphia: Westminster, 1978); also John Koenig; *Jews and Christians in Dialogue* (Philadelphia: Westminster, 1979).

14. Paul regularly approaches Jews first: Acts 13:14; 14:1; 16:13; 17:10, 17; 18:4, 19; 19:8; 28:17, seemingly on principle: Acts 3:26; 13:46; Rom 1:16; 2:9–10.

15. Krister Stendahl, "Notes for Three Bible Studies," in G. Anderson, T. Stransky, eds., *Christ's Lordship and Religious Pluralism,* 7f.

16. *Ibid.,* p. 13. But see also "An Evangelical Conviction" on the same passage, by Waldon Scott in the same volume, pp. 58–74.

17. As reflected most spectacularly in John's stereotypical and at times polemic usage of the phrase *hoi Ioudaioi.*

18. On Samaritans, see M. Gaster, *The Samaritans* (London, 1925); J. MacDonald, *The Theology of the Samaritans* (Philadelphia: Westminster Press, 1964); S. J. Miller, *The Samaritan Molad Mosheh* (New York: Philosophical Library, 1943); J. A. Montgomery, *The Samaritans* (New York: Ktav, 1968[2]).

19. Gerald Sloyan, "The Healing of Division from the North: Jesus and '*Hoi Ioudaioi,*'" unpublished paper presented at the Annual Meeting of the Chesapeake Bay Section of the SBL/CBA on May 3, 1981.

20. Stendahl notes the importance of the distinction between Jesus' mission and that of the Church: "It remains a fact worth pondering that Jesus had preached the Kingdom, while the Church preached Jesus. And thus we are faced with a danger: we may so preach Jesus that we lose the vision of the Kingdom, the mended creation": *op. cit.,* p. 10.

21. E.g. *ibid.,* p. 9. Stendahl noted Acts 3:20, where Jesus has been "designated" as Messiah but has not yet come *as* Messiah.

22. E.g. J. Douglas, ed., *Let the Earth Hear His Voice* (Minneapolis: World, 1975), and W. Scott, "In No Other Name," in *Christ's Lordship and Religious Pluralism,* pp. 58–95.

23. Carl E. Braaten, "The Uniqueness and Universality of Jesus Christ," in *Mission Trends No. 5,* pp. 79–81. Braaten cites 1 Cor 15:22, Col 1:19–20, Eph 1:9–10, Phil 2:10–11, 1 Cor 15:28, and 1 Jn 2:2 in this context.

24. Rosemary Ruether, *Faith and Fratricide: The Theological Roots of Anti-Semitism* (New York: Seabury, 1974). For various responses to Ruether's dramatically-posed theses, see John Oesterreicher, *The Anatomy of Contempt* (South Orange: Seton Hall, 1975); Samuel Sandmel, *Anti-Semitism in the New Testament?* (Philadelphia: Fortress Press, 1978); and most recently, the collection of reactions by twelve Christian scholars in Alan T. Davies, ed., *Anti-Semitism and the Foundations of Christianity* (New York: Paulist Press, 1979).

25. See, among others, Edward Flannery, *The Anguish of the Jews* (New York: Macmillan, 1965), and Frederic Schweitzer, *A History of the Jews* (New York: Macmillan, 1971).

26. John Koenig, *op. cit.,* p. 78.

27. See note 13 above. E. P. Sanders' point that the law (Torah) was never taken in Judaism, biblical or rabbinic, to be a vehicle for "justification" in Paul's sense is also of importance for the understanding of the discussion in Galatians; cf. *op. cit.,* pp. 183–233, 419–430, 447–557.

28. John Koenig, *op. cit.,* p. 56.

29. Krister Stendahl, in *Christ's Lordship and Religious Pluralism,* p. 18.

30. Quoted in H. van Straelen, *The Catholic Encounter with World Religions* (New York: Newman Press, 1966), p. 120.

31. *Ibid.*

32. For taxonomies of contemporary theories, see L. Newbigin, "The Gospel among the Religious," in *Mission Trends No. 5,* pp. 5–10; Owen C. Thomas, *op. cit.,* pp. 15–28; H. R. Schlette, *op. cit.,* pp. 27–40. Most modern theories, from the "evangelical" approach of the 1974 Lausanne Conference to the more "liberal" approach of the Rahner/Kueng school, ultimately go back to these two patristic mainstreams, though with a certain refinement of expression.

33. Clement of Alexandria, *Stromateis,* I, 5. See O. C. Thomas, *op. cit.,* p. 16.

34. Justin Martyr, *First Apology,* 5.

35. See L. Newbigin, *loc. cit.,* p. 6.

36. Hence the great battles that were waged in various periods over the question of how far to go in "accommodating" Christianity to indigenous religious practices.

37. H. R. Schlette, *op. cit.,* p. 29. See, e.g., Karl Barth, *Church Dogmatics* I, 2, 17; and *ibid., The Doctrine of Reconciliation* I, 60, 3.

38. Cited in W. Scott, *loc. cit.,* p. 59.

39. Cf. Samuel Sandmel, *Philo of Alexandria* (Oxford University Press, 1979).

40. Justin Martyr, *First Apology,* 46; *Second Apology,* 10.

41. H. R. Schlette, *op. cit.,* pp. 29f.

42. Karl Rahner, *Theological Investigations* (London: Darton, Longman & Todd, 1966), V, pp. 115–134.

43. Rosemary Ruether, *op. cit.,* p. 124.

44. Origen, *Contra Celsum,* 7.18 (tr. Chadwick).

45. Julian, *Against the Galileans* 253b, 238b, 320b (tr. Wright).

46. Recent archaeological excavations of Jewish and Christian catacombs in Italy have illustrated the sense of communal affinity and peaceful relations that prevailed between Jews and Christians in this period.

47. John Chrysostom, *Homilies on the Judaizers* 1.5, 1.6 (tr. Wilken).

48. "On no detail of Judaeo-Christian relations did the option of Roman officialdom in favor of Christianity work more openly to the disadvantage of Judaism than on the question of conversion from one faith to the other": Edward A. Synan, *The Popes and the Jews in the Middle Ages* (New York: Macmillan, 1965) p. 23.

49. *Ibid.,* pp. 24–29.

49a. The documents in R. Chazan, *Church, State and Jew in the Middle Ages* (Behrman House, 1980) illustrate this development. Cf. esp. pp. 15–52 and 167–276.

50. Pope John Paul II has repeatedly emphasized this theme of the spiritual bond between the Jewish and Christian communities which connects them, he has stated, "at the very level of their respective religious identities" (NC News, March 15, 1979). In a critically significant statement in November 1979, the Pope in three

different ways stressed the continuing validity of the Jewish covenant on its own terms, addressing the Jews as "the people of God of the old covenant *never retracted by God*" (NC News, November 20, 1980; italics added). For a commentary on this papal talk see John Roach, "A Renewed Vision of Catholic-Jewish Relations," in *Origins* (May 7, 1981) 751f.

51. *Codex Iustinianum* 1, 9, 14, 11, 62 (tr. Synan, *op. cit.,* p. 30). For later examples, cf. R. Chazan, *op. cit.*

52. *New Catholic Encyclopedia* IX, 1967, 932. On this period, see also J. Muldoon, *Popes, Lawyers and Infidels: The Church and the Non-Christian World, 1250–1550* (Philadelphia: University of Pennsylvania Press, 1979).

53. Thomas Aquinas, *Summa Contra Gentiles* I, 2 §3.

54. *New Catholic Encyclopedia* IX, 933.

55. Quoted in R. L. Wilken, "The Making of a Phrase," in *Dialog* 12 (Summer 1973) 174.

56. H. R. Schlette, *op. cit.,* p. 14.

57. *Ibid.,* pp. 13–21, nicely summarizes the theological implications. See also Pius IX's *Singulari Quadam* (D. 1647) and the response of the Holy Office to Archbishop Cushing of Boston (1949), specifically rejecting L. Feeney's attempt to interpret *extra Ecclesiam* exclusively, in *American Ecclesiastical Review* 77 (1952) 307–311.

58. Edward A. Synan, *op. cit.,* pp. 66–82. Other preachers, such as Peter the Venerable, Abbot of Cluny, however, were instrumental in whipping up anti-Jewish sentiments that led to the massacres.

59. Owen C. Thomas, *op. cit.*

60. Edward A. Synan, *op. cit.,* pp. 39–43.

61. *Constitutio pro Iudaeis,* Innocent III, 1199; *ibid.,* 229–232. The question of forced baptism of Jews and Muslims (*infideles*), and of their children against their parents' will, became a fundamental one in the development of the concept of sacramental validity in Roman Catholic tradition. Benedict XIV, the "scholars' Pope," devoted no less than three encyclicals to the issue: *Inter omnigenas* (1744, addressed to Catholics living under the Turks in Serbia), *Postremo mense* (1747) and *Probe te meminisse* (1751). This illustrates the significance of the mission question for other areas of Christian thought, such as ecclesiology and sacramental theology. See John A. Gurrieri, "Sacramental Validity: The Origins and Use of a Vocabulary," in *The Jurist* XLI (Washington: Catholic University, 1981) 54f.

62. *Constitutio pro Iudaeis,* 217.

63. *Ibid.,* 49.

64. As Synan, among others, has shown, much of the Christian legislation against Jews in this regard was adapted from earlier Muslim attempts to convert both Christians and Jews living in Muslim societies by the none too subtle means of rigorously imposed economic and social sanctions of second class citizenship. See Edward Synan, *op. cit.,* p. 54.

65. *Ibid.,* p. 59.

66. *Ibid.,* p. 19.

67. *Ibid.,* p. 226. So, too, the medieval *Constitutio pro Iudaeis:* "Although in many ways the disbelief of the Jews must be reproved, since nevertheless through them our own faith is truly proved, they must not be oppressed grievously by the faithful, as the prophet says, 'Do not slay them, lest these be forgetful of Thy Law,' as if he were saying more openly: Do not wipe out the Jews completely, lest perhaps Christians might be able to forget Thy Law, which the former, although not understanding it, present in their books to those who understand it" (230–232).

68. Owen C. Thomas, *op. cit.,* p. 15. Contemporary arguments concerning the necessity of a mission to the Jews based on the "universality" of the Christian proclamation, such as "The Thailand Report on Christian Witness to the Jewish People" (Lausanne Committee for World Evangelization, Occasional Papers, No. 7, June 1980), may thus, in the final analysis, be largely irrelevant to the far more trenchant and complex realities that must be considered in any adequate theology of Christian-Jewish relations.

69. *New Catholic Encyclopedia,* IX, 931.

70. *Ibid.,* 932.

71. *Institutes of the Christian Religion,* I, 3–4.

72. Owen C. Thomas, *op cit.,* p. 18.

73. *Ibid.,* pp. 29–48.

74. See Walter M. Abbott, ed., *The Documents of Vatican II* (New York: Guild-America Press, 1966).

75. An excellent example of this newer form of Christianity relating to other religions can be found in the extensive handbook, *Religions: Fundamental Themes for a Dialogical Understanding,* produced by the Vatican Secretariat for Non-Christians (Rome: Editrice Ancora, 1970).

76. The modern missionary movement has already had the unforeseen effect of providing a tremendous impetus for the ecumenical movement, the search for Christian unity. As missionaries of various denominations tripped over each other in foreign lands, all with slightly different versions of "the Gospel," it soon became apparent that internal Christian disunity posed the greatest immediate threat to evangelization. The practical necessity for a unified proclamation of the Gospel thus became a major factor in the foundation of the World Council of Churches.

77. See Gregory Baum, "Rethinking the Church's Mission after Auschwitz," in E. Fleischner, ed., *Auschwitz: Beginning of a New Era?* (New York: Ktav, 1977), 115–117.

78. Translation in Walter Abbott, ed., *op. cit.,* p. 581. All subsequent conciliar citations are from this edition.

79. On the conciliar notion of religious freedom, see Franco Biffi, "The Right to Religious Liberty," in *SIDIC* 13 (1980) no. 3, 4–9.

80. See the essays by John T. Pawlikowski and J. Bryan Hehis, in Eugene Fisher and Daniel Polish, eds., *The Formation of Social Policy in the Catholic and Jewish Traditions* (University of Notre Dame, 1980) pp. 162–192 and 109–122.

81. C. Curran, *Catholic Moral Theology in Dialogue* (University of Notre Dame, 1976), pp. 125f.

82. Karl Rahner, *Das Christentum und die nichtchristlichen Religionen* (Cologne: Benziger, 1962).

83. Franco Biffi, *loc. cit.,* p. 7.

84. Gregory Baum, *loc. cit.,* p. 123.

85. The dialogical stance is also reflected in the *Constitution on the Church,* n. 16, and the *Constitution on the Church in the Modern World,* n. 22.

86. Here, as Baum suggests, may be a case where *praxis* will ultimately "force" the development of new theory.

87. *Evangelii Nuntiandi,* December 8, 1975 (Washington, D.C.: USCC Publications, 1976).

88. *Ibid.,* n. 21.

89. *Ibid.,* n. 53. The notes cite Justin, Clement of Alexandria and Eusebius.

90. "Statement on Catholic-Jewish Relations by the U. S. National Conference of Catholic Bishops," November 20, 1975. Protestant and Catholic scholars alike are increasingly questioning the propriety, on theological grounds, of efforts to convert Jews, e.g. Reinhold Niebuhr, Franklin Littell, Alice and Roy Eckardt, John Pawlikowski, Eva Fleischner, Rolf Rendtorff, Monika Hellwig, Rosemary Ruether, Krister Stendahl, Paul van Buren, John Oesterreicher, J. Coert Rylaarsdam, Clemens Thoma, and Gregory Baum. Some, like Baum, see historical as well as theological reasons: "After Auschwitz the Christian Churches no longer wish to convert the Jews. While they may not be sure of the theological grounds that dispense them from this mission, the churches have become aware that asking the Jews to become Christians is a spiritual way of blotting them out of existence and thus only reinforces the effects of the Holocaust. . . . After Auschwitz and the participation of the nations, it is the Christian world that is in need of conversion" (loc. cit., p. 113).

91. For texts of these documents, Protestant as well as Catholic, which are vital to the reassessment of the missiological question, see Helga Croner, ed., *Stepping Stones to Further Jewish-Christian Relations* (New York/London: Stimulus Books, 1977); John Sheerin and John Hotchkin, eds., *John Paul II: Addresses and Homilies on Ecumenism, 1978–1980* (USCC Publications, 1980), pp. 16–21, 27, 41, 121, 131, 150–153; M. T. Hoch and B. Dupuy, eds., *Les Eglises devant le Judaisme: Documents Officiels 1948–1978* (Paris: Les Editions du Cerf, 1980).

92. For commentary on the documents, see Michael McGarry, *Christology after Auschwitz* (New York: Paulist Press, 1979), pp. 13–55; Leonard Swidler, "Catholic Statements on Jews—A Revolution in Progress," in *Judaism* (Summer 1978) 299–307. On the current state of theological dialogue and on the question of covenant, see John T. Pawlikowski, *What Are They Saying About Christian-Jewish Relations?* (New York: Paulist Press, 1980), pp. 33–68.

93. In John Sheerin and John Hotchkin, eds., *op. cit.,* p. 152. For commentary, see John Roach, *loc. cit.,* pp. 751f.

94. John Sheerin and John Hotchkin, eds., *op. cit.,* p. 153.

95. *Current Dialogue* (Winter 1980/81) 1, World Council of Churches, Geneva.

96. Rolf Rendtorf, "The Effect of the Holocaust on Christian Mission to the Jews," in SIDIC 14 (1981) no. 1, p. 24.

97. A recent example of the conversionary approach questioned in this paper can be found in "Christian Witness to the Jewish People" by the Lausanne Committee for World Evangelization. Unfortunately, the statement is marred by its negative and at times misleading descriptions of the nature of Judaism (as in its rather confused treatment of the Law, p. 15), its uncritical endorsement of questionable proselytizing tactics, such as "Messianic Jewish Congregations" (p. 11), and the fact that only a single page is given to establishing the necessary theoretical foundation for its quite elaborate program. On more solid grounds, see A. H. Baumann's defense of the mission to the Jews, "Judenmission—gestern und heute," in *Evangelische Mission* (Jahrbuch 1977) 17–39.

98. Quoted in Helga Croner, ed., *op. cit.,* p. 81. The centrality of the people of God concept in Vatican II indicates, I believe, the direction of contemporary Roman Catholic thought.

99. See especially Clemens Thoma, *A Christian Theology of Judaism,* Stimulus Book (New York: Paulist Press, 1980); also Franz Mussner, *Traktat ueber die Juden* (Munich: Koesel, 1979).

100. "Documentation," SIDIC 11 (1978) no. 3, pp. 25–34.

101. *Ibid.,* p. 32. Federici notes that this rejection is in conformance with the agreed statement of the Joint Working Group between the World Council of Churches and the Roman Catholic Church, of May 1, 1970, "Common Witness and Proselytism," designed to regulate "proselytism among Christian Churches," 5 SIDIC (1971/II) no. 14, pp. 14–24.

102. Federici, *loc. cit.,* p. 33. Note the "inner to outer" stages of this list which proceeds from those perceived closest to the Church outward "even" to atheists. This theory of concentric circles, which in some measure flows from the patristic "fulfillment" theory, has had strong influence in contemporary Catholic missiological thought.

103. *Ibid.*

104. *Ibid.,* p. 34. For narratives of the spiritual journey of both Protestant and Catholic missions to the Jews in this century, see R. M. Healey, "From Conversion to Dialogue: Protestant American Mission to the Jews in the 19th and 20th Centuries," and C. Klein, "From Conversion to Dialogue—The Sisters of Sion and the Jews," both in *Journal of Ecumenical Studies* (Summer 1981) 375–400.

# The Mission of Israel: A Theologico-Historical Analysis

*Martin A. Cohen*

## I. THE NATURE OF MISSION

The word "mission" comprehends consummation, conduit and content. It suggests the entelechy that moves all created entities. Upon inanimates at creation's base mission is totally imposed, but every upward step in the animate world expands the creature's involvement. Plants respond reflexively to proximate stimuli; animals react instinctually over an extended range, while humans, individually or clustered, can plan through reason, if not always rationally, for distant ends. The increased volitional and rational involvement in the higher species correspondingly trellises their mission scenes with luxuriant diversification. Yet, at the same time, no will or reason can appreciably alter the given contours of any being's contextual circumstance.

All missions possess a history. They are initiated, launched and directed in time. They leave records of success and frustration. Their combined experience shapes our knowledge of universal history from geology to biology to human events.

Though present in the most rudimentary existence, mission is conceivable only in life's highest. If lower species can somehow communicate their purposes, only the descendants of humanoids can promulgate them through verbalization. Such expression inevitably reflects a world-view, or, as it may uninvidiously be called, a myth. By their very nature the formulations of mission constitute the myth's most cogent apology, arguing its desirability, necessity and often supernal ordination.

Human missions vary greatly. Some are accommodative, others exclusive; some are particular, others universal; some are ephemeral and others perduring. Through all missions there pulses a drive for survival, expansion and dissemination. Given the complexity of human existence, every individual simultaneously participates in various missions and these inevitably conflict. The conflict is resolved by acts of will, whereby individuals and groups, logically speaking, first hierarchize their missions and then blithely underimplement or overlook all subordinate variations. To grasp human history requires a distinction between mission formulations and their implementation, that is, between professed hierarchies of mission ideals and the real hierarchies inferable from action.

Despite the creative role of human initiative, metaphysicians irrepressibly ask the telling question: Is mission range, however broad, ultimately determined by the same teleological tug that dominates lower existence and patently establishes the perimeters of all higher life? Could it be, as Tennyson says, that "through the ages one increasing purpose runs," a purpose progressively discernible as the "thoughts of men are widened with the process of the suns"?[1]

All exclusive missions necessarily respond in the affirmative. Such missions rest upon premises which they regard to be universal and supportive. Around them they weave their myths and upon them they erect their apologies. All are inevitably highly complex, with manifold strands for differential responses to the diverse stimuli of life. All are deeply imprinted with context and experience.

Human missions are all strongly rooted in the life of the world—even if they are religious—and so are their expressions. The determining coordinates of every mission are human and, in most instances, societal. These coordinates include axiology, geography, history (or the social sciences in general), theology (or meta-history in whatever form) and utopianism, especially in missions that are more complex. Involving a conceptualized response to the first three coordinates, the last two of these coordinates proceed to shape subsequent perceptions. To understand any mission an analysis of every pertinent coordinate is essential.

The historical dimension merits an additional word. All too frequently overlooked by students of religion, it provides the indispensable soil for the planting and growth of ideas. History presents a canvas of constant change and challenge, in which no concept of mission or, for that matter, any other idea ever enjoys a total and exclusive primacy in any group. Indeed, the real, as differentiated from the professed, mission hierarchies of any group invariably fall along a broad spectrum of possibilities. In the case of the faith-people Israel, the real mission spectrum usually reveals four nodal types: (1) assimilationists, who wish to "pass over" to the larger surrounding culture, or, as tradition puts it "to be like all the nations"; (2) survivalists, who accept the primacy of the surrounding culture but, for a variety of reasons, seek a distinctive place for some measure of their inherited identity; (3) visionaries, who seek to actualize an idealized perception of their heritage, usually around major themes consonant with the myths of their surrounding cultures; (4) retentionists, who seek to dike their inherited identity against the novelties of their ambiance and excessive proselytic ingress; (5) synthesists, who seek to preserve maximally the spirit and theology of their inherited traditions in forms responding to the crises of novelty.

Of these groups the visionaries necessarily reveal the greatest creativity. Their world-views, and, within them, their theologies of mission, usually, if they run their course, develop into three stages. These stages are chronologically successive and thereafter co-existent. They may be respectively called imminent utopianism, advocating immediate change; expectant utopianism, calling for proximate realization; and channeled utopianism, anticipating eventual fulfillment while concentrating on current stability. The move toward channeled utopianism is necessarily accompanied by the stabilization of the articulating sub-group and the development of its own group of retentionists.

The point is that at all times, even in perceived stability, history, theology and therefore the conception of mission are in flux. We must bear this in mind as we study the Jewish mission.

## II. THE STUDY OF MISSION IN JUDAISM

Human missions may be studied from three perspectives: internal, oppositional and external. Though permitting variations, each of these is precisely bounded. Out of spatial considerations, we must eliminate an analysis of the oppositional perspective on the Jewish mission and concentrate on the other two.

Our vantage point will stand outside of Judaism, in a structure developed from the so-called "scientific method" as utilized in the contemporary social sciences. The remonstrances of many of its practitioners notwithstanding, the "scientific method," or, more correctly, the methodogical clans related through their common secularism, rationalism and empiricism, is ultimately no more objective than any other. Like all other thought constellations, it rests upon assumptive foundations and superstructures, whose validity is establishable only through *petitio principi*. Besides, every approach, "scientific" or otherwise, even if claiming total detachment, can be linked to apologetic ends. For our purposes, the scientific method possesses a dual advantage. On the one hand it is generally accepted as objective in at least the practical realms of modern thought and is therefore eminently suited for broad communicability. On the other, the frequent application of the scientific method to the depreciation of theological concepts and religion in general makes a corrective application to their support all the more desirable.[2]

Without violence to the canons of the scientific method, our analysis of the Jewish mission from without will be avowedly apologetic. It will argue the presence throughout history of an ineluctable destiny, essential to the world and imposed upon the faith-people Israel by historically analyzable forces that form a stunning pattern. Simultaneously it will trace Israel's conceptions of its task and observe the dichotomies between their articulations and implementation.

The very notion of a determined mission stirs queasiness in the religious innocents who in the face of all contrary evidence harbor the delusion of total personal freedom. Even more, it terrorizes timorous Jews of marginal faith who fear that a focus on Jewish mission will reveal a distinctiveness which they would as lief hide behind the reassuring anonymity of their general societies.

Without purpose or mission Judaism is as incomprehensible as it is without any of its other distinctively nuanced theological coordinates. These include a God, Torah, providence, creation, revelation (*Torah min ha-Shamayim*),[3] election, covenant, Israel the faith-people (*K'lal Israel*), the land Israel (*Eretz Israel*), diaspora (*Galut*), reward and punishment, ingathering (*Kibbutz Galuyyot*), messiah (with messianic era), immortality and resurrection. The popular contemporary theological reduction of Judaism to some amorphous platitudes about God and equivalently unprovocative selections from the rest of its theology derive from the assimilative erosions of the general environment in which Jews have lived since the advent of the modern world.

Not only are the categories of Jewish religious thought manifold and distinctive. They are not always connotatively co-terminous with their counterparts in other religions, nor are they always equivalently prioritized. In addition, some cardinal concepts of Judaism, like *K'lal Israel* and *Eretz Israel,* have no counterpart in other faiths, especially Christianity, against whose background much of modern Jewish thought has developed. Judaism traditionally knows of no dichotomy between the secular and the sacred. The compulsion of its thinking into the categories of the secular and the sacred in the modern world has often led to grotesque distortion. It is interesting to note the de-emphasis of the traditional distinction between the holy and the profane by Jewish theologians who have adopted the categories of secular and sacred.

It is axiomatic that exclusive positions entail exclusive missions. Judaism is an exclusive faith. All monotheisms necessarily are, even though, like Judaism, they may be respectful of others and cognizant of the universal accessibility—or inaccessibility—of the mountain peak of truth. But like others, including Christianity and Islam, Judaism can rely only on its own canons to measure its own and others' upward climb.

To analyze the Jewish mission and its conceptualizations, it is instructive to divide Jewish history into two major epochs separated by the cataclysmic *Hurban ha-Bayit,* or destruction of the Temple in the year 70 C.E. The two epochs may be called respectively the formative epoch, in which the faith-people Israel was prepared for its mission, and the probative epoch, in which this mission in its fullness has been exercised and witnessed.

The formative epoch, both scientifically and traditionally within Judaism, begins with the Exodus and the subsequent theophany at Sinai. Its deeper roots, of course, hark back to the dawn of Mesopotamian civilization, and its proto-history to the Patriarchs, whose etiological accounts were somehow early, perhaps at the time of the United Monarchy, incorporated into biblical tradition.

For our purposes, this epoch may be subdivided into four segments: (1) Exodus (with Sinai) and Conquest (ca. 1280—ca. 1000 B.C.E.); thereafter the epicenter of Israel's life is rooted in the land Israel; (2) Monarchy, United and Divided (ca. 1000—586 B.C.E.); (3) Exile and Theocracy (586—168 B.C.E.); and (4) Hasmonean Revolution and Second Commonwealth (168 B.C.E.—70 C.E.).

The probative period begins with the *Hurban,* and what merits denomination as the "second theophany" at Jamnia (Yavneh). Here, too, a division into four segments is useful: (1) the *Hurban* (with Yavneh) and the normalization of Judaism; therefore the epicenter of Israel's life shifts to the *Galut*; (2) the pre-modern world (70—1945), characterized by the legal position of Jews as a special caste on the margin of every society of their domicile and internally by the quasi-autonomous status of Jewish communities under Talmudic law, or, in more modern times, the psychological residue of this status past; (3) the modern world (sixteenth century to date), characterized within Judaism by the process known as the Emancipation; this process involved the grant of full civic equality to Jews under national constitutions in return for their acquiescence to the dissolution of their quasi-autonomous status; (4) the infelicitously named post-modern world, characterized within Judaism by rapid identity reorientation. The terms "pre-modern," "modern" and "post-modern" are taken from a European perspective. The term "modern" refers to the spread within Europe of rationalism, secularism, capitalism, nationalism and other forms that describe a major transformation in its total life. Rising from an earlier dawn, this change spread gradually from West to East from the sixteenth to the twentieth centuries. Since Jews were dispersed throughout Europe during this time, they entered the modern world at different periods. Hence the chronological overlap above in the pre-modern and modern categories. The fact that during these centuries most Jews lived in Eastern Europe means that the majority of the Jews entered the modern world relatively late. The "post-modern" world is characterized by a disillusionment with the promise of modernity, an alienation from the world it created, a despair of its transforming agents and a frantic groping for the meaning of existence in the immediate, the personal and the mystical. Often mistakenly regarded as having begun with the end of World War II and the Holocaust in 1945, its origins hark back to a point no later than the Congress of Vienna in 1815. It developed as the underside of modernity from the many individuals disillusioned with enlightenment, nationalism, socialism and other utopian solutions to the problems of humanity, and, within the faith-people Israel, the identity of the Jew.

In each of these epochs the presence of the mission will be reconstructed by a consideration of the determining coordinates mentioned above. The consideration in each epoch will focus on two broad periods: the regnancy of that epoch's classical expression of mission and the ensuing transition.

## III. THE FORMATIVE EPOCH OF THE JEWISH MISSION

Axiologically, the determinant in the formative epoch was the wilderness ethic. This is the name we give to the Israelites' value system which was conceived in the darkness of Egypt and manifested in Israel's birth at Sinai. Like all other axiologies visceral rather than cerebral, the wilderness ethic, despite eddies of deviation, distortion and contradiction, has bestowed life and perspective upon the institutions, laws, customs and practices of all subsequent Judaism. Reconstructible from its manifestations, the fundamental dimensions of its organic whole may, though not without the deflection inevitable in intellectualization, be analytically articulated as follows:

1. The Ultimate Unity of Being
2. The Intrinsic Purposefulness of Existence
3. The Pervasive Sanctity of Life
4. The Fundamental Centrality of Humanity
5. The Innate Goodness of Individuals
6. The Essential Equality of People
7. The Inherent Perfectibility of Society
8. The Ennobling Duty of Creativity
9. The Sublime Altruism of Compassion

Singly, to be sure, none of these aspects is intrinsically or exclusively Jewish. Every one surfaces with intensity in diverse places and times. Yet the organic harmony of these dimensions can be cogently defended. So too can the equivalence of their organic whole to what the Bible calls *daat elohim,* meaning literally "knowledge of God," but contextually unmistakably denoting affective rather than cognitive knowledge. The Isaianic prediction that at the end of days "the knowledge of the Lord will cover the earth as the waters cover the sea" foresees the welling not of philosophical disquisition but of the spiritual elixir that produces humility, righteousness and love, all sheaved by holiness.[4]

The wilderness ethic lends itself to an explanation as the Hebrews' affective compensation for the Egyptian bondage. It reveals both a determination to live and a trust in an ultimately supportive universe. The forms of its pristine, wilderness embodiment were spare and austere as befitted a nomadic people.

Geographically, the determinant was the thrust of the Exodus. Over its direction the Hebrews could exercise little control. With inland Egypt to the west and south and elsewhere the sea, the Hebrews' only viable route lay toward the Sinai wilderness and thereafter the Holy Land. Located at the heart of the cradle of Western if not pan-terrestrial civilization known as the Fertile Crescent, the Holy Land Israel also forms the only natural bridge between Asia and Africa and the critical overland passageway to Europe. Militarily defenseless against large powers, the Land Israel has been lusted after by every leading nation in world history and has consequently been independent only during deadlocks between the world's primary powers. Once established on this land, the Hebrews were irremediably subjected to its special nature. The Land Israel uniquely exposed the faith-people Israel to the continuous threat or reality of subjugation and bred within it a systemic insecurity. This insecurity made for sensitivity, acuity and restless creativity. It also gave ever newer meaning to the Exodus and insured the survival of the wilderness ethic as the marrow of its myth. The Land Israel also afforded the faith-people Israel continuous contact with the world's latest knowledge and techniques. This turned Israel into a skilled and learned people relying on knowledge and service rather than brute force for its survival.

Historically, the determinant was the nature of Israel's survival. Israel's protohistory evolved at the culmination of the Fertile Crescent's hitherto greatest millennia of change and churning. Its cradle history, from the Exodus to the Exile, took place in the noontide of the first great imperial efforts at full hegemony over the Fertile Crescent. In both periods the descendants of Abraham were extraordinarily positioned to witness the kaleidoscopic appearance and disappearance of polities large and petty, and with them the identity of their peoples and the power of their gods. Yet through the Götterdämmerung of all these states, small Israel, further reduced to the Kingdom of Judah, survived—with its identity and with its God. This experience drove home a twofold lesson: that Israel, as Balaam had said, was "a people that dwells apart, not reckoned among the nations" (Num 23:9) and that its destiny depended not on its might but on forces, or rather a force, beyond its control. Israel was indeed an anomaly.

Theologically, the determinant was Israel's reflection on its experience. Fundamental to this reflection was its conviction of a covenant with its God Yahweh, consummated at Sinai, but viewed retrospectively as commencing with Abraham when the God was known as El Shaddai and ultimately, beyond, to the dawn of humanity. This covenant guaranteed Israel's well-being in return for its performance of Yahweh's covenantally expressed will, or, to put it more precisely within our frame, the fulfillment of its mission.

Although without certain record until its overwhelming reinforcement during the United Monarchy, a cardinal insight of Israel's may well have been present in its earliest history: that Israel's deity was not, like others, an ordinary, parochial god, but rather the universal God who controlled all nations. A corollary naturally emerged: Israel was the covenant people not of one god among many but of the only true God among all. This God had therefore chosen Israel for his covenant from among all the peoples of the earth. Adumbrated by the prophet Amos in the middle of the eighth century, this understanding was more clearly enunciated by Exodus 19:5–6, whose present redaction was roughly contemporary. Described here as God's treasured people, Israel is promised the opportunity to be God's "kingdom of priests and a holy people."

Election and mission are always the obverse and reverse of the same coin. Israel's insight into its election therefore automatically raised three fundamental questions related to its mission: What was the purpose of Israel's choice? On what basis was it chosen? What was its message to be? The answers to these questions received their classical formulation in the words of the literary prophets of Judah, especially Ezekiel and Deutero-Isaiah, whose lives spanned much if not all of the Babylonian exile.

These prophets univocally declare that the goal in Israel's mission was to glorify Yahweh's name throughout the world through his acknowledgment as universal God by all its peoples. "Turn unto me and gain success, all the ends of earth: For I am God, and there is none else. . . . To me every knee shall bend, every tongue swear loyalty" (Is 45:22f).[5]

No less emphatically the prophets declare that the choice of Israel was not a reward for distinction, but an act of grace. For reasons beyond inquiry, Yahweh selected Israel at its birth and therefore before any possible accrual of merit. On the contrary, its condition was lowly. It was a mixed-breed foundling, born of an Amorite father and Hittite mother, and still wallowing in its natal blood (Ez 16). At this time, perhaps even before, Yahweh had chosen her and infused her with his spirit.[6] The purpose of the election was for Israel to be God's servant[7] and, above all, his witness.[8] The imagery of Israel's witness is taken from the court of law, where Yahweh is pictured confidently challenging other gods to produce their witnesses.[9] It was for this mission that Yahweh tenderly nurtured Israel (the unmistakable reference is to the wilderness period). Though he chastised her repeatedly, he protected her against annihilation.[10]

The content of Israel's mission was to provide an example of holiness.[11] Holiness meant a separation, not physically but spiritually. This separation was to be attained by witness rather than missionizing, that is, by the performance of the totality of Yahweh's commandments, ethical, legal and ceremonial, through which the wilderness ethic was concretized. In this way Israel was to be a priest people, "a covenant people, a light to the nations" (Is 42:6, 49:6–8). Quietly, humbly, without cry, bluster or hurt, caring not to quench even a dimly burning wick, Israel was to "teach the true way to the nations," through the resonance of her deeds. In this way it was to bring to the far-off coastlands the example of Yahweh's teaching (or as the Hebrew says, *torah*) "until he has set the right on the earth" (Is 42:1–4).[12] Israel was to strengthen itself for this mission by preparing "to bring back Jacob" to God "that Israel may be restored to him" (Is 49:5), by opening the eyes of the benighted in their midst, and extricating their prisoners—doubtless psychologically as well as physically—from their fetters (Is 42:7; 49:9).

The goal of universal recognition in no way made of Yahweh an international God. Though the God of all the world, Yahweh was simultaneously only the God of the people Israel.[13] The recognition of Yahweh by others implied that they "take hold of every Jew by a corner of his cloak and say, 'Let us go with you, for we have heard that God is with you' " (Zech 8:23). Such recognition in a modern sense does not imply conversion.

That this lofty mission was not in effect zealously pursued by the faith-people Israel every minute of its days is hardly surprising. With its stark honesty the Bible records Israel's propensity to backsliding. It does so not to reveal Israel's extraordinary sinfulness but the paradigmatic human frailty of its people. Of this its noblest spirits were sensitively aware. Like its individual prophets, Israel as God's servant-prophet complained about the difficulties of its task (Is 49:4). The Bible records that some within Israel were prepared to risk their ideal for the fleshpots of Egypt or the sensuousness in Canaan, others to sacrifice toward these ends all but a sliver of their identity, and still others to preserve the expressed forms of their identity with an atavistic inflexibility.

Yet, notwithstanding Israel's similarity as individuals to all other peoples, the fate of corporate Israel was to be different. Israel's loneliness and insecurity militated against its full assimilation to the ways of its surrounding nations. On the contrary it kept ever alive, usually in the form of opposition parties, the defenders of the wilderness ethic and the austere simplicity of its ways.[14] Though some moved in that direction, no government in Israel was ever able to establish an oppressive regime, no assimilative group was ever able to root its way of life, and no retentive group was ever able to withstand the onslaughts of external change. Only those prepared to redefine Israel's role by tempering doctrinaire ideals with inherited tradition by applying the wilderness ethic to the changing externalia of life enabled Israel spiritually, theologically and physically to survive.

When first articulated, the prophetic expression of Israel's mission was imminently utopian. Israel would now be everlastingly vindicated. Yahweh "has redeemed Jacob" and "has glorified himself through Israel," acting through King Cyrus "for the sake of my servant Jacob, Israel my chosen one" (Is 44:23; 45:4).[15] The ingathering from the entire diaspora would now take place. Jerusalem and Judah would be rebuilt, Israel would expand. Its children would be served by kings and nursed by queens (Is 49:23).[16]

The continuing Utopian strain powerfully reappeared in the prophecies of Zechariah and particularly Haggai, who declared that Yahweh would shake the nations and bring them with all their precious substance to Jerusalem's new Temple, whose foundations had just been laid (Hag 2:6ff). Ultimately the mission was substantially channeled into the theocracy, and, within it, the supreme text of all subsequent Jewish life, the Torah, then redacted in essentially its classical form. With its canonization, the Torah became the permanent residence of the wilderness ethic, the place of regular resort for the word of God.

Beginning with Ezra and Nehemiah the theocracy, encouraged by Persia for its own political ends, was strongly retentionist, manifesting this position by a trenchant particularism. Yet at the same time the universalists continued to encourage proselytism. Following the earlier Trito-Isaiah's belief in the full equality with Judeans of "the foreigner . . . who has attached himself to the Lord" (Is 56:3), they expressed their position through the Book of Ruth, which carried a universalistic message so powerful that it contradicted an explicit Deuteronomic injunction (Dt 23:4–7). Its point was to derive the ancestry of none other than King David from a woman of the despised Moabites and thereby argue for the full admission to Israel of all sincere converts, whatever their origin.

Around the same time, late in the post-exilic period, the Book of Jonah, similarly concerned, offers the first instance of a Hebrew prophet commissioned to a non-Jewish people. Even if a fictional character, Jonah symbolizes the basally involuntary and determined aspect of Israel's mission.

The great Utopian determinant, as distinguished from all others in this epoch, derived from the progressive coordination of the Western world through Greek conquest, Hellenistic culture and, incipiently at least, Roman administration, with the influence of all far transcending their political boundaries. The rampage of these changes profoundly transformed the life of the Near East. It shifted the tonality of the Near Eastern world from rural to urban, uprooted countless people and imperiously battered at traditional myths and missions.

Its effect on Judaism was pervasive. Its novelty activated an entire spectrum of response, including a proliferation of imminent utopianism. A reconstruction of the unenduring positions is not necessary here. Ultimately emerging from this luxuriance was the channeled utopianism of the Pharisees, whose tonally urban *mitzva* system, derived from the Torah, vied with mystery cults and other syntheses to provide the individual otherwise potentially disoriented in this world with a sure hope of salvation in a world beyond.[17]

For the faith-people Israel as an entirety, the *mitzva* system emphasized the utopian mission. It envisioned the advent of a Messiah for a world under God, with Zion exalted, the exiles ingathered and the dead resurrected.

This ultimately centrist Pharisaic position was not universally accepted. Its eventual broad support notwithstanding, the centrist Pharisees were bitterly opposed by significantly supported Sadducees, as well as in their own way by Essenes and other groups. The centrist Pharisees themselves manifested continual internal struggle in the diverse adjustments of their utopian position to the realities of external stimuli.

Thus as the Pharisees attained stability, their more sharply defined political divisions included particularists and universalists. The particularists de-emphasized the active mission, while the eventually dominant universalists pursued it so fervently as to elicit a grudging admiration from the evangelist Matthew (23:15).

Under the Pharisees, the faith of Israel became cosmopolitan. It was they who made the tetragrammaton ineffable and called Yahweh by the euphemism Adonay ("My Lord" or simply "Lord" or, by extension "God"). It was their positional descendants who called the individual servant of Yahweh, whether Judean or not, by the name Israel.[18]

By the end of the first century C.E. the Pharisees had converted significant numbers of non-Jews throughout the Western world to Israel's faith. Jewish communities, including proselytes, could be found in many places from the Euphrates Valley westward throughout the Roman world. The Jews of Egypt alone numbered a million. With nearly seven million, the Jews formed ten percent of the total population of the Roman Empire. The size of the Jewish population was further augmented by "God fearers" who were on the road to proselytization.

If the Pharisees nurtured the hope of eventually converting the entire Roman Empire, it was not an arrant delusion. Who knows what continued successes they might have enjoyed if the Empire's stability had continued. The Pharisaic utopia sank with the Empire's decline, and with these events a new epoch dawned in the history of the Jewish mission. Interestingly, it was Christianity, derived from Pharisaic Judaism and regarding itself as the true Israel, which eventually swept the Roman Empire through its pursuit of a utopian inner kingdom rooted otherwise in the wilderness ethic.

## IV. THE PROBATIVE EPOCH OF THE JEWISH MISSION

The critical event inaugurating the new or probative epoch of the Jewish mission was the *Hurban ha-Bayit* (destruction of the Temple in 70 C.E.).

This destruction was emblematic of a crescendoing malaise throughout the Roman Empire. The *Hurban* shattered Israel's general optimism and drove it into a deep despair. Its restabilization was achieved by the Hillelite Pharisees. The Hillelites reinvigorated Israel with the spirit of the wilderness ethic prismed through their classical expression of the *mitzva* system.[19]

During this epoch active proselytization by Jews has been prohibited or discouraged. While even under the strictest prohibitions there have been significant conversions into Judaism, it was obvious by the time of the First Nicaean Council's injunctions that proselytization was not to be the way for Israel to fulfill its mission.

In this epoch the axiological determinant in Jewish life has been the Torah. After the destruction, the scrolls of the Torah replaced the Temple as the principal cynosure of Jewish life and the element most responsible for Jewish survival.

Under the Pharisees and the Hillelites the concept of Torah extended beyond the Pentateuch to embrace first the entire Bible, then its application to the changing circumstances of Jewish experience, then to the record of this "oral tradition" and ultimately to all worthy knowledge.

In this sense the Torah was regarded as the constitution of the universe and therefore, contrary to appearances, a transcendentally perfect text. On the surface, the Torah comprised temporally sequenced accounts; beneath, it was atemporal "without earlier and later."[20] So too it appeared flawed, with omissions, contradictions and superfluities; but these constituted intentional cables of meaning containing guidance for all possible contingencies of human experience. Stored in the Torah text therefore were all the correct concepts, laws and practices that would be conceived in the future, "even what a devoted student would expound before his teacher."[21] The Torah pre-existed the universe and served as its pattern, or, as the rabbis said, "the vessel by which the world was created."[22] The Torah was therefore all miracles, according to Moses Nahmanides (1194–1270).[23] As Judaism's sacred tradition well understood, this vessel's sanctity derived from the precious elixir it contained. This elixir is what we have called the wilderness ethic. To retain its immaculateness, the tradition's sages have often diverged from the Torah text and occasionally contradicted it. The second century sage, Rabbi Joshua ben Karha, even declared that "whoever studies the Torah and revises it not is like a sower who reaps not."[24] And the modern sage, Joseph Baer Soloveitchik (1820–1892), commenting on the blessing that follows the liturgical reading of the Torah, essentially agreed. In the blessing the words "who gave us the Torah of truth" mean, he says, that we have been entrusted with the elucidation of the truth that resides within the Torah, while the words "and planted within us eternal life" also have reference to the Torah, which like a plant grows through endless renewal.[25]

Until the modern world Jews universally regarded the Torah as God's will, whose fulfillment automatically evoked his benign response. In the modern world, this view has continued to prevail in many Jewish circles, despite the often unspoken skepticism that has shattered its universality. As its center, the Torah has been the widest read and most influential text in Jewish life. It has provided the inspiration for endless ethical, philosophical and belletristic creativity.

In the probative period the geographical determinant has been the *Galut*.

With the *Hurban* the Jews became a tonally wandering people. They have not chosen this destiny. On the contrary, wherever Jews have gone, they have struck for rootedness. They have diligently, at times even desperately, sought to integrate into their new societies as rapidly and maximally as possible. Where permitted they have quickly acculturated, and in some instances even adopted customs and ideas at great variance with their tradition. In many places, including the Land Israel, Jews have remained rooted for centuries. And yet, few have been the Jews insensitive to the celerity with which uprootedness could come. Throughout this period, secure or not, all Jews have been potential wanderers, even if, like the prophet Jonah, they have ingeniously sought to conceal their identity.

Invariably the societies Jews have left under the imminence or presence of compulsion have been in the throes of decline or dissolution, while those who have invited them have been new or in the process of renewal.

Nor has the wandering Jew wandered aimlessly. On the contrary the epicenter of Jewish life, measured by the combination of population, wealth and culture, has traced a remarkable line. It has closely followed the developmental pattern of Western civilization. At all times the major Jewish community has been located at the most advanced center of this civilization or close enough to be but one stage away. From the Land Israel it passed to Babylonia and then Western Europe, where it bifurcated into Iberian-Sephardic and Franco-German-Ashkenazic components. The Sephardic center then moved to the Ottoman Empire, where it shared that area's decline, while the Ashkenazic center proceeded toward Eastern Europe, where it remained rooted until the Holocaust. Thereafter Judaism's major center has been located in North America. Throughout Jewish history, subordinate centers, as measured by our canon, made vital contributions to the totality of Jewish life. Today, the State of Israel, because of its traditional centrality in Judaism, contributes disproportionately to Jewish culture and identity.

As a result of their migratory direction, the Jews of the probative period, like the ancient Israelites, have been exposed to the widest horizons of communication, the latest winds of knowledge, the greatest challenges of opportunity, and, not least, the throbbing pangs of an unremitting insecurity.

It is no fortuity that the direction of Jewish wandering has been further conditioned by compatible desires for survival on the part of the Jews and the establishments of their inviting societies.

The wandering Jews have sought an opportunity to survive as Jews with dignity. And their new hosts have needed the Jews for the development of their societies. For this purpose these societies have always been prepared to grant Jews significant privileges in order to encourage their sacrificial labor for the establishment's greater gain. As a result, prominent Jews often enjoyed *de facto* a status equivalent to that of the middle or even high nobility. The notion that Jews have always suffered in every country of their sojourn is incorrect. It stands to reason that they would not have entered and could not long have remained under those circumstances. Even a cursory review of Jewish history reveals that in most lands the years of relative tranquility and superior position enjoyed by Jews have at least equaled those of their degradation and persecution.

The historical determinant in the probative period has been the Jews' ineluctable marginality. In every society of their wandering Jews have constituted a caste with diversely shaped but carefully monitored contours. Rankling though it is to Jews in modern polities who serve with undiluted loyalty and reciprocally expect unqualified integration, the Jews' caste status remains as much a reality today as it was in the pre-modern world, where the clashing religious orientations of their host societies necessitated the grant of permission for them to live quasi-autonomously under Talmudic law.

The caste status of the Jews has developed out of the psychological impact of a unique combination of theological and sociological factors. Theologically, Jews have been isolated by the accumulation of farragoes of hostile texts in both Christianity and Islam. Sociologically, Jews have been spotlighted by their high status and positions of visibility. These have been imposed upon them by the establishment, which has regularly compelled them to implement its oppressive policies. As a result of these factors, the hostility of the disaffected has, with the expected statistical variations, perennially and ubiquitously been directed against the Jews.

Though obviously not without empirical foundation, anti-Jewish feeling possesses a basic mythical dimension. Although the desirable dilation on this point is impossible here, suffice it to say that being Jewish is not an absolute prerequisite for the attraction of anti-Jewish passion. In many societies non-Jews similarly located and envied have been regarded and treated as Jews. Out of such people some societies, particularly in the modern world, have inflated Jews' numbers and power, in some cases in communities where few or no Jews lived.

The establishment in every host society has controlled the extent of Jewish immigration. With the cunning of its position, though not necessarily with malice or conspiracy, it has also determined the range of its Jews' social absorption, economic endeavor and political function.

It has decided how many and what types of Jews would be afforded access to the higher rungs of society, and how many the opportunity to "pass over," and in both categories at what speed and price. It has determined the channels of the Jews' primary economic endeavors (additionally, of course, permitting the involvement of many Jews in support services). Invariably these have entailed greater knowledge than was otherwise abundantly available and greater risk than enough non-Jews were prepared to assume.

Above all, it has decided the political use to which Jews have been put. This use has always depended upon the relative stability or instability of its society, but in either case the primary political function of the Jews has always been to shield the establishment. Utterly dependent upon the establishment's upper echelons, Jews have had no alternative but to accept their fate, or leave for another society where it would be identical.

In relatively stable times, the establishment has utilized its Jews to serve as a wedge against the ambitions of lower echelons of authority and power. Because of the Jews' skills and threatlessness, the establishment could confidently entrust them with responsibilities which, if given instead to other elements of leadership, might menacingly enhance their position. Naturally, lower elements of the leadership—both lay and ecclesiastical—were, visceral attitudes aside, politically opposed to the Jews and did their utmost to stir popular emotions by appeals to theology and sociology. However, in stable times the establishment, for its own interest, has regularly protected the Jews.

In unstable times, however, the same establishment has just as regularly assumed the direction of the popular passions against the Jews in attempts to deflect the natural flow of disaffection into revolutionary behavior. In desperation, when the only alternative was its own demise, the establishment has never scrupled to sacrifice the Jews through persecution, banishment and destruction.[26]

A distinction must be made between the ever-present antipathy to the Jews and its cerebral direction for political ends. The visceral reaction to Jews is best called anti-Jewishness; its cerebral direction is appropriately called antisemitism.

Far from being an incidental excrescence on the periphery of Western civilization, antisemitism has been its most chronic and corrupting disease. It has feverishly flared in direct proportion to the oppression, exploitation, inequality and despiritualization in a society. And it subsides only in direct proportion to the alleviation of these conditions. In every society the degree of antisemitism is thus a faithful barometer of the relative absence or presence of the wilderness ethic. This recognition was already articulated by the great Iberian poet and philosopher, Judah Halevi (1070?–1141), who referred to the faith-people Israel as "the heart of the nations."[27]

Antisemitism and mission are inextricably coupled. Antisemitism is the perversion of mission. The perversion results from a classic case of projection. The mission of Israel entails the effort by an intensely human people, frail and foible-prone like all others, to end all enslavement by enhancing life through actualization, compassion and holiness. Antisemitism inevitably aims to enslave the minds and bodies not only of Jews but of countless others through the pernicious myths of master-faith, master-nation or master-race.

Yet never has antisemitism succeeded in destroying the Jews or saving the guilty society. All such societies have been destroyed, though in modern times one has been quickly revived with outside help, while the faith-people Israel, though beaten, bruised and battered, has like the phoenix revived from its ashes to continue its amazing trek.

The exploitation of antisemitism is always a threat as long as anti-Jewishness exists to any degree. And in Western civilization and in its cultural satellite system which in a practical sense encircles the earth anti-Jewishness will exist as long as there are individuals in any way benighted and oppressed. From this there derives the stunning realization that only in a world suffused with the wilderness ethic can the Jew, as one among equals, rest secure. The mission of Israel is thus inseparable from anyone recognized as a Jew.

The theological determinant in the probative epoch has been Israel's reflection on the *Galut*. Conditioned internally by the other coordinates, this reflection has been further prodded by the Christian explanation of the *Galut* as punishment for Israel's sins. Even though Israel could not accept the Christian claim of its rejection of the Messiah as one of these sins, the principle of the *Galut* as punishment is to be found as early as the Sybilline Oracles.[28] It has reverberated throughout the tradition and has found liturgical expression in the Festival *Mussaf* service.[29]

Yet, for all this, the *Galut* was regarded melioratively by Fourth Ezra[30] as a necessary bridge for the attainment of the good, and by Philo[31] and Josephus[32] as natural and even desirable. And despite its lachrymose strain, the tradition has also revealed the positive aspect in the mission. It has continued passively to anticipate the messianic age, with its universal acceptance of God and Israel's compensatory vindication. Repeatedly expressed throughout this epoch in commentaries and sermons, this goal is representatively evidenced in three aspects of Judaism's liturgy. The first is found in the theology implicit in the *haftarot,* the prophetic portions selected by the rabbis to accompany the fixed cycle of liturgical Torah readings. Here, for example, the Torah portion of holiness (Lev 19:1–20:27) has Amos 9:7–15 (now certainly understood universalistically, regardless of its possibly different pristine meaning) in the Ashkenazic ritual, and the familiar "for the sake of his name" section in Ezekiel 20:2–20 in the Sephardic, while for creation (Gen 1:1–6:8), the *haftara* is the mission in Isaiah 42:5–21 (Sephardic), or to 43:11 (Ashkenazic), taken to mean nothing short of the completion or perfection of the world. The second, the prayer *'Alenu*, known as The Adoration, actually uses the words "To complete the world in the kingdom of the Almighty," in its expression of the messianic goal. Originally a Rosh Hashanah prayer and now recited daily, the *'Alenu* is grounded in Isaiah 45:23. In a similar vein the kabbalists in sixteenth and seventeenth century Safed spoke of the "completion of the world" (*tikkun olam* or simply *tikkun*) as the process involving the assembly of all the sparks of holiness strewn among the imperfections of life.[33] The third is the characteristic High Holy Day prayer, *U'vkhen Ten Pahdekha* ("And Now Set Your Awe"), which prays to God: "May all Your works come to revere You and all Your creatures bow before You, and all form a single band to do Your will with perfect heart."[34] This theme is reflected in the Rosh Hashanah hymn *Vayeetayu*, dating from the Byzantine period and expressing the hope that "all the nations shall come to serve You and proclaim Your glorious name."[35]

So too this epoch explained Israel's election traditionally but within the context of the *Galut*. The explanations univocally point up both Israel's divine instrumentality and representative humanity. The mainstream of tradition places Israel's election before the creation as an act of God's grace[36] and makes the *Galut* the necessary bridge linking it to the ultimate redemption.[37] Israel's wanderings and suffering, the tradition holds, have refined[38] her by teaching her humility,[39] fortifying her against assimilative blandishments,[40] and thus strengthening her bond with God.[41] Israel's dispersion has also helped her mission in three dramatic ways: It enabled Israel to spread God's name "like a flask of perfume."[42] It permitted Israel to survive elsewhere in the world when any of her components was destroyed.[43] And it gave the faith-people Israel greater opportunity "for their numbers to be increased by converts."[44] The sages also saw the *Galut* as a prerequisite for the ultimate redemption.[45]

Above all, the tradition emphasizes Israel's role as witness. The rabbinic sages call attention to the connection between the affirmation of faith in Dt 6:4 ("Hear, O Israel, the Lord is our God, the Lord is one") and the theology of witness. They note that in the traditional Hebrew text the last letter (*'ayin*) of the first word in this declaration ("Shem*a*"—Hear) and the last letter (*daleth*) of the last word ("Eha*d*"—One) are traditionally written or printed larger and that these two letters together spell the Hebrew word for witness.[46] They also explain the words "You are my witnesses, says the Lord" in Is 43:12 to mean "that when you are my witnesses, I am God, and when you are not my witnesses, I am not God."[47] For the tradition the supreme witness of God's unity and purpose, or, as tradition puts it, "to the sanctification of the Name of God," is martyrdom. So strong is this tradition that the thirteenth century *Book of the Pious* promises the righteous who have given their lives "for the sake of God's Name" a greater post-terrestrial recompense than the fully righteous fortunate enough to live in less demanding times.[48]

No less did this entire epoch emphasize the exemplification of Torah as the basis for Israel's mission. No theme in the entire literature of Judaism's sacred tradition is treated with such frequency and thoroughness. The third century Talmudic sage, Rav Ulla, said that the purpose of the Babylonian diaspora was to enable Israel "to eat dates (i.e. to have the leisure afforded by Babylonia's plentous resources) and to devote itself to the Torah."[49] Through Torah Israel was to be a holy nation. The tradition leaves no doubt that holiness derives from the observance of the totality of the commandments, ethical, legal and ceremonial,[50] obviously as these were understood in any given age, for in no age, certainly after the *Hurban ha-Bayit,* could all the commandments be observed. And to judge from Rabbi Simlai's (third century C.E.) resolution of the essence of all the commandments to Amos' "Seek ye me and live" (5:4) or Habakkuk's "The righteous shall live by his faithfulness" (2:4)[51] as well as from other passages urging an *imitatio dei*[52] there is even less doubt about the tradition's recognition of what we have called the wilderness ethic as the Torah marrow of Israel's life. It is instructive to note in this connection the by no means surprising influence of this thinking on the Book of Titus: "For the grace of God has appeared . . . instructing us to deny ungodliness and worldly desires and to live sensibly, righteously and godly in the present age" (2:12).

Through its holiness Israel was to serve as an inspiration for all human beings, "so that of their own accord they will come and learn from them."[53] This is made possible not only by Israel's essential humanity (as opposed to antisemitism's projection of difference) but also by the Torah's equal availability to the entire world. "Why was the Torah given in the wilderness?" the sages ask. And they answer, "Because had it been given in the Promised Land, the tribe on whose territory it was given might have said of the others, 'I am superior to you.' It was given in the wilderness, for there all were equal."[54] The rabbinic statement that the proselytes' guiding stars were present at revelation suggests another reason for its occurrence in the unclaimed wilderness.[55]

For the tradition, it is not Israel that makes the Torah; it is the Torah that makes Israel.[56]

That Israel had to be reminded that the Torah was the source of its mission is evidenced by the Targum to Isaiah 42:7, which advises that the "blind eyes" are Israel's eyes which are removed from the Torah[57] and no less by the Talmudic aphorism, "Correct yourself first and then correct others."[58]

## V. THE UTOPIAN DIMENSION AND THE IMPACT OF MODERNITY

The utopian dimension in the probative period has comprised the progressive coordination of the world through European conquest, Western culture, and, incipiently at least, American diplomacy, with the influence of all far transcending political boundaries. The kaleidoscopic changes of modernity have profoundly transformed the life of the entire world. They have increasingly shifted its tonality from urban to cosmopolitan. No less than those generated by the ancient Greeks, Hellenists and Romans, their accompanying disorientations have challenged inherited myths and missions.[58a]

The modern world has reversed the earlier subordination of the secular to the religious. The secularity of its primary world-view has pervaded every dimension of its existence, including the affective axiologies and cognitive constructs of its religions. Particularly dysfunctional for religion has been the apotheosis of secularly grounded ethics and reason and their divorcement from revelatory systems. This has led to a general desacralization of religions and a neutralization of their secularly unpalatable claims. Particularly noticeable in this desacralization is the effective denial of providence, a denial often palliatively couched in the euphemisms of novel theologies.

On Israel, faith and people, the impact of modernity has been especially pronounced. As a minority longing for normalization, Jews touched by the Enlightenment eagerly anticipated full civic enfranchisement, or, as they came to call it, the Emancipation. Emancipation in its fullest sense has been the dream of all modern Jews, to such an extent that many have fantastically equated it with the millennium, even as indisputable evidence to the contrary has mounted. With this delusion Jews for decade after decade have been lured sociopolitically by the mirage of assimilated anonymity and religiously by the sirens of alien thought. Furthermore, the political dethronement of the Talmud has led to the abandonment of its foundational theology and the erosion of its radical axiology. The Torah, formerly its legal and spiritual cynosure, has been functionally relegated to the backwaters of Jewish concern. The majority of contemporary Jews are essentially ignorant of Torah and tradition and have little faith in their transcendental dimensions. It is for this reason that the question of "Jewish identity" has arisen with the modern world.

It follows that except by religious retentionists the traditional concept of Israel's mission, especially its inner mission, has been largely overlooked, and that sublimate substitutes have been quested for its energies. Two such points of attraction have been found in the secular environment. Although both have been laboriously overlaid with ideas culled from the tradition, each umbilically derives from a secular ethic, whose distortive coloration of every contemporary definition of Jewish identity and mission, except the extreme retentionist, is apparent even to the unpracticed eye. The first of these is universalism and the second is nationalism. At their extremes, the first has reduced the faith-people Israel into a faith indifferent to peoplehood, while the second has procrusteanized it into a nation largely indifferent to faith.

The utopian determinant has had three major phases, chronologically successive but thereafter overlapping. These may be respectively denominated Enlightenment (or non-Jewish nationalist) utopianism, socialist utopianism, and Jewish nationalist (and within it Zionist) utopianism. Enlightenment utopianism has been strongest in Western Europe and its cultural satellites, socialist utopianism has been strongest in Eastern Europe and its cultural satellites, while Zionism, though broadly rooted, has received most of its strength from Eastern Europe.

The crisis of identity has nowhere struck more tempestuously than among Jewish intellectuals. From this segment two divergent streams have emerged, one of deracinated individuals, highly marginal and ideologically pendular with respect to their heritage, and the other of determined idealists devoted to the radical change or the radical retention of the inherited past, but in either case less than fully faithful to the flexibility and relevance of its inherent élan.

These intellectuals have advanced innumerable definitions of Jewish identity. These fill the entire spectrum from a doctrinaire assimilation to a doctrinaire retention of pre-modern Jewish life. Some of these definitions are more "secular," while others are more "religious," but these categories, being foreign to Jewish life, inevitably interpenetrate. Often they have provided the basis for new institutions of Jewish expression. Fiercely competitive, these have stirred bitter animosities, whose polemical distortions have beclouded their own and their opponents' full worth.

Their positions are recorded in more abundant detail than their counterparts in the formative period. Their variegated richness is insufficiently recognized, particularly outside of the Jewish community, where there is a tendency to consider only a handful of individuals as the normative representatives of modern Jewish thought.

Our spatial limitations permit little more than the cataloguing of some of the authors of these positions. Though intricately interconnected and therefore resistant to decisive separation, they may be usefully if arbitrarily divided into "secular" and "religious," and then into assimilationists, survivalists, visionaries and retentionists.

Though variously structured in accordance with their incorporation of secularity, they all reveal the influence if not at least the partial presence of Judaism's traditional mission.

On the secular side, Jewish assimilationists in quest of messianic peace run the gamut from cowering inaction to conspicuous involvement in the most comprehensive world-view that appears to hold out a reasonable promise of their personal apocalyptic exodus (or "pass-over") from Judaism.

The survivalists have sought a measure of Jewish separateness within the cultural confines of their geographical context. They may be divided into socialist utopians, like Aaron Samuel Liebermann (1845–1880), Arkadi Kremer (1865–1935), Samuel Gozhansky (1867–1943) and Julius Martou (1873–1923), who advocated a Jewish group separateness within their otherwise universalist socialism; the Bundists (members of the "General Jewish Workers' Union in Lithuania, Poland and Russia" founded in 1897, and its satellites elsewhere), with their orientation toward socialism, diaspora autonomism and opposition to Zionism; the cultural autonomists, like Chaim Zhitlowsky (1865–1943), Simon Dubnow (1860–1941), Israel Zangwill (1864–1926), and, in a sense, Micah Joseph Berdyczewski (1865–1921), who called for the "transvaluation" of Israel from a Torah-centered to a nation-centered people; and cultural pluralists, like Horace Kallen (1882–1974), whose general humanism and cultural egalitarianism was accompanied by a dedicated Hebraism and defensive Zionism.

The visionaries include various grades of utopian Zionists. On the one hand we have utopians profoundly influenced by Jewish messianism. These include Elhanan Loeb Lewinsky (1857–1910), in his *Journey to the Land of Israel in the Year 2040* (in Hebrew, 1892); Edmund M. Eisler (1850–1942), in his anonymously published *A Picture of the Future* (in German, 1885); Theodor Herzl's *Old New Land* (German, 1902), the most renowned of the utopias, whose motto "If you will it, it is no fable" became the Zionist slogan. The visions of Ahad ha-Am, pseudonym for Asher Zevi Ginzberg (1856–1927), are reconstructible from his many works, and that of Henry Pereira Mendes (1852–1937) in his addresses and sermons.[59] On the other hand we find the utopian blended with the practical, as in Moses Hess (1812–1875) who rejected the value of the *Galut* and lionized the Land Israel as the keystone of a world utopia; A.D. Gordon

(1856–1922), who saw the Jews as the embodiment of humanity and through their own nationalism capable of realizing the fulfillment of the moral law in such a way as to serve as an example to all humanity; Judah Leon Magnes (1897–1948), who saw the Land Israel as the indispensable spiritual center for the fulfillment of the people Israel's teaching mission; and, not least, Theodor Herzl, whose *Old New Land* blended with the practical program of *The Jewish State* (1896).

The retentionists may be divided into the religious, cultural, socialist and diplomatic Zionists and, in a special category, Reconstructionists. The religious Zionists representatively include Jehuda Alkalai (1798–1878), who believed that the messianic age could be imminently achieved through human redemption of the Land Israel; Zevi Hirsch Kalischer (1795–1874), whose *Quest for Zion* derived out of a similar desire to initiate the millennium "from below"; and, above all, Abraham Isaac Kook (1865–1935), who belongs to both—and neither—of the categories "secular" and "religious." Kook connected the concept of election to Jewish nationalism, and then, through its example, the actualization of all humanity.

The retentionists also include reiterations of the traditional pre-modern position in the modern world. The most passionate of these is to be found in the tract *The Remnant of Israel* (in Hebrew) composed by the distinguished head of the rabbinical academy at Volozhin, Naphtali Zevi Judah Berlin (1817–1893).[60]

The cultural Zionists, a vast group, are divisible into the spiritual Zionists, like Leo Pinsker (1821–1891), Ahad Ha'am (1856–1927), who saw the Land Israel as a spiritual center for world Jewry, and the exclusive Zionists, like Jacob Klatzkin (1882–1948), who enunciated the concept of the rejection of the diaspora (*Shlilat ha-Galut*), though he lived and died in it. The socialist Zionists, most prominently Ber Borochov (1881–1917), synthesized Jewish nationalism with the socialist class struggle. The diplomatic Zionists include the so-called "political" Zionists whose main thrust was the acquisition of a haven in the Land Israel (among these was Theodor Herzl (1860–1904), whose attention at first was not limited to the Land Israel), and the "practical" Zionists like Menaham Ussishkin (1863–1941), Otto Warburg (1859–1938) and Jules Simon (1875–1969), who additionally insisted on educational, economic and cultural blueprints as the basis for political requests.

Reconstructionism, founded by the centenarian Mordecai M. Kaplan (born 1881) provides an unusual combination of the "religious" and "secular." Although its synagogue component is indispensable, it regards Judaism as a civilization and makes the people-Israel superordinate to its faith. Though retaining the vision of universal societal perfection, it abandons the supernatural and transcendental elements in tradition.[61]

On the religious side, Jewish assimilationists run the gamut from conversion out of Judaism to the adoption of a universalist faith which they occasionally rationalize as a deritualized Judaism. Perhaps the most notable example in the latter category is Ethical Culture, founded by Felix Adler (1851–1933) in 1876.

The survivalists saw as their mission the creation of palatable apologies for Judaism on the foundation of contextually dominant philosophies. In almost all cases they abandoned the traditional concept of mission. Under the influence of Kant, some, like Moritz Lazarus (1824–1903), and Hermann Cohen (1842–1918), particularly in his Marburg period, de-emphasized metaphysics and based their Judaism on nineteenth century German ethics, allowing it to inform their residual concepts of mission. Under the influence of Friedrich Schelling (1775–1854), and Georg Hegel (1770–1831) thinkers like Solomon Formstecher (1808–1889), Samuel Hirsch (1815–1889) and Nachman Krochmal (1785–1840) variously founded their theology on spirit. With the possible exception of Krochmal, who identifies Judaism with the "absolute spiritual," they proceeded to neutralize Judaism's traditional mission. On a contrary course we find the irrationalism and anti-idealism of Solomon Steinheim (1789–1866), influenced by Christian Weisse (1801–1866) and Immanuel Fichte (1797–1879), the existentialism of Franz Rosenzweig (1886–1929) influenced *inter alios* by Martin Heidegger (1889–1971) and positing a radically racial Jewish bond and the distinctive existentialism of Martin Buber (1878–1965), whose philosophy of relationship bypasses *Torah* and the *mitzva*-system for a covenantal relationship with God which points to the universal mission.

The visionaries largely represent the groups that came to be known as Reform Judaism. For all their often unrecognized theological divergence, they have traditionally coalesced in their abandonment of Torah and inner mission for a heightened emphasis on the universalist mission, which on closer observation reveals the unmistakable influence of Enlightenment utopianism and romantic nationalism. Almost unexceptionally they follow the dictum of Reform Judaism's first great ideologue, Abraham Geiger (1810-1874), who affirmed that throughout history "Israel never lost the awareness that it embraced the whole of mankind and that its labors were on behalf of humanity as a whole."[62] This was in no small measure a response to emanicipation, which extended the sphere of Jewish activity beyond the gates of the Jewish community to the broader society of nation and humanity. Numerous other distinguished thinkers, among them Samuel Holdheim (1806–1860) and Samuel Adler (1809–1891) in Germany (Adler also in the United States), Claude G. Montefiore (1858–1938) in England, Kaufmann Kohler (1843–1926) and Samuel S. Cohon (1888–1959) in the United States, and Leo Baeck (1873–1956) who lived in all three countries, emphasized the universalist view.

Evident in the discussions on the Messianic question at the critical rabbinical conference held at Frankfort-on-the-Main in 1845,[63] this view was enshrined in the principles of the Philadelphia Conference of 1869,[64] the Pittsburgh Platform of 1885,[65] and the Columbus Platform of 1937.[66] It also inspired passionate petitions, particularly in the Confirmation services of the principal Reform orders of prayer, including *The Daily Prayers for American Israelites* of Isaac M. Wise (1819–1900),[67] the *Book of Prayers for Jewish Congregations* of David Einhorn (1809–1979),[68] the *Israelitish Prayer Book* by Marcus Jastrow (1829–1903) translated and revised by Benjamin Szold,[69] *The Ritual for Jewish Worship* (1884) by Max Landsberg (1845–1928),[70] and the various editions of *The Union Prayer Book for Jewish Worship.*[71]

Because it was conceived in Enlightenment universalism, this articulation of mission was understandably averse to a separate Jewish nationalism. That this position, however, was accidental to Reform Judaism rather than substantive is evidenced by two considerations: first that similar non-nationalism or anti-nationalism was expressed by other elements of the Jewish community, including the neo-Orthodox Samson Raphael Hirsch (1808–1888), and at one time much if not most of the pre-modern rabbinate, and, second, that beginning early in the twentieth century and under the impact of descendants of Eastern European Jews, including Samuel S. Cohon, Reform increasingly incorporated both ideal and practical Zionism.

The retentionists are best exemplified by the groups that are known as Orthodox, a term first appearing in connection with the faith of Israel in 1795. The theological positions within this group differ appreciably from one another. Yet they all essentially follow Moses Mendelssohn (1729–1786) in their exaltation of Judaism as a "revealed legislation" and their insistence on the punctilious observance of its unchangeable, or minimally changeable regulations. This emphasis on retentive orthopraxy, symbolically manifested by the conversion of the traditionally supple *halakha* (derived from the root *HLKh,* and meaning "procedure") into fixed legal decisions, has become the cachet of the modern Orthodox group. In its extreme it follows the pronouncement by Moses Sofer (1762–1839) that any innovation, even if insignificant from the standpoint of traditional law, is prohibited for no other reason than that it is an innovation. Important contemporary thinkers, like Jehiel Weinberg (1885–1966), Joseph H. Lookstein (1902–1979) and Joseph Soloveitchik (born 1903) have creatively articulated a halakhic conservatism for the modern context of life, usually on an at least implicit claim of their group's exclusive authority as halakhic decisors.

Within this framework, modern Orthodoxy most strongly adheres to the traditional concept of Torah and the mission of Israel. That its concern in this area is not confined, as some would have it, to the inner mission, but includes as well the universalistic one, is perhaps best evidenced in significant commentaries like those of H. Hertz (1872–1946), M. S. Segal (1876–1968) and E. S. Artom (1887–1965)[72] and above all in the expressions of the important school, often called Neo-Orthodox, founded by Samson Raphael Hirsch.

At the same time a strong sense of traditional mission was not absent from the Reform perspective of Judaism. It was never more eloquently articulated than by Samuel Schulman (1864–1955), rabbi of Temple Emanu-El in New York from 1927 to 1935. Says Schulman:

> The conception of . . . the Torah as governing life . . . has not triumphed. We should first put our own house in order and then proceed to do something for others. . . . What we need is faith, piety . . . a revival of the religious sentiment as such.

He continues:

> A righteousness without God is self-righteousness, and is just as ethically imperfect and eventually disintegrating, as is a God-consciousness without righteousness, which is self-seeking and tends to degenerate into formalism and superstition, and may become morally dangerous. We need the re-emphasis, on the basis of a living faith, according to a law of right and duty. We must go back to the conception of a Torah, as a government of life.

He perorates:

> The modern Jew and the modern man must learn again that there is such a thing as a "thou shalt" and learn again that there is such a thing

> as "thou shalt not," governing his daily life, which commandments and inhibitions are the expressions of the prophetical ideas of justice and love.

And he concludes:

> Our mission is to be the living witness to God and the spiritual power in the life of the nations. . . . Our duty is to witness to the true religion for the sake of humanity.[73]

## VI. THE MISSION OF ISRAEL IN THE "POST–MODERN" WORLD

From many perspectives the "modern world" came to an end in 1945. Its "post-modern" component has lingered on like a lambent flame in its mortal throes. The turning point was World War II and synechdochically the Holocaust. The Holocaust exposed the spiritual bankruptcy of the modern world, for all its rational achievement and dithyrambic promise. With the crumbling of its illusory props, the Western world has been gripped with an adhesive despair, which has perhaps nowhere been better expressed than in the oxymoronic theology of the death of God.

At the heart of the world the faith-people Israel has poignantly experienced this despair. The devastation of the house of Israel in the Holocaust has sunk the people Israel into a crisis of faith paralleled only, though by comparison faintly, in the wake of the *Hurban ha-Bayit.* This malaise has accelerated the process of theological desacralization. Not unrelated to the basally Christian death-of-God theology is a new radical denial of Providence by defiant assertions of unbridled individual freedom. This is nowhere better discernible than in a contemporary humanistic-racistic perception of tradition. According to this perception, any statement about the ultimate verities of life by people calling themselves Jews and reasonably definable as such through descent represents a valid theological position within Judaism, regardless of its consonance with the mainstream or even eddies of tradition. With such perception, the traditional aristocracy of Israel's learning, founded on the premise of universal truths, has been leveled by the mobocracy of whimsical opinionaires.

No small part of the contemporary Jewish despair derives from the Holocaust's explosive puncture of all the modern utopias, secular as well as religious. Except to the expected random recalcitrants, the Holocaust has pellucidly revealed, on the one hand, the impossibility of complete Jewish integration in any society, and, on the other, the insufficiency of *de jure* national sovereignty in a post-nationalist world. From the heart if not the zenith of Western European civilization, it has all too vividly brought home the irrefutable reality that the Jew remains as marginal, as isolated and as vulnerable as ever. Stunningly, it leaves no alternative but to conclude that the Jew's security lies not in doctrinaire secular universalism, nor in doctrinaire secular particularism, unquestionably beneficial as both may be, but rather and only in the extent to which the wilderness ethic is embodied in the warp and woof of universal society. Only when all can sit under their respective vines and fig trees will there be none to make the Jew afraid.

As in the past, the new epoch that has been dawning over the embers of the modern world brings with it the hope of every morning. This epoch appears already to be characterized by an incipient unification of the planet earth through communications, geopolitics and geoeconomics. Though the new world is still in its infancy and locked in inevitable struggle with the vested structures and ideologies of the past, it is not difficult to descry its breathtaking possibilities for the actualization of human potential.

Jewish experience suggests the need for a cautious approach to the new epoch's implicit opportunities, assuming of course that it is not engulfed by the moribund recklessness of the old. Theologically, on the basis of current need and the example of its predecessor epochs, it suggests the desirability of a synthesis of the spectral extremes within the modern utopian determinant. Such a distillation would restore the centrality of Torah and the traditional mission in language and goals consonant with contemporary needs.

That these ideas have increasingly been rooting is evidenced in the poetic synthesis included in the *Sha'arey Tefillah,* the *Gates of Prayer,* the most recent prayerbook of Reform Judaism. Among its declarations the following encapsulates Israel's mission:

> The revelation at Mount Sinai is shrouded for us by the mists of antiquity. But this we know: that it released a torrent of spiritual energy that transformed Israel into a people of priests and prophets, bringing enlightenment to humanity. It inspires and guides us still, and it will redeem the world.
>
> Sinai was only the beginning. The Torah has never ceased to grow. In every age it has been purified and enlarged. It has a permanent core and an expanding periphery. It expands as the horizon of our vision grows.

> Nor are God's revelations confined to Israel. He has been the inspiration of the great and good among all the families of the earth. His love and guidance reach out to all the world.
>
> Let us then give thanks for the wise and noble of every age and people who, by word and example, have shed light on our way; but above all for the prophets and teachers of Israel, who shine as the brightness of the heavens and, having led many to righteousness, are like the stars for ever.
>
> What is Torah? It is what God has revealed to us, and what we have come to understand about God. It is the ideas and ideals, the laws and commandments, that make up our religious heritage. It is the experience of Abraham, the legislation of Moses, the vision of the Prophets, the commentary of the Rabbis, the insight of the Mystics. It is the questions we ask, and the answers we receive, when we seek to understand God, the world, and ourselves.
>
> One event stands out above all others in the memory of our people: When God revealed the Torah, no bird chirped, no fowl beat its wings, no ox bellowed, the angels did not sing, the sea did not stir, no creature uttered a sound. The world was silent and still, and the Divine Voice spoke: "I am the Lord your God."[74]

This restatement of tradition in modern language recognizes Israel's providential purpose, distinctive role, and Torah foundation. Above all, it repudiates all attempts to dilute their expression into palliative conformity. It thus represents a reaffirmation of the mainsprings of Israel's faith.

*E pur si muove.*

## NOTES

1. A. Tennyson, *Locksley Hall,* 1.137.

2. See, for application of the same methodology, my earlier articles "Are the Jews the Chosen People?" in *Dimensions* (Spring 1968) 1–5; "The Mission of Israel after Auschwitz," in Helga Croner, Leon Klenicki eds., *Issues in the Jewish-Christian Dialogue,* Stimulus Book (New York: Paulist Press, 1979), pp. 157–180; "Record and Revelation: A Jewish Perspective," in Lawrence Boadt, Helga Croner, Leon Klenicki eds., *Biblical Studies: Meeting Ground of Jews and Christians,* Stimulus Book (New York: Paulist Press, 1981), pp. 147–171.

3. Several of the concepts are cited here in transliterated Hebrew to call at-

tention to their specific nuances which are obscured by their conventional English translation.

4. For a more detailed interim discussion, see my article, "Record and Revelation," pp. 160f.

5. See also, v.g., Is 40:8; 41:9; 44:6; 45:6; 48:12; 40–55 *passim*; Ezek 20.

6. Is 42:1; 43:1, 21, 24; 46:3; 49:1, 5.

7. Is 41:8; 42:1, 18f; 44:1, 21; 49:3; 52:13ff. On the analogy of Israel to the prophets, see also Is 49:2; 50:4; 51:16.

8. Is 43:10, 12; 44:8f.

9. Is 43:8; 45:20; 50:8.

10. Ezek 20; Is 47:6ff; 48:9f. Cf. Is 60:10.

11. Reconstructed from the Holiness Code (Lv 19:1—26:2), of exilic redaction, plus passages like Is 48:17–19; Ezek 16 and 20, esp. 20:18–20; and other prophetic parallels.

12. That this torah was the "Torah of Moses" is axiomatic for Judaism's sacred tradition. See, e.g., Isaac Abravanel *ad loc.*

13. On this, see the insightful study of H. M. Orlinsky, "Nationalism-Universalism and Internationalism in Ancient Israel," in H. T. Frank and W. I. Reed, eds., *Translating and Understanding the Old Testament: Essays in Honor of Herbert Gordon May* (Nashville/New York: Abingdon, 1970), pp. 206–236; reprinted in H. M. Orlinsky, *Essays in Biblical Culture and Bible Translation* (New York: Ktav, 1974), pp. 78–116.

14. On the political dimensions of this prophetic stance, see my article "The Prophets as Revolutionaries," in *Biblical Archaeology Review* 5 (1979) 12–19.

15. See also, v.g., Is 46:13; 51:3ff; 52:1ff; 54:17.

16. See also other prophets, including the unknown authors of Is 2:2–4 and Mi 4:1–4.

17. For a new approach to this period, see M. A. Cohen, *Two Sister Faiths: A New Approach to the Origins of Rabbinic Judaism and Christianity* (Worcester, Mass.: Assumption College, 1982).

18. On the utilization of the term *Adonay* see, e.g., S. Zeitlin, "The Origins of the Pharisees Reaffirmed," in *Jewish Quarterly Review* (NS) 4 (April 1969) 255–267, although Zeitlin posits too early a date for Pharisaic origins. On the term "Israel" see Zeitlin's "Israelites, Jews in the Pauline Epistles," in *loc. cit.* 58, 1 (July 1967) 72–74, and his earlier essay, "The Names Hebrew, Jews and Israel: A Historical Study," in *loc. cit.* 43,4 (April 1953) 365–379.

19. This subject is treated at greater length in my aforementioned article "Record and Revelation."

20. TB *Pesahim* 6b.

21. TJ *Peah* 1,17a; TJ *Megillah* 4,74d; TJ *Hagigah* 1,76d.

22. *Abot* 3,14.

23. Moses Nahmanides, "Sermon: 'The Torah of the Lord Is Perfect" (He-

brew), in *Kitvei Rabbenu Mosheh ben Nahman,* B. Chavel, ed. (Jerusalem, 1963) I, pp. 129–175, esp. p. 153.

24. TB *Sanhedrin* 99a.

25. J. D. Soloveitchik, *Sefer bet Ha-Levi* (Wilna, 1911), p. 57.

26. This role of Israel did not go unnoticed. At the height of Medieval Iberia, Isaac Arama in *Akedat Yizhak* to Dt 28:68, H. J. Pollak, ed. (Pressburg, 1849) V, p. 28a, clearly articulated its positive aspect and wisely left the reader to imagine its adverse counterpart.

27. Judah Halevi, *Kitab al Khazari,* H. Hirschfeld, ed. (London: Cailingold, 1931) Part II, para. 36. For a later and somewhat different recognition of the same principle see Samuel Usque, *Consolation for the Tribulations of Israel* (Portuguese), M. A. Cohen, tr. (Philadelphia, 1965), p. 219. Usque here sees Israel as the pattern and quintessence of humanity.

28. *Sybilline Oracles* 3:26 f.

29. Joseph H. Hertz, ed., *Daily Prayer Book* (New York, 1948), p. 85.

30. 4th Ezra 3:32–34; 6:59; 7:3–16.

31. Philo, *De Legatione ad Gaium,* F. H. Colson, ed. (Loeb Classical Series, Cambridge, Mass. & London, 1962), p. 143. See also *ibid., Vita Mosis* II.20.

32. Josephus, *Antiquities* 4, 115f.

33. Gershom Scholem, *Major Trends in Jewish Mysticism* (Jerusalem: Schocken, 1941) pp. 273ff.

34. Ben Zion Bokser, ed., *High Holyday Prayer Book* (New York, 1959), p. 47.

35. "All the world. . . .", I. Davidson ed., *Otsar Ha-Shirah Veha-Piyyut* (The saurus of Medieval Poetry) (New York: Ktav, 1929/1970) II, p. 186 entry #201; and S. Krauss, *Studien zur Byzantinisch-Juedischen Geschichte* (Vienna, 1914), p. 41. See also the commentators, v.g. Eliezer of Beaugency (fl. 12th century) to Is 42:1.

36. See, e.g., *Genesis Rabbah* 1, 4 and *Tanhuma,* Noah, 12. Other parts of the tradition for a variety of purposes, including apologetics, place the election of Israel at a later time, as, for example, traditionally, the wilderness; see, e.g., Kaspi, *Adnei Keseph* to Amos 3:2, I. H. Last, ed. (London, 1911) p. 82; or Jacob, whom God chose because he was "a perfect man." See also E. Mihaly, "A Rabbinic Defense of the Election of Israel," in *Hebrew Union College Annual* 35 (1964) 103–143, esp. 107.

37. See also M. Friedman, ed., *Sifre* (Vienna, 1864) 73a ff., and commentators like Isaac Abravanel to Is 42:8.

38. See, e.g., *Numbers Rabbah* 5, 16, and the classical expression in the *Prayerbook of Saadia Gaon* (I. Davidson, S. Assaf, B. Joel, eds., 1941), pp. 77f.

39. Levi Yitzhak of Berditchev, *Sefer Kedushat Levi* (Warsaw, 1902), p. 141 to Lv 19:1.

40. *Sifra, Behukotai* 8, 4f; *Pesikta Rabbati* 21, 15; *Midrash Psalms* to 5:6.

41. *Genesis Rabbah* 33, 6.

42. *Canticles Rabbah* 1, 4. See also *Genesis Rabbah* 41, 9.

43. TB *Pesahim* 87b; see also *Genesis Rabbah* 41, 9; and M. Friedman, ed. (Vienna, 1900), *Sedar Eliahu Rabbah,* chap. 11, p. 54.

44. TB *Pesahim* 87b; see also *Canticles Rabbah* 4, 2; and *Sifre* 32ff.

45. *Canticles Rabbah* 2, 8; *Pesikta Rabbati* 15, 71b; *Pesikta de Rav Kahana* 47a–48a.

46. TB *Pesahim* 87b.

47. *Midrash Tehilim* to Psalm 123:2.

48. Jehuda Wistinetzki ed., *Sefer Hasidim* (Frankfurt/M., 1924), p. 86.

49. TB *Pesahim* 87b–88a. See also Azariah Figo, *Binah la-Ittim* (Venice, 1653), Part 2, Sermon 42, folios 12a–b.

50. *Sifra* 91d; see also 93d.

51. TB *Makkot* 23b–24a. In this connection, the JPS translation (Philadelphia, 1978, *Prophets*) of the Habakkuk passage is noteworthy: "But the righteous man is rewarded with life for his fidelity" (p. 855).

52. See, e.g., the commentaries to Lv 19:1 and the beautiful expression of *imitatio Dei* in ed. M. Friedman, *Sifre debe Rab,* (Vienna, 1864) f. 85a. For later sermonic material on the subject, see, e.g., J. Krantz, *Ohel Jacob,* Vol. 3 (Pressburg, 1852) pp. 40a ff. See also Sforno on Ex 19:5; 26:3, and Dt 33:3; and Isaac Frances *Pnai Yitzhak* (Salonica, 1743) f. 140a, col. 1.

53. *Numbers Rabbah,* Hukkat 19, 26.

54. J. Z. Lauterbach, ed., *Mekilta,* Bahodesh II, 198f. See also TB *Shebuoth* 39a and *Numbers Rabbah,* Hukkat 19, 26.

55. TB *Shabbath* 146a; *Exodus Rabbah* 28, 6 and *Ets Hayyim* to the Tanhuma *Yitro* 11.

56. This is explicitly stated in *Exodus Rabbah* Ki Tissa 47, 3. See also, e.g., *Genesis Rabbah* 41, 9; and Abravanel to Ex 19:3ff.

57. *Targum* to Is 42:7.

58. TB *Baba Meziah* 107b, and elsewhere.

58a. Considerations of space preclude our analysis of the theological legacy of the various pre-modern stages in the development of the utopian dimension.

59. For a synopsis of Henry Pereira Mendes' writings, which are especially rare, see *H. Pereira Mendes: A Biography* (New York, 1938), pp. 37, 42f.

60. See Naphtali Zevi Judah Berlin, *Shear Ysrael* (Warsaw, 1894), printed with the author's commentary to the Song of Songs, pp. 115–134, esp. pp. 119f, on Israel's separation/holiness, universal mission and the irrelevancy of religious conversion (as opposed to value acceptance) for its fulfillment.

61. Because it is as yet embryonic, we are omitting from consideration here the segment of humanistic Judaism with its affirmation that the "Judaism of the twentieth century has become a secular 'religion' " (Sherwin T. Wine, *Humanistic Judaism,* Buffalo, 1978, p. 10), its claim that "the category of the sacred is inappropriate" (p. 25), its concession of a Jewish distinctiveness only in the 'trivia' of ceremony and language" (p. 45), and yet its recognition of the uniting bonds of Jewish

history, custom and ritual. It defines "the humanistic Jew as an individual of either Jewish or non-Jewish descent, who believes in the ultimate value of self-respect and in the principles of humanism, community, autonomy and rationality" (p. 121).

62. Abraham Geiger, *Das Judenthum und seine Geschichte* (Breslau, 1865[2]) I, p. 40. For another translation, see M. Wiener, *Abraham Geiger and Liberal Judaism* (Philadelphia, 1962) p. 183.

63. D. Philipson, *The Reform Movement in Judaism* (New York, 1931), pp. 173ff.

64. *Ibid.,* pp. 353ff.

65. *Ibid.,* pp. 355ff.

66. *CCAR Yearbook* 47 (1937) pp. 97ff.

67. See, e.g., *Minhag America* (Cincinnati, 1856), pp. 14f.

68. See, e.g., *Olat Tamid* (New York, 1896) pp. 87f. See also *Olat Tamid: Gebetbuch fuer Israelitische Reform Gemeinden* (New York, 1858[6]), p. 453.

69. See, e.g., *Avodat Ysrael* (Philadelphia, 1910), First Part, pp. 14f.

70. See, e.g., *The Ritual for Jewish Worship* (Rochester, 1897), pp. 44f, 128f.

71. See, e.g., *The Union Prayerbook for Jewish Worship* (New York, 1961) I, pp. 34f, 183; II, pp. 262, 345.

72. See, e.g., their commentaries to such passages as Ex 19:5; Lv 19:1; Dt 7:6.

73. *CCAR Yearbook* 29 (1919), pp. 295ff.

74. *Gates of Prayer* (New York, 1975), pp. 696ff.

# A Contemporary Understanding of Mission from a Protestant Orientation and Tradition

*David M. Stowe*

The missionary impulse in Christianity is abundantly documented in the history of nearly all Churches and deeply rooted in their Scriptures. It is true that Protestantism was slow to pick up the missionary impulse after the Reformation. Eastern Orthodox folk churches have sometimes seemed content to express a merely culture religion. But over the centuries the missionary impulse has clearly prevailed. After a slow start, there was an explosion of Protestant missions in the eighteenth and nineteenth centuries, and today there is a revival of the ancient Orthodox missionary commitment.

It is also true that the missionary imperative is not uniformly stressed throughout the Christian Scriptures. There is a good deal of ethnic religion in the Old Testament, a concentration on the distinctiveness and the earthly fortunes of the chosen people of God. But in many ways the Old Testament does witness to a missionary impulse, beginning with Genesis 12:2–3 where God's promise to Abraham is not only that "I will bless you and make your name great" but that "you will be a blessing" and "by you all the families of the earth will bless themselves." When Jesus sent forth his disciples on mission, he was only doing what his Jewish contemporaries did in traversing "land and sea to make a single proselyte" (Mt 23:13).

One of the best ways to understand the New Testament is to see it as a record of the full release of the missionary impulse in Old Testament religion. This occurred in many ways and on many levels. Christ was interpreted as the servant Messiah who should be "a light to the nations" (Is 49:6). It was the necessities of mission which helped convince the young Christian community to discard elements of ritual law which separated Jewish people from Gentiles and hindered conversion. In experiences of what the Christian understood to be the Holy Spirit they were driven out into mission. The first great history of Christianity, the twin volumes of Luke-Acts, is a missionary history.

The substance and style of the mission carried on by ecumenically oriented Christians today, whether Protestant, Roman Catholic, or Orthodox, is perhaps best understood in the light of a crucial passage in the Book of Acts (17:16–34). Here in an address to the Areopagus in Athens, St. Paul, the first great missionary, sets the Christian faith squarely in a context of the total history of the planet Earth.

> (God) made from one every nation of men to live on all the face of the earth, having determined allotted periods and the boundaries of their habitation, that they should seek God, in the hope that they might feel after him and find him.

Here humankind is identified as a biological unity with a unique place within the sweep of what we would today call cosmic evolution. But although humanity is clearly one, it has developed in highly varied ways in its various "habitations"—regions, cultures, epochs. All of these cultures, known and unknown, are part of God's plan for bringing persons everywhere to that maturity of spirit by which they might feel after God and find his purpose for his world. Each great culture functions like a spiritual school where mankind learns something about how God is working out his purpose to the world. In this way, Paul admits the worth of the great religious quests which lie at the center of the various cultures.

In Acts 17:30, however, there comes a dramatic change of emphasis.

> The times of ignorance God overlooked, but now he commands all men everywhere to repent, because he has fixed a day on which he will judge the world in righteousness by a man whom he has appointed, and of this he has given assurance to all men by raising him from the dead.

The long-separated strands of human history are to be drawn into one culture. A humanity which has had many histories is now to have one history. The misunderstandings of God's purpose and the rebellions against his will, which are mingled with the achievements of the many cultures, are to be exposed and corrected. And all of this is to be related to a man named Jesus of Nazareth. His life, teachings, death, and resurrection as a living force among his followers are to become the hinge of all history, the norm and standard for all human existence.

Today, 1,900 years later, Christians see a certain striking realism in Paul's words regarding the unification of humankind. He does not say—and it obviously is not the case—that all the variety in the cultures and the distinctive sense of community held by a vast number of peoples is to be eliminated. That multiplicity continues, perhaps even grows in some respects. But essentially it is a phenomenon within a larger tidal movement of human history, powered by a desperate need for world order and exemplified in growing economic interdependence.

We are seeing the cultures of mankind, in their many "habitations," drawn together in a most remarkable way. Architecture, one of the most comprehensive of the arts, everywhere reflects Scandinavian, Japanese, German, American, and other forms. Western classical music, singers of many folk musics, rock and jazz music with their African and European and Creole roots—all are parts of a universal musical language. Increasingly, cookbooks carry recipes from many countries of the world. Satellites weave a web of almost instantaneous global communication through radio, television, and newspapers. Vastly broadened college curricula and the fantastic expansion of tourist travel, as well as highly developed patterns of international trade—all testify that in truth "all men everywhere" form the context for human life and decision.

The really crucial affirmation, however, is Paul's other assertion that Jesus of Nazareth is to be the center of this world civilization, multiple in its group loyalties and pluralistic in its cultures. The essential and decisive conviction of Christians in the twentieth century as in the first is that "Jesus is Lord" (1 Cor 12:3).

But what does that conviction mean in terms of missionary action? Christian groups answer in differing ways. For a few Christ's Lordship means the imposition of a "Christian way of life," some variety of American or other presumptively Christian folk culture, a full-blown cultural and religious imperialism. Others recognize that cultural, liturgical, and even theological variety will obtain in the pluralistic world civilization which is coming, but believe that all persons must eventually acknowledge Jesus Christ and become members of some kind of Christian Church. But for the ecumenically oriented Churches an explicit verbal and doctrinal confession and a denominational belonging are not the central concern. For them what matters is the extension of Jesus' teaching and spirit, of his vision of God and of God's will for humankind.

The missionary activity of this kind of ecumenically oriented Protestantism is a very considerable factor in the world religious scene today. It is estimated that there are some 50,000 Roman Catholic "foreign missionaries," i.e., missionaries working in cultures other than their own, and some 55,000 Protestant missionaries. Of these some 12,000 are North American Roman Catholics, and some 35,000 are North American Protestants. Among the Protestants about 5,000 are sent by agencies related to the National Council of Churches. For the world the proportion of ecumenically oriented Protestants would probably be similar. Roman Catholic missionaries reflect all shades of opinion about the aim and style of mission, but a substantial proportion of the North Americans would certainly reflect an "ecumenical" stance sensitive to the pluralism of cultures and religions. It is estimated that all North American Protestant agencies spend some $655 to $700 million annually on personnel, program, maintenance, and fund-raising. Of this $130 to $150 million would be spent by the ecumenically oriented Protestant agencies, a proportion somewhat higher than their proportion of missionary personnel.

In other words, the ecumenically oriented agencies of mission, related to what are sometimes called "mainstream" or historic denominations, are in some ways a minority factor in Christian foreign mission today. Yet their activity is large and widespread, and it has special significance because it is linked with the great denominations which in spite of the current "evangelical revival" still represent by far the largest sector of the Christian population, in North America and throughout the world.

The importance of this ecumenical mission sector is underlined by the fact that "missions" are by no means confined to the activity of professional missionaries in foreign countries. The "home missions" of the Churches in aggregate are probably two or three times as large in funds and personnel as the "foreign missions." Indeed, it is hard to know where ordinary Church life ends and "missions" begin. For mission includes three main components. One is a vast array of what might be called *social services,* at home and abroad, programs which seek to provide for the needs of people beyond the membership of the Churches. These social services recall the activity of Jesus in healing and in feeding the needy. Another sector of mission focuses on *social change,* the reshaping of economic, political, and other social structures and practices to conform more nearly to the teaching and spirit of Jesus and his predecessor prophets of Israel. The third element might be called *evangelism,* the more specifically and identifiably religious task of awakening religious concern, focusing religious devotion on the God revealed in Jesus Christ, and fostering moral and spiritual values and commitments commensurate with the Lordship of Christ. These elements of mission are identifiable but hardly separable. In almost any specific enterprise of mission there is some blend of more than one and often all three, although many mission agencies and missionary personnel are specialized in one or another.

The social service dimension of Christian mission, at home and abroad, actually makes up the bulk of the effort. In one liberal denomination the total income of the Church, for all purposes at all levels including local congregations, is about $225 million per year from its 1.8 million members. Related to that Church although not controlled by it are some 125 agencies for homeland social services with total annual budgets ranging up toward $1 billion annually. These include hospitals and community health programs, homes for the aged and other institutions serving the aging, services to the developmentally disabled, neighborhood and community centers, and services to children in need of special care because of family inadequacy or other reasons. In education there are some forty-five colleges, seminaries, and academies related to the Church although, again, largely self-supporting and having independent boards of trustees.

Ministries to Indian Americans have been an important part of home missions historically and they continue in many forms. Many younger people leave the reservations to look for better educational and employment opportunities in such centers as the Twin Cities of Minnesota, Chicago, and Rapid City, South Dakota. Here the Church helps with problems of housing, employment, and recreation, and with personal adjustments of many kinds.

Meanwhile, ministries continue to be needed on the reservations, where life can be almost indescribably stagnant and corrupting. Crowded into inadequate housing, with nothing to do but play basketball or sleep during the day, free at night to roam, many young men may not even have money to get drunk as a release from their sense of meaninglessness. Sucking gas fumes or drinking white gas may provide such release at minimum cost. It may be easier to have children outside of marriage than within since they will then be supported from public funds.

Mission scholarships are granted to ambitious young people. Funds are provided for Indian Youth Workshops where cultural anthropologists help these young people understand their own heritage, learn how Indian communities relate to government at several levels, and understand what it means to be an Indian and an American.

Some of the other historic "frontier" missions also continue. In Alaska, pioneers are still breaking virgin sod and clearing forests. Along the inland Passage are scattered isolated fishing villages. Farther back in the wilderness, missionaries work with the Eskimos and Indians. Evangelism, education, and medical care are all needed on these frontiers.

In regions of the border South, missionaries live among isolated mountain communities to strengthen Churches, set up schools, and provide medical care by hospitals or through circuit-riding nurses and midwives. The poverty of Appalachia is challenged by development projects and community organization.

The need for mission outreach at home has always been vividly apparent when masses of people have arrived in this country from their homes in Europe or Asia. Although the number of immigrants coming to America decreased during the generation following World War I, a massive influx from Latin America is underway today. Large numbers from half a dozen Asian countries are gaining. All these groups call for helping ministries from the Churches.

Black Americans, whose ancestors arrived in America long ago, must still hammer at the gates of opportunity for open housing, equal education, equal employment. For a century the Churches' missions among black Americans have focused on educational opportunities. After the Civil War, schools and colleges were founded for black freemen by Church agencies. To meet needs in the areas of health and community welfare, Churches have helped to provide hospitals and community centers.

There is a whole array of rural missions in America. Some are directed to farm families fighting to wrest a living from marginal lands. They may work as sharecroppers in the cotton-raising South, live on cutover timberlands in Minnesota, or struggle to make a living on rocky New England acres. Larger parishes, providing a staff of specialists in rural ministry for an entire countryside, offer one kind of answer.

The Churches also face a responsibility for the more than two million migrants who each year travel from place to place harvesting seasonal crops. Pay is poor, life is rootless, and children often suffer terribly in the pattern of migrant labor. Many belong to minority groups, thus having a double handicap. To these people the migrant ministries of the National Council of Churches and of denominational mission agencies render service. Such missions try to secure better living conditions, special educational provisions for migrant children, and general community acceptance. There are child care centers, elementary schools, teenage clubs, worship services, Sunday and weekday church schools, classes for adults in literacy and homemaking, recreation for all ages, family nights, and welcome centers. The Churches are increasingly engaged in social and political action that attempts to right the basic injustices suffered by migrants. Aid to union organizing efforts is basic.

Then there are missions to the alien world of those who must spend part of their life behind bars—in prisons, mental hospitals, or correction centers. Others are less tangible but no less real—the bars of illness that prevent free passage in and out of hospitals, sanatoriums, and other institutions where the sick in mind or body are cared for. Theological seminaries and other training centers prepare men and women for the unusual kinds of communication needed in prisons or in hospitals and teach them to recognize some of the signs which indicate developing problems or increasing hope.

In overseas mission there is a similar massive involvement in programs of social service, in all the varieties of health, education, and welfare. In many countries mission schools brought the first opportunity for modern education. The extraordinary proportion of present-day African leadership which was trained in mission schools is vivid testimony to that effort. Similarly, Christian hospitals and other medical programs continue to provide much of the health care in many third world countries, following the introduction of modern medicine by missionaries. Today these programs are shifting toward emphasis upon community health, toward preventive rather than curative medicine and toward community-based rather than institution-centered programs. In this they are in the vanguard of emphases favored by the World Health Organization.

In many developing countries the need for service for the handicapped and disabled is scarcely recognized. Christian missions are sponsoring pilot programs for the blind, the mentally retarded, those with other physical handicaps, and social welfare centers for the deprived and destitute.

One of the principal targets of mission today is world hunger. Two billion persons representing half the world's population live in areas of nutritional deficiency. Nearly half of these suffer daily or recurrent hunger. Explosive population growth points toward even more widespread suffering in the years ahead. Other factors contributing to the problem are such cultural patterns as caste, the pressures of trade and finance, political instability, natural disasters, and the sheer complexity of concerted international action. Christian people are making a concentrated attack on these problems, with Church agencies working alongside secular and government agencies.

In this complex picture agricultural missions play a vital role. In many countries otherwise good development schemes for food production are failing at the grass-roots level. By helping to fill in with programs intermediate between large-scale government efforts and the rural family, organized missions help the large schemes to succeed.

This may be done by fostering cooperatives and credit unions. Another basic contribution is made through the training of young farmers and their wives in more effective production. Basic to more productive farming is the right relation of the farmer to the land he tills. Large landholding and the correlative farm tenancy pose serious problems, both for the development of the people and for a sound economy. Obviously, governments must take major responsibility for land reform but the rural poor can be organized to demand it. Once land is made available, mission efforts can assist in the selection of families, the providing of subsistence during the relocation period, the establishing of schools, cooperatives and credits, and the offering of technical advice.

In the twentieth century, mission agencies have been prominent in efforts to meet emergency needs created by war, political turmoil, or natural disasters. Near East relief before and after World War I was followed by China relief in the following decades. Then after the outbreak of war in 1940, masses of refugees in Europe and Asia called for emergency help and resettlement. In addition, there were great floods in India.

In 1946 a unified agency called Church World Service came into being, representing much of American Protestantism. In 1948 the World Council of Churches was born. Within it was a major program responsible for far-reaching programs of mutual aid among Churches of the world, and of service to refugees, DICARWS (Division of Inter-Church Aid, Refugee and World Service). Under the umbrella of these two great agencies of service are many specialized programs such as CROP (Christian Rural Overseas Program).

The amount of aid that is channeled through such service agencies is impressive. In a period of fifteen years, CROP food and self-help materials totaled 150 million pounds, with a value of fourteen million dollars. Church World Service distributed well over four billion pounds of foods, with a value of nearly thirty-two million dollars. In addition, nearly 75,000 tons of clothing, bedding, and shoes were made available to needy people, a contribution worth another one hundred and fifty million dollars. To this could be added the value of medicines, drugs, and other health supplies totaling seventy million pounds and worth some twenty-four million dollars.

While Christian missionary work is often identified most strongly with these service activities, there is a second dimension which is becoming more and more prominent as people everywhere, especially the disadvantaged, recognize that they have needs because they are part of intrinsically unjust social systems. It is *social change* even more than social welfare they demand.

In its traditional missionary work the Church recognized a responsibility for doing something about social evils. In the nineteenth century Arab slave traders were still spreading death and misery across large areas of what was truly a dark continent of human suffering. David Livingstone's work is well summarized in the epitaph which marks his tomb in Westminster Abbey:

> Brought by faithful hands over land and sea,
> Here rests David Livingstone. . . .
> For thirty years his life was spent
> In an unwearied effort
> To evangelize the native races
> To explore the undiscovered secrets
> To abolish the desolating slave trade of Central Africa
> Where with his last words he wrote,
> "All I can add in my solitude is,
> May Heaven's richest blessing come down
> On anyone, American, English, or Turk
> Who will help to heal
> This open sore of the world."

However, it is only recently that the Church as a whole has discovered that it has a responsibility *as a Church* to become involved in missions of social change. In 1908 the Federal Council of Churches declared its stand

> For the abolition of child labor.
> For a release from employment one day in seven.
> For a living wage as a minimum in every industry, and for the highest wage each industry can afford.
> For the protection of the worker from dangerous machinery, occupational disease, injuries, and mortality.
> For the principle of conciliation and arbitration in industrial dissentions.

The missions of the Church in social action sometimes produce stormy reactions. When principles, no matter how "Christian" they appear to be in theory and discussion, are actually applied where economic, social, or political interests are threatened, they become controversial.

One school of Christian thought today holds that such controversy and conflict should be welcomed as clearing the air and moving toward necessary social change. The traditional Christian objective of reconciliation must come only with serious struggle. These theologians maintain that because of human sinfulness, self-interest can never be purged by "spiritual" means and idealism alone. Self-interest gets itself embedded in power structures and can be modified only when countervailing power is brought to bear upon it. This is why the dispossessed and the weak must organize themselves for the exertion of power on behalf of their own legitimate interests. Without justice, love cannot do its proper work.

The list of social change missions in which the Churches are involved is a long and growing one. Agencies specifically focused on issues of racial justice have flourished since the civil rights struggle of the 1960's, when the influence of the Churches was a decisive factor at many crucial points. But beyond the achievement of the right to vote, integrated education, and access to public facilities lies the vast problem of black poverty, linked with discrimination in employment. The Churches continue to be involved in this battle as its scope widens and deepens.

The social change agenda of Protestant missions is almost endless. One denomination's social action magazine in a recent two-year period dealt with such issues as:

freedom of choice in abortion
sex education for youth
anti-semitism
civil and religious liberties
private wealth and public poverty
gambling
gay rights
reform of the funeral industry
cybernation
agribusiness vs. the family farm
sexism in church and society

Recently, two items have moved up near the top of that list. One is the effort to reverse the arms race and the increasing militarization of

American life, indeed of the global society. Church action was a major factor in the final American decision to liquidate the Vietnam War. Some of that energy has been remobilized to counter a renewal of the cold war and the accelerating arms race. This entails involvement with such flash points as the Palestinian issue and the proper relation of the security of Israel to the rights of Palestinians. In general, the ecumenical Churches have tried to affirm equally the right of Israel to exist within secure borders properly drawn, and the right of Palestinians to some kind of national entity compatible with their sense of peoplehood and their claim to ancestral lands now occupied by Israel.

The other major agenda of social change mission is human rights, at home and abroad. In a number of repressive situations overseas the indigenous Christian Churches, often the product of Western missions, have been leaders in the human rights struggle. This is particularly true in Taiwan, the Philippines, South Korea, and many Latin American countries where the Roman Catholic Church is prominent.

In some of these societies the Roman Catholic Church has rather dramatically shifted from being the prop and sanctifier of exploitative and repressive elites to being the champion of the poor and their rights and liberties. That shift is linked with the rise within the last two decades of what is generally called "liberation theology." Although quite similar in many ways to so-called "black theology" of the United States, liberation theology is largely a product of Latin American Christianity. Aided and encouraged by mission agencies, it has more recently become popular in differing forms in Asia and in Africa. In North America it finds resonance with the long-established social gospel tradition of the ecumenical Churches, and in Europe with a Christian socialist tradition coming down from the nineteenth century.

Liberation theology is strongly rooted in the Old Testament although its proponents find New Testament warrant as well, particularly in the passages dealing with the kingdom of God. Above all, the Exodus from Egypt provides the fundamental paradigm. A people is liberated from bondage by the will and action of their God, who takes the side of the oppressed against the oppressor. Their slavery had fundamentally economic roots: "What is this we have done, that we have let Israel go from serving us?" (Ex 14:5).

Liberation theologians characteristically adopt a Marxist interpretation of social dynamics, relating oppression to class structures and liberation to class struggle. They call for a clear identification with the poor and oppressed against the rich and powerful, and accept the necessity for revolutionary measures including violence if necessary to achieve new social structures.

There are, of course, numerous passages in the Hebrew prophets which support such a theology with its corollary that the essential mission of the people of God is to achieve social justice. The New Testament warrants are less commanding. There are downright quietistic passages which have long been cited by Christians who are either committed to the status quo or who believe that religion is essentially concerned with salvation in the life after death and/or in the miraculous transformation of the world by the Second Coming of Christ.

New Testament teaching which encourages a liberationist stance is usually based on prophetic precedent. The inaugural sermon of Jesus in the synagogue at Nazareth is a classic example:

> And there was given to him the book of the prophet Isaiah. He opened the book and found the place where it was written,
>
> "The Spirit of the Lord is upon me,
> because he has anointed me to preach good news to the poor.
> He has sent me to proclaim release to the captives
> and recovering of sight to the blind,
> to set at liberty those who are oppressed,
> to proclaim the acceptable year of the Lord."
>
> And he closed the book and gave it back to the attendant, and sat down; and the eyes of all in the synagogue were fixed on him. And he began to say to them, "Today this scripture has been fulfilled in your hearing" (Lk 4:17–21).

The current prevalence of these liberationist themes is strikingly illustrated by the agenda of the World Conference on Mission and Evangelism held at Melbourne, Australia, in May 1980. This was the latest in a series of landmark assemblies held first by the International Missionary Council and then by the World Council of Churches after the merger of the two organizations. Approximately once in each decade since 1910 mission leaders from around the world—and now predominantly from the third world—have gathered to assess the state and the challenge of mission. At Melbourne the overall theme was "Your Kingdom Come," with four major sub-themes: good news to the poor, the kingdom of God and the struggles of the world, the Church witnesses to the kingdom, and the crucified

Christ challenges human power. Clearly the agenda was social change, in one form or another.

This is not to say that evangelization was not part of the agenda at Melbourne. Indeed, for the planners and many participants the element of evangelization was inseparable from these matters of social concern and social action. One historic mission agency has expressed that integration of the evangelical with the social component of mission in its definition of evangelism:

> Evangelism is word and deed which testify to and participate in the acts of God, and call forth the response of conversion—conversion being understood as the continuing reorientation of individuals and communities to the willing service of God as known in Jesus Christ.[1]

The Old Testament root of this definition of conversion is in the Hebrew word *shuv,* "return." The "continuing reorientation" of persons and the societies in which they live involves a constant turning back to the will and ways of God, and to a commitment to his purposes for the world. The New Testament term for conversion is *metanoia:* "change" of ideas, attitudes, intentions, commitments. Conversion, then, has not so much a sociological reference as it has a moral and attitudinal reference. It is not primarily concerned with religious labels and moving from one religious community to another, but with deeper changes in values and loyalties and life-style. The significance of these deep spiritual factors is eloquently stated by a great Hindu philosopher and Indian political figure:

> The supreme task of our generation is to give a soul to the growing world-consciousness, to develop ideals and institutions necessary for the creative expression of the world soul, to transmit these loyalties and impulses to future generations and train them into world citizens.[2]

In other words, humankind must find a common set of moral values, a common standard of human greatness, a common conviction about the purposes embedded in the universe. Every great civilization of the past has had a religious core. The world civilization of the future must also have a spiritual core, so noble, so universal, so practical that it will be adequate for all humankind.

Christians believe that Jesus' faith in God, Jesus' description of the true way of life, and Jesus' spirit provide the only truly adequate basis for a healthy world civilization. Numbering almost a quarter of the world's population, the Christian Church in its many branches exists in practically every country on earth. No other international community has such potential ability to draw together all ages, races, nations, and classes. Christians believe that through mission essential new powers, new standards, new motives, and new character can be released in the world.

What then about the assumption that the aim of mission is to convert people from other religious allegiances to Christianity, to bring them out of their inherited and often ethnic faith into the Church, to elicit a verbal confession of faith in Christ? Such is the most evident motive and style of the large so-called "evangelical" sector of missionary activity. Roman Catholic and Orthodox missions have traditionally had this aim, on the ancient theological premise that "outside the Church there is no salvation."

But for the ecumenically oriented missions today the picture is different. A story in the *New York Times,* under the dateline of El-Maten, Algeria, begins: "An American missionary doctor has built a modern hospital in this primitive Kabylia mountainside hamlet." It then goes on to say, "The 30-year-old bearded physician, from Storm Lake, Iowa, considers himself part of a new wave of missionaries now coming to Africa in increasing numbers. These missionaries are concentrating almost entirely on helping the Africans build better countries. 'Proselytizing is a dead dodo today,' said Dr. Dierwechter, whose informal attire goes unnoticed among the ragged town folk here."

If not exactly dead as a dodo, it is true that missions focused on bringing "heathen" into the Church is out of style in many ecumenical circles. One Catholic missiologist, asked about the classical and long-unquestioned theory of mission that focused on the extension of the Church as the central aim of mission, replied that Church growth is not an authentic aim of mission at all. A former general secretary of the International Missionary Council, Bishop Lesslie Newbigin, who is certainly very evangelical, rejects missions which simply fish in a pond, the world, and lift people out to put them into a fish bowl called the Church.

Obviously, unless salvation is a purely transcendental and non-ethical conception, being a Church member in no way guarantees it. Jesus spoke contemptuously about those who say, "Lord, Lord," but do not do God's will. He says also in the parable about Dives and Lazarus that a great gulf in eternity between lost and saved is simply the extrapolation of a great separation defined by wrong social and moral attitudes in this life.

Many mission leaders today would approach the question of Church growth by suggesting not that it is the aim or *end* of mission and evangelism, but that it is an essential *means* of mission. It is one way in which a community is created at least theoretically committed to doing God's will. In other words, it is necessary for the Gospel to be embodied institutionally in order that God's mission in the world may go forward. In order to be effective the Gospel must be embodied in some social, indigenous, permanent, and universal form.

In the 1920's John Dewey made a visit to Peking that had tremendous influence upon leaders of the new China. One evening in a gathering of missionaries Dewey said in a burst of candor,

> Until I had lived in a country where Christianity is relatively little known and has had few generations of influence upon the character of the people, I had always assumed as the natural reactions of any normal human being in a given situation the reactions which I now discover you only find among people that have been exposed for many generations to the influence of the Christian ethic.[3]

Recently a Japanese pastor spent five years as a parish minister in Hamburg, Germany, and then returned to Japan. In a very interesting interview he commented first upon the purely nominal character of Christianization in German society. But then he went on to describe a profound subconscious effect to which he assigned high significance:

> In Germany people are very critical of the social order in a way not found in Japan. I can describe my meaning by describing a pair of scales. On the one hand there are the practices of society; on the other, in Germany, is the individual conscience acting as a censor. In Japan we lack that censor; the other side of our scale is weighted with obligations and "oughtnesses" developed out of our old feudalistic society.[4]

So we identify the Church as an indigenous and yet universalizing social institution where the symbols and the story of divine love are preserved and recounted and the Bible continually reaffirmed as the norm of thought and life and faith. It is also a place where the terms of the Gospel are defined by action and example as well as by theological debate, terms like "God" and "love" and "neighbor."

In this way Christians may affirm Church growth as the aim of missions, but only in a very particular and provisional sense: Church growth as a *means* to the *end of mission.* The Church is seen as an institution or community explicitly seeking to make meaningful and believable three propositions: that God is love; that persons, though sinful, are made in God's image; that Jesus Christ is both the norm of human life and the revelation of God's purpose to make all men sons of God and brothers of the Son of God. The Church is not a colony of the saved but attempts to be a community of the saving.

So far we seem to have said almost nothing about the issue which is often thought to be crucial for missions: the relationship of Christianity to other faiths. Recall, however, that we began with the Athens speech of St. Paul which does center on this very point. He talks about the great religiousness of the Athenians, with altars to many gods, symbolizing the religious diversity of humankind in its many societies. He suggests that there are two problems with this religious pluralism. One is idolatry. It is terribly easy to be captured by a false or inadequate conception of God through making images, as the Athenians and most of the world's peoples have done. Once made, these images, even though they have the value of making the divine seem real and present, invariably tempt their worshipers to false or inadequate understandings. In his criticism Paul continues the Old Testament condemnation of idolatrous worship, from the worship of the golden calf at Sinai to Isaiah's ridicule of the man who takes part of a log to roast his dinner and then makes a god with the other part, to which he then prays, "You are my god—save me" (Is 44:13–17).

The other problem with the religions is ignorance, says Paul. He cited the Athenian altar to an Unknown God. What they already worship with vague and dim understanding he is now prepared to make clear to them: Jesus as the true and adequate revelation of the "unknown God's" real character and purpose.

On the one hand, there is genuine religious seeking in all the religions. Anyone anywhere can worship the true God by following faithfully the insights of conscience and the best leadings of one's own religious nature (see Rom 2:9–16). On the other hand, there is also much ignorance and idolatry. Only by taking Jesus Christ as the spiritual and moral norm can one be sure how to offer "willing obedience to the purposes of God." Hence, the proper stance for Christians in mission is neither an uncritical affirmation of all religions nor a doctrinaire dismissal and rejection. There is no room for Christian triumphalism as if in the Church and in Christian theology there has come a final and perfect reflection of God's will. All persons, of whatever religious sign, are called to "change," to conversion, because all are under the continuing judgment of God as he has been revealed in Christ.

The suggestion is not so much that Christians are to judge other people but that our missionary task is to call them to self-judgment. We help them to examine themselves and their beliefs as they are actually being examined by a divine judgment, a judgment according to what is seen and heard in Jesus.

Nothing in this procedure prejudges how much conformity to Jesus Christ as norm, as Lord, there may be under any religious label. As a matter of fact, formal designations of religious affiliation are often very misleading. The blatantly racist white Citizens Councils of the South required that members must believe in the divinity of Christ! Much more useful, as we examine Christianity vis-à-vis the other faiths, is to look for the actual moral and spiritual actualities in any given religious allegiance. What is the ultimate concern or norm that determines the spiritual, ethical, and social life of the believer? We may often find persons who certainly have "repented"—changed their thinking—under the power of Christ's teaching and example and who yet wear surprising labels. One man, for instance, was an active participant in the life of his local church, an effective lay preacher, an ardent disciple and servant of Jesus Christ whom he gladly named as Lord. Yet he was never baptized out of his inherited Muslim belonging. He wanted to be under the Lordship of Christ within the Muslim community, and thus possibly a bridge to other Muslims.

These reflections point to one practical conclusion: the proper spirit or mode of mission as directed to another person in his non-Christian faith is essentially the same as our style and spirit in theological discussion among Christians. Both mission and theological debate are efforts to participate in that action by which God is bringing all persons under the judgment of Christ as Lord, both in belief and practice. The proper mode of such theology as well as of missionary evangelism is dialogue. Note that we are saying "mode" or "spirit," not a "method." We do not need question-and-answer periods, or eyeball-to-eyeball confrontations, or buzz sessions, or group dynamics in order to exemplify the mode of dialogue. Preaching, lecturing, and many other forms of communication can be dialogical in spirit, in mode, and in style.

The Commission on World Mission and Evangelism of the World Council of Churches has well described this dialogical approach. The basic need of all persons is for the Gospel, whether they know it or not. The individually and actually felt need of anyone, under his particular circumstances at any given moment, also requires sympathetic and informed understanding on the part of one who would speak of the Gospel. Whatever the circumstances may be, the intention in every human dialogue should be to become involved in the dialogue of God with persons, to move our partner and ourselves to what God in Christ reveals to us, and to respond to him.

Around the world there are some fifteen centers for the study of other religions, many of them encouraged by the World Council of Churches. At all these such dialogue is going forward: at the famous Tao Feng Shan Center in Hong Kong; at the Christian Institute for the Study of Religion and Society in Bangalore, India, which publishes an excellent journal embodying much of this dialogical material; at Colombo and Kyoto and Beirut and many other points in the Far East, Southern Asia, and the Middle East.

In 1763 John Woolman, the great Quaker mystic and prophet, was led to make a missionary journey among the Pennsylvania Indians. It was an extremely dangerous journey because there was fighting on the frontier. He records how for several days he was confined to his tent in the woods by heavy rain, and how he spent the time reflecting on his mission there. He wrote in his *Journal:* "Love was the first motive; and thence a concern arose to spend some time with the Indians that I might feel and understand their life and the spirit they live in, if happily I might receive some instruction from them, or they might be in any degree helped forward by my following the leadings of truth among them."[5]

It would be hard to find a better description of the spirit in which Christian evangelism ought to work. Because we love our fellowmen we undertake to be with them. With them we witness and learn, giving and receiving, going forward hand in hand to explore the great options for human life and faith in the spirit of Jesus Christ. A particularly delicate and important question within this general issue of Christian mission to those of other faiths is the question of missions to Jews. Several comments can be made. One is that Christianity and Judaism have an extraordinary kinship. They share the Hebrew Bible. The Founder of Christianity and most of his first followers were Jews. They have a long, intertwined, and often tragic history. This calls for great sensitivity on the part of Christians, and also great humility in view of many Christian offenses against the Jewish people. It certainly calls for great respect for Judaism, since from one point of view Christianity can be seen as the universalized and missionary form of Hebrew faith. Few, if any, ecumenical churches carry on "missions to Jews." They feel that there are other, needier fields of work.

At the same time, they do make efforts to foster Jewish-Christian dialogue, through the National Council of Churches and in other ways. Because of the preoccupation of Jews with the fortunes of the State of Israel and the long-drawn-out Palestine crisis, these dialogues tend to focus on such political concerns. Another focus is on the explanation of Judaism and its practices to Christians, on the plausible theory that Jews can pick up a good deal of general knowledge of Christianity from the culture—from Christmas, Easter, and the rest—while Christians must make an effort to learn about Judaism. These exercises, however, seldom reach a serious exchange on fundamental questions of faith. Whenever such deeper dialogue does occur, it is potentially a missionary situation, in both directions. Conversion, a reorientation of ideas and of loyalties, may happen.

Ecumenical mission today is based on such dialogue and equally on a concept of partnership. Partnership as a style of mission and a source of strength for mission is rooted in the Christian understanding of God. There is a revealing story about how Jesus once found himself powerless in his own home town: "He could do no mighty work there . . . because of their unbelief" (Mk 6:5). Without the partnership of faith, without responsive, venturing human beings with whom and through whom to exercise his power, the God who worked so effectively through Jesus at many other times was blocked from bringing hope and healing.

This partnering God has created a world in which the imperative of partnership is inescapable. Great nations which possess and mobilize enormous power are finding that they can in no way go it alone. Nor can churches. For more than a century the stated aim of many mission agencies has been the establishing of "self-governing, self-supporting, and self-propagating churches." But, say many Christians in mission-founded churches, selfhood must not be interpreted to mean separation, to deny our need of others and the refusal of assistance from Christians of other countries. That is not God's plan for his Church. His plan is unity and mutual interdependence.

In mission policy discussions, some have said that Japan is wealthy now and does not need missions from American churches. Japanese Christians have responded that the mission of the Church is not to be based on the idea that rich nations help out of pity for the poor nations. There must be a mutuality of mission in which the Churches in both countries are strengthened. Everywhere in the world the Church needs co-workers from other countries for the enrichment of its Christian life and experience.

"Everywhere" includes the United States. Mission agencies are increasingly involved in fostering missionary effort by third world Christians in America. This two-way exchange reflects the great needs of the United States as a "mission field" and the resources that partnership can bring.

As the 1980's begin, Churches are moving toward some new dimensions of missionary partnership. One of these is greater depth in partnership. "Depth" means getting beyond official Church cooperation to an active involvement with the people themselves. For example, the revolutionary idea has emerged that ordinary people are not just consumers of missionary health care. They are really the primary agents of health. They must help themselves to health, taking responsibility for the community's sanitation and hygiene, for basic nutrition and essential inoculations—all the things that are most fundamental for health. That means that the professionals—doctors, nurses, and their clinics and hospitals—become auxiliary rather than primary.

In a similar way, mission in theological education has moved toward a people's partnership. Local leaders are encouraged and enabled to pursue theological studies on a part-time basis in their own localities and at their own academic levels—sometimes quite low, sometimes very high. The seminary—its faculty and curriculum—comes to the student, on his or her own terms, rather than bringing the student to a brick and mortar institution. Leadership selection and formation is fostered at the local level. Theological reflection is carried on right within the ongoing life of congregations.

Another new dimension of partnership in mission today has to do with the reach out—the range—of partnership. Roman Catholics have become significant partners with Protestants in many places. In the Middle East, partnership with the ancient Orthodox Churches is developing.

The increasing range of partnership was exemplified at the Assembly of the World Conference on Religion and Peace in 1979. This event brought together many kinds of Buddhists, Christians, Hindus, Jains, Jews, Muslims, Shintoists, and Sikhs from forty-five countries and all ideological blocs. These members of many faiths decided to join forces first of all to generate a worldwide mass movement for disarmament, especially nuclear disarmament.

A second commitment was to promote more just international economic relations. Finally, these partnering faiths agreed to intervene in selected conflict situations involving human rights. They will build small multi-religious task forces of experts on the issues, who will try to discover ways to achieve greater justice without recourse to violence.

Christians believe that all this is part of the wisdom and will of God. Partnership is the way his power is released—not just partnership with Church leaders but with all the people of the congregations, and not just with Christians like ourselves but with all Christians. Nor is the partnership confined to Christians. We welcome as partners all those who are open to the leading of the Spirit which was in Jesus—a Spirit which moves like the wind, blowing where it will. That Spirit is at work to make effective in all human life the divine intention "to unite all things in Christ, things in heaven and things on earth"—a partnership whose depth and range we are still only beginning to comprehend and which calls for caring involvement and generous support.

## NOTES

1. Formulated by the United Church Board for World Ministries.
2. Sarvepelli Radhakrishnan, *Eastern Religions and Western Thought* (New York: Oxford University Press, 1941), p. vii.
3. From a personal letter by Henry Smith Leiper who at the time was a missionary in China, later Associate General Secretary of the World Council of Churches.
4. From a report by Paul R. Gregory, Pacific Regional Secretary, United Church Board for World Ministries.
5. *The Journal of John Woolman* (London: Headley Bros., n.d.), p. 171.

# A Reformed, Evangelical Perspective of Mission

*Richard R. DeRidder*

## I. DEFINITION OF TERMS

Every theologian functions out of as well as within a specific theological matrix. It is impossible to do otherwise. The conclusions reached will obviously build upon the past and provide bridges to the future. This essay is written from a Reformed, Protestant, non-conciliar, Evangelical perspective. Some may prefer the word "Calvinist" in place of "Reformed," but the Reformed tradition is heir to and has profited from other traditions as well as its dominant Calvinist orientation. This is especially true in the present day, for much mutual sharing and cross-fertilization is taking place. The name "Reformed" will also be used in contrast to other major traditions such as Baptist, Methodist, etc. These will not be ignored, however. The designation "Protestant" refers to that branch of contemporary Christianity which stands in contrast to and alongside the Roman Catholic and Orthodox branches of the Christian world. Although many Reformed Churches are active participants in the conciliar movements, the specific reference of this essay is to the largely non-conciliar Churches, sometimes designated "evangelical." Evangelical and conciliar are not mutually exclusive, however. Each non-conciliar Church has its own reasons for non-affiliation with the conciliar movement, and attempts to provide alternatives within the evangelical orientation of these Churches have not proven spectacularly successful. The term "Evangelical" is used in the sense of contrast from theologically liberal-oriented churches.

## II. THE SCRIPTURES

The Church is inconceivable without the Scriptures. From the Bible the Church receives the revelation of God which provides its reason for being, its charter, and the basic principles of its continuing mission and goal. Perhaps nothing is more important to the Church and its well-being than the Scriptures it holds, confesses, and preaches (apart, of course, from the person of God himself and of Jesus). For the development of its own life as well as for the success of its mission, it has been a basic principle of Protestantism that every people should have the Bible in its own language at the earliest possible date. Stephen Neill suggests that Bible translation is not a Protestant fad but a universal principle of universal obligation which any missionary enterprise will neglect at its own peril.[1] The result has been that Protestant missions have always been active in Bible translation and distribution wherever such work has spread.

This is still true today. The Bible societies have produced translations of the Bible in whole or part in nearly two thousand languages, while currently hundreds of translation teams are busily employed in producing additional translations.

Controversy continues, however, as to the "most accurate" translation. New translations have appeared in recent years, each of which in its turn sparked additional discussion as to acceptability, accuracy, etc. At the same time answers to questions relating to the infallibility and inspiration of the Scriptures continue to divide evangelicals from non-evangelicals and even from each other. But what use is made of these Scriptures? And how is the Hebrew Bible being used among Protestants? How does the contemporary Christian Church evaluate and use the Old Testament?[2] In order to validate its claim to being in the will of God, the early Church had to claim the Old Testament as its own. A. A. Van Ruler has pointed out that our answers to questions concerning the Christian Church's use of the Old Testament are decisive for an understanding of Jesus Christ in his historical character, as well as the Jewish context in which he lived and out of which he spoke. It will also decide for the Church how it views the saving acts of God in history and will be determinative for the answers we give to the relationship of the Church to the chosen people of God.

> Our whole understanding of the kingdom of God—and therefore also the catholicity of the Christian faith, the Christian church, and Christianity—is determined by what we think of the Old Testament and how we handle it.[3]

I refer to this matter because these questions are so central to the way in which Christians and Jews relate to one another. Various views of the Hebrew Scriptures are current in Protestant circles. Some deny the validity of the Hebrew Scriptures for the New Testament and interpret the Old Testament as a record of Israel's dismal failure to be true to God and his covenant. In less rigid attitudes the Old Testament is seen as inferior to the New Testament, a position which regretfully fails to take account of the grace God mediates and mediated to men in the past. This position sometimes takes the form of the judgment that the Old Testament is merely a source book to prove the validity of the New Testament and that its meaning is exhausted when this function has been fulfilled. Among Reformed Churches the unity of the two Testaments is fairly maintained. John Calvin in his commentary on Hebrews 1:1 seeks the unity of the Old Testament and New Testament in God and not in Christ. Following Calvin it is distinctive of Reformed theology, both in thought and life, to work back through Christ to God. Unless and until the Christian Church is able to work with its Scriptures as a whole and understands with the early Christian Church that the Old Testament is an indispensable and irreplaceable basis for the Church's mission to the world, it will proclaim only a truncated, imperfect witness.

The God who discloses himself in the Hebrew Scriptures is the God of the whole world (universe). The frequent references to the creation accounts in Genesis 1 and 2 in Jewish literature together with the emphasis placed on God's activities in creating and sustaining his world sometimes stand in stark contrast to the Christian emphasis on man's fall as told in Genesis 3. The difference between these two starting points is not one which can be ignored but touches the heart of our attitude toward the world and our fellow men.

God is the God of all men, for all mankind descended from his creation of our primordial parents, Adam and Eve. If he is not this universal God, he is merely a tribal deity, one among many, and men would be free to create new gods for themselves as necessity and occasion might warrant. But no man possesses that liberty. The Jewish insistence on the unity of God is on target.

The common Christian reading of Genesis 1–3 frequently disregards the significance of the world as created good and life in this world as a joyful fellowship and walk with God, as will be noted in greater detail later. It is a misrepresentation of God and his mission to say otherwise or to make the future the sole focus of the joy of the believer. The day-to-day life of man is lived under the grace and blessing of his Creator and Redeemer. God's world is still "good" and man's life is one of endless potential to live out the joyful life and experience, the *shalom* of God. Man lives out of the grace of his Creator.

The answer to the question "What do you think of the Old Testament?" is crucial to Jew-Christian relationships. It is quite untrue to limit the significance of the Old Testament to that of preparation for the New, or to say, as is frequently said, that the New Testament fulfills the Old. Both Testaments are necessary and cannot be weighed the one against the other. God's mission, begun with the dawn of human history, moves forward through all time to the present and will continue to the end of time. Having inaugurated his kingdom in Eden, God will bring it to completion at the end of the ages.

## III. THE COVENANTING GOD

What then is the significance of Abraham and his descendants in God's redemptive program? Why was there an identifiable people, elect of God, in the Old Testament? And what is the significance of the continued existence of this elect and holy nation, the Jews? Christians have been forced to answer these questions today because of what has occurred in the worldwide dispersion of the Jews, the Holocaust, as well as the establishment of the State of Israel.

When the Old Testament is taken seriously as part of the forward movement of God's redemptive plan for his world, it is immediately apparent that Abraham and his descendants have a special and continuing destiny under God. Genesis 12:1–3 speaks to God's continuing concern for the nations, a theme developed in and central to the first eleven chapters of that book. In Abraham all the nations would be blessed (Gen 13:1–3.)[4] Later repetitions and enlarging of the scope of that covenant promise make it very clear that Israel exists for the sake of the world. God's covenant with Abraham and Israel is for the sake of the nations which will find blessing through Abraham. Christianity may never forget this, nor may the Jews ever ignore it. Whatever happens, a blessing and mission was conferred on Israel which no other people can claim, and that is the "you only have I known out of all the peoples of the earth" (cf. Dt 7:6ff.; Am 3:2).

## IV. THE UNITY OF JEW AND GENTILE

But this special calling of Israel and its place in God's mission include the sharing of its treasures so that Gentiles too may participate in what it means to be the people of God. The fellowship of disciples of Jesus drawn out of all the peoples of the world, Jews as well as Gentiles, is seen from the Christian perspective as the direct result of the redemptive work of Jesus. The clearest statement of this is found in Ephesians 2:12–19.

> Remember that you were at that time separated from Christ, alienated from the commonwealth of Israel, and strangers to the covenants of promise, having no hope and without God in the world. But now in Christ Jesus you who once were far off have been brought near in the blood of Christ. For he is our peace, who has made us both one, and has broken down the dividing wall of hostility, by abolishing in his flesh the law of commandments and ordinances, that he might create in himself one new man in place of the two, so making peace, and might reconcile us both to God in one body through the cross, thereby bringing the hostility to an end. And he came and preached peace to you who were far off and peace to those who were near; for through him we both have access in one Spirit to the Father. So then you are no longer strangers and sojourners, but you are fellow citizens with the saints and members of the household of God.

The great mystery that Jesus has revealed is the fellow-citizenship of Gentiles *with* Israel. This is not *in place of* Israel, however. Nor is it to the *exclusion of* Israel. It is *with* Israel, as Paul makes abundantly clear in Romans 9–12. Abraham, for Paul, is himself the prototype of Gentile Christians (Rom 4). It is evident that the election of Israel was intended for the purpose of the universal covenant of God promulgated through Abraham (Gen 12:1–3 and elsewhere). Israel's election does not stand by itself, as does no election. It is for a purpose.

Salvation is meaningful, therefore, only if it is all-inclusive and embraces all mankind. The unity of Israel and the Gentiles belongs to the confirming signs of messianic fulfillment. No matter how one views the tensions of world history (Old Testament or New Testament), the Christian Church with believing Israel has learned to know that Jesus is not the

Messiah unless he is the Messiah for the Jew as well as the Gentile, and that if Jew and Gentile remain separate this is at heart a denial of Jesus' messiahship. What is so important to observe is that everyone who is saved is redeemed in no other way than through the will and work of the one God whose will and plan for man is the same for all in all ages. This will and purpose of God are first of all covenant action. God created a people, Israel, by his sovereign choice. Even when the New Testament Church adopted titles and names for itself from the Old Testament, it did so in the clear understanding that this did not exclude Israel. Jew and Gentile are now both inseparably connected by his sovereign, redemptive plan to unite all things in heaven and earth to himself.

Markus Barth has expressed the debt of the Church to Israel in this way:

> What the Christians owe to Israel, what they learn from Israel, and what they hope for Israel, this they also apply to their conversation with every man.[5]

The Jews are essential for the growth and development of the Church, those who lived before us, live among us and around us. The proclamation of the Gospel of the kingdom did not herald some new form or administration of Jewish nationalism but it heralded the creation of the one new people of God from among Jews first and also from the Gentiles. This new people does not supplant the former but is the realization and fulfillment of it.

The consequence of this is that no one people can claim Jesus Christ as its own, singular possession. Jesus Christ belongs to all mankind, as God intended. And although he was proclaimed "to the Jew first," the Church has always maintained with Paul the "and also to the Gentiles." There is not one Gospel for one people and a different Gospel for yet a different race or nation. Or to put this in yet another way: if there is a way of salvation possible outside of Jesus Christ, then we must all unite together in all honesty to proclaim that way to mankind. The Christian insistence on the validity of the apostles' dictum that "there is no other name under heaven given among men by which we must be saved" (Acts 4:12) is grounded in the unity of God and his mission and purpose for the world. Jakob Jocz insists that a Church without a message for the Jews lacks a message for the Gentiles also. He further requires that in addition to speaking the Gospel, Christians must live that Gospel.[6]

In spite of what ought to be from a scripturally oriented position, the actual situation is that mission to the Jews has been in serious decline among most branches of Christianity. At the Edinburgh World Missions Conference in 1910 no less than ninety-five societies were identified at that time which had 804 people engaged in mission to the Jews. Today, large sections of the Christian Church have abandoned all concern for witness to Jews and fail in every respect to communicate the good news by word and often even in deed. Dialogue has replaced witness, but as Christians listen, they may never fail, as Verkuyl insists, "to bring up the matter of Jesus Christ and his kingdom which both has come and is coming."[7]

What voices remain today, insisting on the attention to witness that is the duty of the Church to the Jews, are often heard from the dispensational and pre-millenarian Christians. The thesis, most often expressed as a judgment against non-dispensationalist Christians, that only dispensationalism has something to offer the Jew is utterly false and untrue from a scriptural viewpoint. When Jews are looked upon only as the hands on God's time clock to determine where God is in history in his dealings with Gentiles, then the Jew is made into a symbol only and he is no longer regarded as a person who is the object of God's seeking, electing, covenant love.

It is also difficult to explain why in the long history of Jew-Christian relationships there has been scarcely any effort to establish uniquely Jewish Christian congregations. The propriety of doing so is not challenged in most instances. The responsibility to find a genuinely scriptural basis to what one's Jewishness means when Jesus is known by faith as one's Messiah has certainly been given little attention. The unwritten but often subtle requirement to give up one's Jewishness when becoming a Christian is contrary to Scripture and understandably serves as a stumbling block in the way of acceptance of Jesus Christ as Savior and Lord. Although some effort has been made to correct this (such as the messianic synagogue), such efforts have received practically no attention from the churches.

## V. GUIDELINES

What guidelines can be identified which from an evangelical Christian point of view may be useful in developing the kind of relationships between Christians and Jews today?

1. It must first of all be remembered and carefully observed that every effort must be made to establish a relationship of openness and trust between the two communities. Neither community is innocent when one

considers the history of their mutual relationships. That does not excuse either community from its duty to the other, however. There have been very deep wounds inflicted upon the Jewish people in the name of Jesus and from false constructions of Christian theology. For these we are deeply sorry. It is not necessary to repeat that history here: others have detailed it sufficiently from their own perspectives either as Jews or Christians. Although antisemitism has not been limited only to Christian cultures and peoples, it has been a factor determinative of attitudes in Christian societies in which Jews have lived. In our own day we are appalled by the antisemitism in Arab and Muslim lands in their relations and attitudes to the Jew and the State of Israel. This fact alone should urge us on to do a thorough housekeeping in our own Christian milieu. Only a complete openness to one another, while realizing that we cannot undo the past, will keep us from recreating that past.

2. Such trust must become the basis of dialogue. Only persons who know each other can hold a dialogue; otherwise our conversations can only take the level of hurling invectives and countercharges or simply debate which confirms each in the thesis he is defending with no intention of changing one's own mind. Both Christians and Jews have witnessed and experienced the positive benefits of dialogue and can speak meaningfully of its benefits. So long as from the Christian perspective dialogue is engaged in to tell someone else something he does not affirm, know, or had rejected, it will get nowhere. Dialogue is a two-way street. When dialogue results in long lists of differences it only serves to make the breach between the two communities wider. Christians and Jews have much to learn from one another. Such learning is not limited to social concerns, theological definitions, or interpretations of history.[8]

Contemporary Christian scholarship is once again giving attention to the Jewishness of the Gospel. Jews are serving Christians in other ways than merely exegeting the Old Testament for them. Jewish scholars (such as Rabbi Philip Sigal) are assisting Christians to understand their New Testament from other than the traditional development of Christian theological constructions developed by the Church in the Christian era. Increased cooperation of Jews and Christians in the study of both Old Testament and New Testament will not only reveal basic differences between them (especially on the understanding of who Jesus is), but will reveal, as Dr. Sigal has affirmed, that there is nothing in the Christianity of the New Testament which is inconsistent with the Judaism of Jesus' day, including the virgin birth and the resurrection of Jesus. He also points out that there were other viable alternatives in that same time and that the rabbinic Judaism which developed parallel to Christianity followed other valid choices. Which of the two is the genuine heir of the Old Testament covenant heritage remains a point of difference, of course.

Dr. J. Verkuyl gives a significant illustration of the way in which mutual cooperation can be mutually beneficial. He points out (as does Rabbi Sigal) that both Jews and Christians have their *halakoth* and that when Jews see Torah as God's invitation to join him in walking a path and living a life of responsibility and caring for each other, we Christians often forget that the New Testament has much similar material. He further points out that we Christians so quickly assume that the only purpose of passages such as the Sermon on the Mount is to bring us to our knees crying, "God, have mercy on me!" The New Testament, however, is a call to join with Jesus as his disciples, finding our joy in doing what he has taught us (Jn 15:9–17) and teaching others to do the same (Mt 28:19–20).[9] It comes as no surprise, therefore, that the members of the early Christian Church were known as "followers of the way" (cf. Acts 9:2; 19:23).

All of this points up another significant difference of emphasis between Jews and Christians. Evangelical Christian theology oftentimes appears to be preoccupied with the matters of sin and its forgiveness. These remarks are not intended to question the correctness of the Christian witness to sin and redemption. These are indeed at the very heart of the work of Christ. What we must remember, however, is that the redemption God wrought for man in Jesus concerned not just his suffering and death. The life he lived (and now lives after his resurrection) is likewise an integral part of his ministry on our behalf. He lived our life; he died our death. Neither can be omitted without losing the efficaciousness of the other. A redemptive work which only focuses on the future and does not see the joyful grace and freedom to live for God in his world today is not true to the Gospel.

This difference appears in yet another way. Jewish thought reflects in large measure a concentration on the creation and God as Creator (e.g., Gen 1–2). Christian theology more frequently begins with Genesis 3 and the fall of man. The difference is not insignificant. When one begins with the Creator, then life under the Creator takes on meaning. This is and will always remain his world. God surrenders his prerogatives to no one, neither Satan nor man. God remains sovereign. In that light even Genesis 3, though witnessing to radical changes, is not just curse but is an assurance to man and woman, to humankind, that life under God is possible and the world is not shut to God's working by grace. Was man to serve God by guarding and tilling the garden (Gen 2:15)? He will still do so (Gen 3:17–

19) although the ground (not man!) bears a curse for his sake. Was "Woman" (Gen 2:23) now called "Eve" (Gen 3:20) because she was the mother of all the living? She will be saved in her childbearing! Our primal parents can leave the garden, not with heads bowed low but with heads held high, eyes directed heavenward and feet walking hitherto untrod paths into a strange and many times hostile world because they carry with them the promises of grace!

It is encouraging, therefore, to note that among Reformed Christians in the Netherlands, Canada, and the United States Christian theologians and philosophers are working at making real for Christians what it means for every sphere of life to be Christian and are defining ways by which God's creation-ordinance applies to all of life.[10] In this exercise they are being true to the Creator's purpose for man, and consistent with the early Christian Church's basic orientation. When interrogated for their faith, it is interesting to note that the prayers of the early Jerusalem community (as recorded by Luke in Acts) begin with an appeal to the Creator!

Closely related to this entire viewpoint is another of the profound lessons we Christians can learn from the Jews, that is, how to live joyfully in God's world. Some forms of Christian doctrine tend to look on this world as only evil and the quicker we can get out of it the better, or at least things are not going to be much better until Jesus returns and recreates this world. The Jews have always seen the world as under God's control and exercised the freedom God gives man to ask him hard questions as to where God is when the only path they are permitted to walk is from home to concentration camp and extinction. We Christians must learn that the answers we have do not always fit the questions we ought to be asking.

3. A third guideline is found in the worldwide dispersion of the Jews and the worldwide spread of the Christian Church. The Jewish people are found throughout the Christian communities. Is it God's purpose that each forever remain in his own ghetto (a ghetto, it must be remembered, shuts one in and keeps the other out)? Christians too struggle with the problems of identification and assimilation. Can we not see in the Jewish people some guidelines and seek help from them as to how one can maintain his basic loyalties and precious heritage in the midst of an often hostile world? The world is simply not Christian. Secularizing powers are hard at work also among Christians to lead if possible to a denial of God's ultimacy. The challenges and temptations of alien life-styles have long been experienced by the Jews.

This worldwide spread of the Christian Church and the widespread dispersion of the Jews throughout Christian communities in the world must be recognized as a providential setting which should make the Church aware of its responsibility to be a living witness to the Jews. The continued existence of the Jewish people concretizes God's purpose for the world (Gen 12:1–3) through this people whose glory includes that it was from them that Messiah Jesus was born (Rom 9:5). The Lord of the Church who controls the history of mankind calls us through the tragic and dramatic events of our modern history to be aware of the urgency of the Jews' continuing need for the Gospel.

4. It has been encouraging to note that evangelical Christianity has in recent years begun to identify with the causes of justice and righteousness in our age. Evangelical Christianity has for a very long time criticized the conciliar churches for their orientation to such concerns because of what seemed to many to result in a lack of address to the Gospel. It was like a breath of fresh air when, gathered at Lausanne, Switzerland, the Covenant adopted there included this reference to "Christian Social Responsibility."

> We affirm that God is both the Creator and the Judge of all men. We therefore should share his concern for justice and reconciliation throughout human society and for the liberation of men from every kind of oppression. Because mankind is made in the image of God, every person, regardless of race, religion, colour, culture, class, sex or age, has an intrinsic dignity because of which he should be respected and served, not exploited. Here too we express penitence both for our neglect and for having sometimes regarded evangelism and social concern as mutually exclusive. Although reconciliation with man is not reconciliation with God, nor is social action evangelism, nor is political liberation salvation, nevertheless we affirm that evangelism and socio-political involvement are both part of our Christian duty. For both are necessary expressions of our doctrines of God and man, our love for our neighbour and our obedience to Jesus Christ. The message of salvation implies also a message of judgment upon every form of alienation, oppression and discrimination, and we should not be afraid to denounce evil and injustice wherever they exist. When people receive Christ they are born again into his kingdom and must seek not only to exhibit but also to spread its righteousness in the midst of an unrighteous world. The salvation we claim should be transforming us in the totality of our personal and social responsibilities. Faith without works is dead.[11]

Verkuyl, speaking of the Jews' emphasis on the Messianic kingdom, says:

> Throughout its history Christianity has so spiritualized and individualized its understanding of the messianic kingdom that it is in need of a

good lesson from Judaism, which tries to give shape and form to the kingdom in *this* world by emphasizing justice and righteousness in the here and now. Fortunately the message is getting through to some Christians.[12]

## VI. LIBERATION THEOLOGY

Thus far our attention has been directed almost exclusively to Jew-Christian relationships. There is, of course, far more that engages the Christian Church today in its relation to the world and the conception with which the Church operates in its mission. Among the purposes of the previous sections has been the desire to emphasize that the Church (in God's mission comprised of Jew and Gentile) is committed to mission, and that this mission makes no distinctions as to race, geography, language, etc. A part of the aftermath of World War II (theologically speaking) has been the number of theological movements spawned by mankind's conscience seeking an answer to the hard questions with which an often evil world confronts it. Although several of these movements are already memories, liberation theology is among those that remain and continue to engage the Christian community.

Evangelical Christians were slow to respond to the voices of liberation which were calling for both practical and theoretical application of a biblical ethic to society and its deep sicknesses. Even when evangelicals as late as 1974 responded with the Lausanne Covenant, the response quoted earlier in this essay was both inadequate and incomplete and revealed an underlying duality that continues to characterize much evangelical missiological reflection on the subject. While Lausanne acknowledged "Christian presence in this world" as "indispensable to evangelism," its call to *diakonia* was deficient in that it saw "responsible service in this world" as the *result* of evangelism instead of an integral part of it. Both are part of our Christian duty, but they cannot be so neatly separated into cause and effect.[13] *Kerygma* and *diakonia* are equally primary in the Church's relationship to the world. Emphasizing one at the expense of the other can only lead to a false dualism. Evangelical criticism of liberal theology as emphasizing *diakonia* at the expense of *kerygma* is validly met by the countercharge that *diakonia* among evangelicals frequently suffers as a result of an unwarranted tension created between *diakonia* and *kerygma.*

Evangelical Christians had very good reasons for hesitating before yielding to the temptation to jump on the liberation bandwagon. Everything that was described as Christian was not so. Reflection on the source from which some forms of liberation theology drew their calls to affirmative action soon proved that every appeal, even to the Bible, is not necessarily biblical. Non-Christian philosophies, Marxism, and varied political ideologies as well as the Bible were appealed to in order to gain ideological support. Meanwhile, North American Christians could only listen deeply pained to the criticisms by the theologians of liberation as we were shown the frequently unacknowledged, unconfessed (even unrealized) paternalism and imperialism so intricately woven into the fabric of Western culture and Christianity. Defense of the faith is easier for Western Christians than living out that faith as true prophets of God set in his kingdom for such a time as this. Early responses of evangelical Christians seemed to be directed consequently to correction of the doctrinal errors of the voices for liberation rather than to applying a critique to itself in the light of God's mission.

Significant changes have taken place in the past few years. The understandable suspicions which haunted evangelical discussions of the subject of liberation do continue, and quite properly so in some instances. However, there are many hopeful signs that a number of Christian leaders have been and are listening to the distressing cries of those who are the victims of oppression, injustice, and sometimes Christianly baptized ideologies and political theories naively assumed without reflection as being consistent with a practiced Christian creed.[14] What is emerging from all this is not merely a re-evaluation of what mission is all about when carried out in another culture whose transgressions seem so blatantly clear, but also an increasing awareness that there are basic demonic structures operative in our own society and culture which must likewise be dealt with both by affirmative action and by prophetic speech. Salvation is more than making a kingdom that is not of this world into a kingdom that is of no earthly use to any world. Salvation is more than a total reorientation of the individual to God from the former way of life; it is a kingdom come and coming, real and present, seen as well as unseen. For this evangelical Christianity can thank the theologians of liberation, for while criticizing others, evangelicals necessarily had to engage in self-critique.

## VII. CONTEXTUALIZATION

A result of liberation-thinking that is having a marked influence upon evangelical missiology is found in the affirmation of the "contextual nature of theology."[15] The term is new to mission theology, although the roots of the concept go far back in the previous century and its definitions of and goals for what became known as the indigenous Church. It is striking that many evangelical missiologists still operate with these nineteenth century definitions in planning mission strategies and defining the goals of mission. Only the form has changed. Now that Western imperialism and paternalism in their former garb are no longer possible, a new form of Western Christian imperialism has made its appearance in the control of theological education by the Western missionaries in emerging churches. What is so easily overlooked is that by the control of the education and training of the emerging national leaders a Church polity, liturgy, and creed can be subtly and innocently imposed on the Church which is as lacking in indigeneity as were some of the applications of the three "self" formulae: self-governing, self-supporting, self-propagating.

Evangelical response to liberation theology's call to liberate culture and to respond affirmatively to the issues of human development and social justice has been remarkably silent and inadequate. Interestingly, evangelical anthropologists and sociologists have been far more aggressive than evangelical theologians in formulating some sort of response and/or definition. No one quarrels with the statement that the content of the gospel must be effectively communicated to the cultural context. What needs to be emphasized (after being recaptured in the service of God's mission) is the duty of all believers to be prophets, priests and kings and to apply Scripture as judge and savior to the whole texture of our culturally bound life. The Reformed concept of the kingdom of God, it would seem, which calls all mankind to respond meaningfully and with integrity to live a full-orbed kingdom life-style in covenant obedience with the whole covenant community, requires a "comprehensive enterprise where the Gospel is shared in depth and out of the depth of man's need and life situations, so that the knowledge of Christ may one day truly cover the earth as the waters cover the sea."[16] The covenanting God lays his claims on the total life of his people who must walk by that covenant in the cultures of the world.

## VIII. THE NEW RELIGIONS AND CULTS

Christianity as a whole is under attack in the present day from a variety of sources. Not the least of these is the attack from the non-Christian religions and multitudinous cults. Whereas formerly Christians conceived of the world as its mission field and the major world religions as beyond its borders, this is no longer true. In fact, the West (and Christianity everywhere) has become the mission field of these major faiths which are winning adherents from within the very bosom of the Church itself. The very existence of the Christian community is under attack, perhaps as never before.

Besides the varied representations of the major world religions and their adaptations, a host of cults have sprung up. Estimates place the number of these at around three thousand, a figure conceivably realistic when one reads the almost endless lists of exotic names by which many of these have called themselves. Many disappear as quickly as they spring up. Others seem to have greater enduring power. Some are born out of men's imaginations; others are indebted in large part to established religions; still others have grown out of the Church itself. It is not just Christianity that is threatened by these new religions and religious movements. The propagandists for the cults threaten every loyalty which men have adopted. It is apparent that these movements are here to stay for a very long time.

Evangelical Christianity responded both early and strongly to this new fact of our time. The response was frequently in terms of Christian doctrine, however. It was soon apparent that doctrinal orthodoxy and thorough indoctrination in the faith was no guarantee that a person (especially the youth) would be immune to the appeal of these movements. What was needed was an understanding of why people were turning from established religion as found in the churches to the call of a new allegiance and orientation. For these answers the disciplines of sociology, psychology, anthropology—in short, the social sciences—needed to be harnessed in the service of the Church, information centers needed to be set up, and ways of reclaiming those who had joined the cults needed to be developed. The progress has been slow and characterized by many failures. The surprise that the Church could itself be another religion's mission field has not been completely grasped even now.

It is, therefore, interesting to note that the Lausanne Committee's Consultation on World Evangelization held in Pattaya, Thailand, in June 1980 addressed itself directly in one of its major study sections to the subject of Christian witness to mystics and cultists. This is evidence of an awareness that Christianity cannot be satisfied merely to be defensive but must grasp the initiative in countering these movements and initiate an offensive over against them. It would be regrettable if in the future this offensive would take the form merely of a Christian apologetic and neglect to respond to the question why people are seeking their answers outside traditional Christianity. The tragedy of Jim Jones and the People's Temple was clearly inspired by evil. But people will continue to be destroyed and human dignity denied to mankind unless some address coupled with affirmative action is made to the root problems distressing the human soul. No person has the right to play God to another or to demand obedience and loyalty reserved for God alone. From an evangelical Christian viewpoint this is one of the more serious forms of threat confronting the Christian Church today. Not to meet this threat head-on will mean that the world itself is left only the option to be further depersonalized, dehumanized and demonized.

## IX. THE SEARCH FOR UNITY

One final observation needs to be made regarding mission as viewed from an evangelical, Reformed perspective. Evangelicals have been notably fearful of identifying with any attempts to promote Christian unity among all branches of the Christian Church. Even among themselves evangelical Christians find it very difficult to agree on a basis on which united action can be taken. The vivid personalism and immediacy of experience, the exhilaration of their certainties, the thrill of their protests or their non-conformity, as Kenneth Cragg describes this,[17] are sometimes more sectarian than admitted. Unfortunately, such a stance hardly gives credence to the ages-old confession of "I believe in one, holy, catholic and apostolic Church." When this is forgotten or ignored, mission and the pattern of our address to the world will see its duty fulfilled in inviting others to join themselves with our "institution" on the basis of an acceptance of an alternative creed to their own.

The Christian has no liberty to make the house of doctrinal faith a closed society. The heart of the Church is found in its commission, for there its deep relevance for the world is revealed. The creed which the community has received in trust must always be accessible to belief and hospitable to discipleship. A price will have to be paid perhaps in many ways when the Church proclaims the uniqueness of Jesus Christ. While it maintains its own divine right to witness, it affirms just as loudly that admissibility to the faith in Christ is equally the universal birthright of mankind. This it may never permit to be curtailed or suspended.

The Bangkok Assembly (1973) summarizes well the challenge of the Christian Church:

> Our attitude to people of other faiths arises out of our understanding of God's will that all man [sic] shall be saved. Therefore we urge our mem-

ber churches to go forward with eager faith, with greater love for our fellowmen, with prayer for guidance and with confidence that God is at work among all people to make his saving love available for all in every generation and to build the kingdom of His love, which we Christians see manifested in Jesus Christ.[18]

## NOTES

1. Stephen Neill, *A History of Christian Missions* (Baltimore: Penguin Books, Inc.), p. 209.

2. This is a question which A. A. Van Ruler describes as having "a fundamental bearing on theology." His book, *The Christian Church and the Old Testament* (Grand Rapids: Wm. B. Eerdmans, 1971), addresses this issue. (Translated from the German *Die Christliche Kirche und das Alte Testament,* published by Kaiser Verlag, Munich, 1955.)

3. *Ibid.,* p. 10. I am also deeply indebted to Rabbi Philip Sigal whose book, *The Emergence of Contemporary Judaism;* Vol. 1: *The Foundations of Judaism from Biblical Origins to the Sixth Century A.D.* (Pittsburgh: The Pickwick Press, 1980), has been immensely helpful to me in developing an appreciation for the roots of Christianity in the Judaism of Jesus' day.

4. Cf. Richard R. De Ridder, *Discipling the Nations* (Grand Rapids: Baker Book House, 1974), a reprint of *The Dispersion of the People of God* (Kampen: J. Kok, 1971); Johannes Blauw, *The Missionary Nature of the Church* (New York: McGraw-Hill, 1962).

5. Markus Barth, *The Broken Wall* (Chicago: The Judson Press, 1963), p. 139.

6. Jakob Jocz, *Christians and Jews* (London: SPCK, 1966).

7. Johannes Verkuyl, *Contemporary Missiology* (Grand Rapids: Wm. B. Eerdmans, 1979), p. 136.

8. *Ibid.,* pp. 362ff., describes three forms of dialogue: "First, there is a dialogue with the goal to bring about better mutual understanding. Second, some dialogue aims at producing cooperation in dealing with the most urgent problems facing society regionally and universally. Third, other dialogue strives to aid missionary communication on both sides." He adds, "There is a distinction, not an absolute separation."

9. *Ibid.,* pp. 142ff.

10. It is encouraging to note that there are many Evangelical scholars within the Reformed tradition who are engaged in applying the scriptural perspective of God's purpose for man in the world as found in what is called the "creation mandate" (Gen 1:28). Institutions such as Calvin College in Grand Rapids, Michigan, the Free University of Amsterdam, the Netherlands, and Dordt College in Sioux Center, Iowa, are among the schools which offer this perspective and continue to reflect on how faith in God relates to every aspect of human life in this age.

11. *The Lausanne Covenant* (1974), Section 5.

12. J. Verkuyl, *op. cit.,* p. 143.

13. Harvie Conn, in Carl E. Armerding, *Evangelicals and Liberation* (Grand Rapids: Baker Book House, 1977), p. 68.

14. The bibliography is extensive and easily compiled.

15. Aharon Sapsezian, "Theology of Liberation—Liberation of Theology, Educational Perspectives," in *Theological Education,* IX, 4 (Summer 1973), 254.

16. Orlando Costas as quoted by Harvie Conn, in Carl E. Armerding, *op. cit.,* p. 106.

17. Kenneth Cragg, *Christianity in World Perspective* (New York: Oxford University Press, 1965), p. 211.

18. "On Dialogue with People of Living Faiths," in *Bangkok Assembly 1973:* Minutes and Report of the Assembly of the Commission on World Mission and Evangelism of the World Council of Churches, December 31, 1972 and January 9–12, 1973, p. 80.

# Contemporary Roman Catholic Understandings of Mission

*Michael B. McGarry*

Roman Catholic mission thinking over the last fifteen years presents an exciting vista overlooking the main currents of fundamental theology.[1] The nature of the Church, salvation, grace, the meaning of Christ—all these influence any Catholic discussion of mission; at the same time, none of them remains unchanged by the interaction with the new trajectories of missionary thinking. In the Catholic tradition, there are many depositories for contemporary mission discussion, and all of them must be visited in order to have a proper panorama of Catholic thought. These include such diverse resources as the Vatican II documents, papal encyclicals, scholarly monographs and articles, letters home from the missionaries, and native peoples' writings from missionary lands. In such a reading of missionary thought, reports emanating from missions in the third world often grate against the logical, coherent theories of Church documents. For example, one missionary in the field boasts of no converts over a number of years (his is a mission of "presence"), while another Catholic resource claims a new-found urgency to bring all peoples to Christ.

How, then, does a Roman Catholic deliver a consensus of contemporary Catholic thinking in the Church? Is there even such a consensus to be found? Surely he or she must review the resources mentioned above and then note the theological trajectories therein. The inquirer finds out where theory and practice overlap and projects what consequences entail from particular directions. Such will be our method.

In this essay, I suggest that contemporary Catholic thinking on mission is best understood in response to the following pressing issues: (1) the fundamental questions and arguments confronting modern Catholic missionaries; (2) the direction of official Church teaching on missionary activity; (3) the Catholic starting points for a theology of mission; (4) the relationship between mission and liberation; (5) the question of Catholic mission and the Jews.

## I. FUNDAMENTAL QUESTIONS TO MISSIONARIES

There are at least four interrelated concerns which have challenged the traditional Catholic missionary enterprise. These have been rehearsed in many places,[2] but we repeat them here to set the context within which all missionary discussion seems to be taking place today. These questions are variously put, but, in the main, they are the following:

A. Are not the missions an ecclesiastical anachronism of the European colonial expeditions? Attempts by one nation to invade another for territorial aggrandizement have fallen into bad repute. Should not the Church, then, respect religious boundaries as carefully as nations are expected to respect political boundaries? Catholic missionaries, one hears, bring in the worst of first world accoutrements and do not allow native religions and cultures to grow and thrive. Missions, in a word, are no more than religious colonialism.

B. Independent of direct missionary concerns, one hears that a new Catholic attitude towards other world religions makes traditional missions superfluous. That is, there is a more positive evaluation of how God works not only in non-Christian individuals but through their religious traditions as well. God's grace is fully present in, and indeed works through, Hinduism, Buddhism, Taoism, etc. Once we acknowledge this, our posture vis-à-vis other religions is really one of dialogue, not of proselytism; of listening rather than of teaching; of calling them to be faithful to their own traditions as we call ourselves to inner conversion.

C. Since Catholics have outgrown their dictum *extra Ecclesiam nulla salus* (outside the Church there is no salvation), one can rest assured that non-Christians will not be lost if they do not become Catholics—and if they are already saved, what more does the missionary enterprise have to offer?

D. Still others suggest that the scandal of Christian division precludes for the foreseeable future mission in foreign lands. First world sins of imperialism and economic injustice, combined with the obvious lack of unanimity among Christians, should postpone any claim which European Catholicity can make on foreign shores.

Other refinements of these questions may be offered, but they present the main arguments which confront contemporary Catholic missionaries and mission theory. Many would claim that against such a formidable attack, Catholic missions have suffered a loss of nerve from which they are only recently mustering cogent and persuasive counter affirmations. It is these efforts at a positive contemporary Catholic theology of mission which will occupy us for the remainder of this essay.

## II. CONTEMPORARY OFFICIAL TEACHING

### A. Vatican II

For a positive contemporary theology of mission, a Catholic, like all Christians, goes first to the Bible. However, Eugene Fisher has examined mission in the Hebrew Scriptures, the New Testament, and particularly Romans 9–11, so, while referring in passing to the more dramatic passages later on, we will bypass a comprehensive treatment of biblical and other traditional data. We will begin, then, by focusing on Church statements influencing (and influenced by) contemporary Catholic notions of mission.

For the Roman Catholic, the watershed for all contemporary thinking on the Church and its missionary activity is, undoubtedly, the documents of Vatican II.[3] They are quite lengthy and commentary on them is voluminous.[4] Reference to the Council's teaching on mission will have to be cursory at best, but this very brief glance should not imply that the documents are not extremely influential in the subsequent discussion of this essay. Indeed, one would not be far off the mark by saying that Vatican II is the most significant historical factor to urge the Church into rethinking its missionary task.

The Council's explicit attention to mission is found primarily in four documents: the *Dogmatic Constitution on the Church,* the *Decree on the Church's Missionary Activity,* the *Declaration on the Relationship of the Church to Non-Christian Religions,* and the *Declaration on Religious Freedom.*

1. The first in importance of all Vatican II documents is the *Dogmatic Constitution on the Church.* In it, one finds the primary images of the Church to be "light to the world," "service," and "sacrament." It is the task of the Church to bring "all men to full communion with Christ" (n.

1); the Church "receives the mission to proclaim and to establish among all peoples the kingdom of Christ and of God. It becomes on earth the initial budding forth of that kingdom" (n. 5). At the heart of biblical images in the Constitution is the image of "the people of God" (Chapter 2). According to the Constitution the mission and the object of the mission are universal:

> All men are called to belong to the new people of God. . . . It follows that among all the nations of earth there is but one people of God. . . . This characteristic of universality which adorns the people of God is a gift from the Lord himself. By reason of it, the Catholic Church strives energetically and constantly to bring all humanity with all its riches back to Christ its head in the unity of His Spirit. . . . All men are called to be part of this Catholic unity of the people of God. . . . For all men are called to salvation by the grace of God (n. 13).

The document goes on to show how all parts of humanity are related in a *positive* fashion to the Church for salvation. In other words, membership in the Church is intimately linked with salvation, but membership is a very widely defined notion. The Church is necessary for salvation which is inseparable from Christ's role as the one Mediator of salvation. Interestingly, the Council Fathers speak of the Jewish people as those who remain "most dear to God, for God does not repent of the gifts he makes nor of the calls he issues." Later in the same paragraph, the document asserts that the "Church painstakingly fosters its missionary work," but the document does not elucidate any specific relation of this mission to the Jewish people (n. 16). Chapter 2 closes on a strong missionary exhortation which summarizes the observations contained in the foregoing: "The Church simultaneously prays and labors in order that the entire world may become the people of God, the body of the Lord, and the temple of the Holy Spirit" (n. 17).

2. The *Decree on the Missionary Activity of the Church* develops the implications of the more dogmatic/theological observations of the *Constitution on the Church.* As one might expect, this Decree is quite clear in saying that the Church's mission is to convert all unbelievers to be members of the Church. Even more strongly, it asserts that "the pilgrim Church is missionary by its very nature" (n. 2) and that the missionary task is "to plant the Church among those peoples and groups where it has not yet taken root" (n. 6).

Are there any exceptions? As the Council puts it: "All must be converted to him (Christ) as he is made known by the Church's preaching. All must be incorporated into him by baptism, and into the Church which is his body" (n. 7).

3. The third, and obvious, document from Vatican II which forms the backbone of any contemporary Catholic thinking on mission is the *Declaration on the Relationship of the Church to Non-Christian Religions.* Within the great world religions, "the Catholic Church rejects nothing which is true and holy in these religions." Holding firmly that only in Christ is the fullness of religious life, nevertheless the Church "respects" the other religions for the truths contained therein (n. 2). With regard to the Jews, the document is more elaborate and provocative. Significantly, the Council Fathers did not call for a missionary program aimed at the Jews; rather they recommend "mutual understanding and respect which is the fruit above all of biblical and theological studies, and of brotherly dialogues" (n. 4).

4. In the *Declaration on Religious Freedom,* God's universal intention for all to be saved by membership in the Catholic Church is stated quite explicitly:

> We believe that this one true religion subsists in the catholic and apostolic Church, to which the Lord Jesus committed the duty of spreading it abroad among all men (n. 1).

With regard to evangelization, the document upholds human dignity and freedom: when spreading religious beliefs, "everyone ought at all times to refrain from any manner of action which might seem to carry a hint of coercion or of a kind of persuasion that would be dishonorable or unworthy" (n. 4).

The foregoing is only a representative sample of the teachings of Vatican II on mission. We present them here because they form the backdrop against which subsequent documentation and theology must be seen. Furthermore, the theology of mission contained in these documents represents the consensus of worldwide Catholic teaching. The documents and debate to which we will turn our attention momentarily are efforts to bridge the consensus of official Catholic teaching with new missionary perceptions and situations.

By way of commentary, one can see that Catholic teaching on missionary activity as found within representative Council documents is indeed quite clear and univocal: God wills all to be saved; this salvation comes through Christ and him alone; the Church is the one mediator of salvation and all—without exception—are obliged to join it once they are convinced of the truth it bears; and, the Church, missionary by its very nature, is required to work to convert all to its fold. Only with effort does one find other strains: the call for dialogue with other religions, the respect which the Church has for the elements of truth to be found in other religions, and the disavowal of dishonorable and coercive means to advance the Gospel.

As thorough and comprehensive as the documents of Vatican II are, they have not staved off further and trenchant debate. Contemporary Catholic discussion on mission has proceeded in many directions. To follow those directions can be a frantic task. It is true that conciliar documents store up the groundswells of historical movements, stabilize and express the state of the question, and broach the salient questions for the future. But theological debate erupts all over the globe, arising out of particular needs and situations and orbits back to Rome in both echo and tension. For the sake of order, then, we will locate the debate in the following areas: Church Documents Since Vatican II; The Question of Starting Points: Salvation, Christ, and Church; Mission and Themes of Liberation; Roman Catholics and a Mission to the Jews.

**B. Other Voices from Rome: Documents Since Vatican II**

1. The single most important document on mission theology since Vatican II is Pope Paul VI's apostolic exhortation "On Evangelization in the Modern World."[5] (Cf. Fisher's article in this volume.) This document has become the active blueprint for modern Catholic evangelization efforts. It is clearly and persuasively written, and sensitive to modern trends, but insistent on the fundamental Christian duty to share one's faith. At the heart of the document is Pope Paul's characteristic concern about human liberation, which is tied at every step to a passion for justice and full human dignity. Imitating Christ the evangelizer, the Christian strives to proclaim the kingdom of God, the core of which is salvation, the "liberation from everything which oppresses man." The Church evangelizes in order to convert "solely through the divine power of the message it proclaims, both the personal and collective consciousness of people, the activities in which they engage, and the lives and concrete milieux which are theirs" (n. 18). Going beyond the documents of Vatican II, Pope Paul underscores the intimate link between evangelization and full human liberation, including explicit attention to socio-economic development (nn. 31–38).

The beneficiaries of this Gospel message include the Church itself, those who have strayed from the truth, and "the immense sections of mankind who practice non-Christian religions" (n. 53). Interestingly, the exhortation does not mention the Jewish people specifically, and, indeed, the description of other non-Christian religions, as those who for centuries have sought God in a fundamental way, does not apply to the Jews. Christians believe that God sought out the Jews and chose them as his own. It would be reading too much into the document to say that Pope Paul meant to exclude the Jews from the Christian missionary venture, but it is also instructive that he did not see fit to include them as specific beneficiaries of the Gospel message.

Toward the end of this lengthy document, Pope Paul candidly addresses the lack of fervor for mission which he observes in the Church. This lack of fervor he blames on those who equate missionary work with importing a foreign truth or with a violation of religious liberty. Some other critics have asked, "Why proclaim the Gospel when the whole world is saved by uprightness of heart?" (n. 80). To these challenges Pope Paul counters that it is a Christian's duty to share the word and "the right of his fellow men to receive from him the proclamation of the good news of salvation." Not denying that God's saving grace is mysteriously present to non-Christians, nonetheless, Pope Paul asserts that the compelling fact is that Christ has "commanded us to transmit this revelation to others with his own authority" (n. 18).

Pope Paul, in this exhortation on evangelization, presents a nuanced and sensitive description of the Christian missionary mandate in line with, but also going beyond, the Second Vatican Council. He frankly admits that the Catholic missionary zeal has been blunted by various theological opinions falsely claiming conciliar foundation. Nonetheless, to all challenges against the traditional missionary mandate to convert all nations, Pope Paul responds with the simple command of Christ: "Go out to the whole world; proclaim the good news to all creation" (Mk 16:15). This presents something of a departure from traditional missionary reasoning in that Pope Paul never suggests that non-Christians will not be saved or that those outside the Church are beyond God's saving grace. Rather he freely asserts Christ's saving grace among all peoples. At the same time, he affirms the salutary dimensions of the great religious traditions. But the urgency of the missionary task is founded, not on the danger of the non-believer being lost, but on both Christian obedience to Christ's explicit command and the right of the non-believer to hear the good news.[6]

2. Pope John Paul II, in his first encyclical, *Redemptor Hominis,*[7] speaks, in a very short section on the Church's mission. While denying nothing of what Pope Paul affirmed, Pope John Paul centers the mission-

ary thrust of the Church not so much on Christ's command, but in the nature of the human person: the missionary attitude begins with

> a feeling of deep esteem for "what is in man," for what man has himself worked out in this depth of his spirit concerning the most profound and important problems (n. 12).

This anthropological center of gravity is to be found throughout the encyclical. The human person—not in the abstract but in the real world—is the center of the Church's attention,

> because man—every man without any exception whatever—has been redeemed by Christ, and because with man—with each man without exception whatever—Christ is in a way united, even when man is unaware of it (n. 14).

This is an extraordinary statement—that all *have been redeemed* in Christ—and it reflects as much as influences a fundamental theme which runs through contemporary Catholic discussion on mission in the modern world: universal salvation, and the attendant and necessary question: If God wills all to be saved, what is the Church doing when it missionizes? Much of the current debate leads in the direction of human liberation and a missionary "posture of presence." To these trends and directions, we will turn after we look at the central relationship between mission and salvation.

## III. WHICH IS THE FIRST QUESTION? SALVATION, CHRIST, AND CHURCH

From tracing official Catholic contributions to the theological discussion, we now turn to a more thematic and systematic consideration of the main vectors in the Catholic discussion of mission today. As in most areas of inquiry, the art of asking the right questions is crucial to a coherent and satisfying solution. This is provocatively true with regard to the question of the Church and its mission. Accordingly, what seems to determine the different theological solutions to the question of mission is not whether the various participants take the Scriptures seriously, but rather what question they put to the Scriptures, and, as importantly, what question they presume the mission of the Church is answering.

For instance, if one starts with the premise that the Church—explicit membership in the Church—is necessary for salvation, then the mission is the Church's attempt to include everyone in its fold so that all may be saved. Or, if one starts with Christ—without whom no one comes to the Father—then mission becomes an introduction to the one mediator of salvation. If one starts from the will of God that all be saved (1 Tim 2:4a), then misssion is the announcement of a reality already present, a bringing to awareness that God has saved them. If one starts with an understanding of the biblical mandate to feed the hungry and give shelter to the homeless, then mission is foremost a task of identifying with and helping the poor in deeds of justice. If one begins with Christ's command to teach all nations, then mission is obedience in faith to Christ.

In short, is mission fundamentally an ecclesiological, Christological, moral, or soteriological question? Surely it is something of all these, but it would indeed take a masterful theological juggler to keep at least the following scriptural tennis balls in the air at the same time:

> No one can come to me unless the Father who sent me draws him (Jn 6:44).
>
> I am the way, and the truth, and the life; no one comes to the Father, but by me (Jn 14:6).
>
> All authority in heaven and on earth has been given to me. Go therefore and make disciples of all nations, baptizing them in the name of the Father and of the Son and of the Holy Spirit, teaching them to observe all that I have commanded you; and lo, I am with you always, to the close of the age (Mt 28:19–20).
>
> Truly, truly, I say to you, unless one is born of water and the Spirit, he cannot enter the kingdom of God (Jn 3:5).
>
> It is acceptable in the sight of God our Savior, who desires all men to be saved and to come to the knowledge of the truth (1 Tim 2:3b–4).
>
> And I have other sheep, that are not of this fold; I must bring them also, and they will heed my voice. So there shall be one flock and one shepherd (Jn 10:16).
>
> The true light that enlightens every man was coming into the world (Jn 1:9).
>
> The story of the rich man and Lazarus: no mention of faith with regard to salvation (Lk 16:19–31).
>
> The story of the Last Judgment: judged not according to faith in Christ, but by whether one has fed the hungry, clothed the naked, etc. (Mt 25:31–46).
>
> Truly, truly I say to you, unless you eat the flesh of the Son of man and drink his blood, you have no life in you; he who eats my flesh and

drinks my blood has eternal life, and I will raise him up at the last day (Jn 6:53f).

Father, forgive them; for they know not what they do (Lk 23:34).

There is no salvation in anyone else, for there is no other name in the whole world given to men by which we are to be saved (Acts 4:12).

In the study which follows we will see that theological trends rest for the most part on one or a combination of several of the preceding scriptural texts. The degree to which they ask questions to these passages determines in large measure their conclusions.

**A. Salvation as Starting Point**

Probably no theme is so central to the current Catholic discussion on mission as the concern for the nature of salvation itself. To ponder the nature of what Christ has done for us—salvation—is the vocation of all Christians. Simply put, the Christian plumbs ever deeper, through prayer, study, and attention to the Spirit, into the mystery of salvation. Many modern theologians, emerging from a narrowly defined understanding of Church membership and a theology that emphasizes salvific grace through the sacraments alone, have framed the question of salvation in terms of God's will that all be saved. Or they have reflected on the claim that God's saving grace is operative everywhere. Representative of theologians who emphasize universal grace and God's will that all be saved are Karl Rahner[8] and Richard Cote.[9]

Karl Rahner locates the foundation for his emphasis on two scriptural texts: 1 Timothy 2:4 and Acts 17:23. These expressions that God's will as revealed in Jesus Christ destines all for salvation color all of Rahner's reflection on the salvation of those outside Christianity. The core of Rahner's position is as follows:

> If, on the one hand, we conceive salvation as something specifically *Christian,* if there is no salvation apart from Christ, if according to Catholic teaching the supernatural divinization of man can never be replaced merely by good will on the part of man but is necessary as something itself given in this early life; and if, on the other hand, God has really, truly and seriously intended this salvation for all men—then these two aspects cannot be reconciled in any other way than by stating that every human being is really and truly exposed to the influence of divine, supernatural grace which offers an interior union with God and by means of which God communicates himself whether the individual takes up an attitude of acceptance or of refusal towards this grace.[10]

It is not our place here to repeat Rahner's intricate and detailed argument. The bibliography in note 8 is sufficient for that. We do allude to it at this length, however, because Rahner's emphasis on God's will that all be saved—and its attendant articulation in the theory of the "anonymous Christian"[11]—has profoundly affected the way Catholic theologians now look upon the missionary task. In more than a few essays and monographs which this writer studied, the authors cited Rahner's claim that the missionary should not approach the non-Christian as if grace had not already preceded him. Indeed, Oblate missionary Richard Cote's concise book *Universal Grace: Myth or Reality?*[12] is little more than a further systematization of Rahner's thought filtered through the experience of a North American missionary in South Africa.

Cote provocatively labels the second part of his book "Universal Grace Taken Seriously." He is fully candid in drawing out the implicit consequences of Rahner's emphasis on the universal salvific will. If everyone is graced, what is the difference between Christian and non-Christian? If salvific grace is operative before the Christian missionary gets there, why go in the first place? What is left of mission when you have outlined an extensive theology of universal grace?

> In this view (of universal grace) the Church's mission does not consist in bringing Christ to the world; having been sent by his heavenly Father, Christ not only comes continually to the world, but through the Spirit he is at work *where* he wills and *when* he wills. It is the church's task to recognize Christ at work and to preach the good news of this recognition to the poor. Its mission consists essentially in proclaiming the acceptable year of the Lord. In this it participates in the mission of the Holy Spirit, without whose light it is impossible to recognize Christ and exclaim, like the disciple whom Jesus loves: "It is the Lord!" For the church, mission means, above all, this: that behind the phenomena of the world and within them the Face of the Lord is encountered and recognized; and thus his saving presence is made known in the history of the world.[13]

Even more far-reaching than the assertion that God is present in individuals is the claim that Christ's saving grace is present in and through non-Christian religions; in other words, non-Christian religions are in some sense salvific:

> The actual religions of "pre-Christian" humanity too must not be regarded as simply illegitimate from the very start, but must be seen as

> quite capable of having a positive significance. . . . A lawful religion means here an institutional religion whose "use" by man at a certain period can be regarded on the whole as a positive means of gaining the right relationship to God and thus for the attaining of salvation, a means which is therefore positively included in God's plan of salvation.[14]

The positive evaluation which Cote and Rahner give to non-Christian religions does not go unchallenged in the debate: one finds other evaluations of the salvific content of these religions. As Richard McBrien rightly points out, the Vatican II documents are not so optimistic about the other religions which are "lesser, relative, and extraordinary means of salvation."[15]

Even in this cursory survey one can see how emphasizing the universal salvific will shakes the very foundations of mission theology. After all, if we are not bringing salvation, what are we bringing?

Many scholars answer this question by saying that "salvation" requires a definition more nuanced and variegated than just whether one is going to "get to heaven." That is, salvation is made up of many dimensions, the fundamental of which is rendered and given in God's universal saving will, namely, ultimate, eternal life. Another crucial dimension of salvation, however, is the *realization* that one is saved. As Cote put it, salvation is a process. This, he states is found in Scripture:

> The total reality of salvation has its beginning in our radical solidarity with Christ, its progressive unfolding in a living, personal fellowship and friendship with Christ, and its consummation in glory. . . . This growth rises in ascending stages from baptism to explicit, credal confession of faith, to recognition of the authority of the visible church, full participation in its sacramental life, and ultimately to the attainment of eternal blessedness. . . . If the church is to carry out its mission in the world, it must be prepared to take the risk of "recognizing" Christ wherever he is and under whatever form he may appear.[16]

One does not have to search very long for important challenges to such a presentation of salvation. Rahner, Cote, and others firmly establish their positions on a couple of scriptural verses, but they virtually ignore other verses which speak of the crucial and determinative choice one makes in deciding for or against Christ. Furthermore, the advantage one gains by recognizing salvific elements in non-Christians may come at the price of neglecting the question of truth[17] or neglecting the very real differences, indeed contradictions, among major world religions.[18]

In fact, the world religions claim views of reality which are radically at odds with one another. For instance, many world religions do not recognize a need for salvation at all. To be grateful for being found, one has to know that one is lost; to rejoice at being saved, one has to experience, at some level, the need to be saved. The search for an absolute savior—which Rahner claims is part of the quest of graced humanity—must at some level be provoked by an experience of being in need. That universal experience neither Rahner nor Cote demonstrates. Finally, in those theologians who wrestle with some notion of God's universal saving will, one seldom finds treated the fate and relation to the missionary task of those who are without religion or inactive in the traditions in which they were reared. Recent evangelization efforts in the United States very sensitively aim at the so-called "unchurched"; is there an analogous term for those inactive Buddhist, Taoists, and—to use an archaic term—pagans?

Most certainly the new thought on salvation has spawned all sorts of obstacles for the Church's missionary enterprise. Indeed when mission was cast in terms of bringing salvation to others, the task—the obligation—was fairly clear. But if salvation is such that it is available to those outside the Church, then how does one rescue the Church's missionary activity? Perhaps then, salvation is not the right starting point.

**B. Christ as Starting Point**

What happens if Christ, and not salvation, is the starting point for one's discussion of mission, that is, if one starts not with 1 Timothy 2:4, but with John 14:6: "I am the way, and the truth, and the life; no one comes to the Father but by me"? If one shifts from talking about salvation and misssion to talking about Christology and mission, the consequences may be quite different. Many Catholic scholars, reflecting on what sort of obligation to mission a Christian has, see in their commitment to Christ a corresponding, implicit obligation to bring all to Christ. After all, not only is Christ the only way to salvation (Jn 14:6), but he himself commanded no less than that all nations be baptized (Mt 28:19–20).

Two recently published volumes show the strong connection between explicit faith in Jesus as Lord and the Christian obligation to preach that faith.[20] Evangelical Waldron Scott neatly sums up the issue:

> The missionary movement—traditionally focused on cross-cultural evangelism, conversion, church-planting, discipling, and service—has been and continues to be for evangelicals an authentic expression of the Lordship of Christ in a religiously pluralistic world.[21]

Fervent faith in Christ, for the Catholic Christian, is not only a question about whether one thinks Jesus is the absolute fulfillment of Old Testament prophecies or whether Jesus was in some way God—an "observer's Christology"—but whether one is committed to Jesus. And it is the commitment to the person of Jesus which one wishes to share in the mission. When put in terms of a personal relationship with Jesus, the task of the missionary is clear and its urgency is all the more pressing. The missionary introduces the non-believer to Jesus and this relationship—should the person embrace it—is enriching, salvific, and joyful. If one has met full satisfaction, full meaning in Christ, it would be most difficult not to have strong missionary zeal. To refuse to share what one has found to be the answer to life's questions then becomes not so much a matter of respect for another's faith but an act of selfishness that one has not shared what is precious with the other. Avoiding judgment of another's faith, the Christian believing passionately in Jesus cannot but witness to his faith.

What one finds, then, in the current debate on mission is that the persons urging the strongest case for some form of the traditional mission are those who cast their argument in decidedly Christocentric terms. Indeed, those who begin to whittle away at the missionary task do so by redefining the universal salvific efficacy of Christ. That is, they claim that what Jesus brings—enlightenment, meaning, salvation—people find in other great religions in their own culture. Since salvation is to be found in these other religions, then one does not have to answer a need to convert them to Christ since they have already found him, or at least they have found salvation. Such writers[22] question Christ's uniqueness, but not his specialness. They focus on his particularity in history, which particularity parallels, but does not surpass, other great religious personages, such as Buddha or Mohammed.

Hans Küng, among other theologians, severely criticizes all such efforts to relativize the claim and person of Jesus, although just where his critique leaves the Catholic missionary exigence is unclear. Küng claims that Christ's uniqueness does not mean exclusivity, but he strongly defends the view that Christ alone is the bearer of salvation for the world. Küng recognizes in those who would relativize the Christian claim an inadequate respect for the question of truth. He calls such syncretistic tendencies

> a crippling dissolvent, agnostic-relativistic indifferentism, approving and comforming other religions indiscriminately, which at first seems to be liberating and creative of happiness, but finally becomes painfully monotonous since it has abandoned all firm standards and norms.[23]

Thus, never giving up the Christian belief in the uniqueness of Christ's role in the history of the world, the Christian mission becomes

> an independent, unselfish Christian ministry to human beings in the religions. . . . Christian missionary activity . . . would clearly be concerned not only with religions but with believers. . . . In a word, then, there would be neither arrogant absolutism, not accepting any other claim, nor a weak eclecticism accepting a little of everything, but an inclusive Christian universalism claiming for Christianity *not exclusiveness, but certainly uniqueness.*[24]

Karl Rahner, in his theory of anonymous Christianity, responds that the yearning for a universal savior, found in all persons, is satisfied only by Christ. Nonetheless, the salvific grace which Christ brings is present and available to all even before they confess their faith in him because the might of the cross precedes all efforts to describe the necessity for each person to believe. To the charge that he has diluted Christ's uniqueness, Rahner replies that to begin with the omnipresence of Christ's salvific grace is not to relativize Christ's uniqueness, but to underscore it. The debate between Küng and Rahner revolves around the *meaning* of salvation in Christ. Many others locate the Christological center of gravity for the Church's missionary task in the obedience which the Christian should have to the *command of Christ* to teach all nations, as found in some of the Gospels.[25]

### C. The Meaning of Church and Its Relation to Mission

Closely related to those who begin the missiological discussion with Christology are those who begin with ecclesiology and conduct their discussion in this theological arena. One can readily predict what sort of missiology one will develop if one begins with the axiom taken from a letter of St. Cyprian in the third century and infamously repeated by Boniface VIII in 1302: "Outside the Church there is no salvation."[26] In such a view, the Church's missionary work is tantamount to a rescue operation, saving those outside the Church from damnation by converting them to become members of the Church. Few there are today who baldly hold such a doctrine, and, indeed, the letter of Pope Pius XII to the Archbishop of Boston (Denz. 3869–72) repeated the Church's long-held position that God, in his mercy and design, could save those outside the Church if they were in ignorance.

Even if a literal understanding of the necessity of Church membership for salvation is not widely held today, one cannot deny the intimate link between one's ecclesiology and the missionary exigence of the Church. As Adrian Hastings has pointed out, it is

> somewhat misleading to say that the Church has a mission, as if the existence of the Church comes first. In truth, it is because of the mission that there is a Church; the Church is the servant and expression of this mission. . . . In so far as the Church fails to live up to the demands of mission, it is effectively failing to be Church.[27]

One could explore many models of the Church[28] which have been profoundly affected by the Church's missionary self-understanding. These would certainly include such notions as the people of God, pilgrim Church, and the Church as essentially missionary.[29] For our purposes, however, no other model of the Church has affected, and expressed, a new emerging missionary self-understanding so much as the Church as sacrament to and of the world.[30]

Bishop Patrick Kalilombe, biblical scholar from Malawi, enumerates the various metaphors for Christian witness in the New Testament, all of which express some kind of relation to and for the world, but do not necessarily include a need to convert the world: "light," "salt," "leaven," a "city on a mountaintop," and (as in Vatican II) "light to the nations."

> It would seem therefore that the Church's destiny is to be inserted into the heart of the world as a sacrament. . . . By looking at the Church and by hearing its prophetic utterances, the rest of the world is challenged by the judgment of God on them, a judgment that, like light, reveals the dross and the good metal, and like fire burns the dross and refines the precious metal. If this is so, the Church's preoccupation should be less with mere recruitment of numbers, and more with authenticity and efficacy of its witness in the world.[31]

The Second Vatican Council mentions Church as sacrament in at least three of its documents: the *Dogmatic Constitution on the Church* (nn. 1, 9, 48), the *Pastoral Constitution on the Church in the Modern World* (n. 42), and the *Constitution on the Sacred Liturgy* (n. 2). Karl Rahner claims that the understanding of the Church as sacrament is a reflective consideration of the fact that the visible Church makes up such a small number of those living in the world today, coupled with the theological facts that the Church is the necessary means of salvation and that God wills all people to be saved.[32] The Church, then, stands as the visible invitation and proclamation of Christ's offer of grace given to the world. The mission—the raison d'être—of the Church becomes not so much to make converts so that the Church will grow and people will be saved, but rather to be a witness of God's saving presence among all peoples who have already been graced in a prevenient way by God's universal salvific will and by the effects of the paschal mystery.[33] This notion of Church as sacrament affects, first of all, the Church's own self-understanding, and, secondly, the perception of the Church by the world. This new self-understanding is such that the members point beyond themselves to the one who has called them together as his body and for whom their lives bear witness to his patient and loving care.

Among those for whom Church as sacrament functions as the primary ecclesial model, one finds frequent references to mission as "witness" and "service." As one Jesuit missionary working in India is described:

> He does not preach, does not administer the sacrament of baptism, does not seek to make converts to the Catholic Church. He is concerned rather with what he calls community building. (In his own words) "Mine is action to help the exploited and neglected masses of people to become conscious of themselves, conscious that they are somebody, that they matter, and are to be counted. Call it humanization, if you like. . . . My work is meant to help them become persons!"[34]

In another place, a missionary reflects on the direction of his missionary service which the Church as sacrament suggests:

> A sign (sacrament) performs its function not by containing, but by communicating; not by annexation, but by representation. . . . Sign is a humble image, sanctuary a haughty one; sign is an image of service, sanctuary an image of separation; a sign is cooperative, a sanctuary is competitive; a sanctuary finds within itself any action which is really important, a sign points beyond itself to where the action is. . . . Failure to take account of sign and sanctuary as competing images of the Church explains much of the distress and confusion with the new theology of mission.[35]

In this section, then, we have looked at three distinct, but related, starting points for a new Catholic theology of mission: (a) bringing salvation to an unsaved world, (b) bringing Christ to a world that does not know him, and (c) mission in terms of the Church as sacrament to the world. The first two emphasize, with different degrees of urgency, the need to convert the other. In the first, the missionary Church brings salvation, many of whose components precede the mission, but full realization of which comes only with a faith-filled commitment. The second starting point, Christ, demands conversion from the viewpoint that only through explicit personal relationship with Christ can one be fully human and fully saved, or from the viewpoint that Christ commanded that all be converted. The third starting point rests heavily on the assumption that saving grace is to be presumed in and through other religious traditions and that the Church is to be first a servant to the world, living the truth while not necessarily demanding all to participate in membership. The first two take the issue of religious truth very seriously; that is, Christianity's claims involve a commitment to certain truths, which commitment is gift and is salvific. The third suspends, for the most part, the debate about competing truth claims and takes very seriously the Christian call to service as found in Matthew 25 and the parables such as the Good Samaritan and Dives and Lazarus.

Obviously, the preceding sketches of mission theology, with their different starting points, are not mutually exclusive; indeed proponents of any one would protest loudly that they are concerned about those things which characterize the others. What we offer here are the primary concerns and the trajectories of the various movements in theoretical Catholic theology of mission today. What are often more interesting than the strictly theoretical approaches of professional theologians are the experiences of Church leaders in mission lands. To these practical situations we now turn.

## IV. MISSION AND THEMES OF LIBERATION

Perhaps no movement in contemporary Roman Catholic theology has received as much attention as that movement loosely referred to as "liberation theology."[36] Those who use the term frequently have in mind a missionary or Church presence in third world countries which speaks not only the words of religious salvation, but also, and sometimes more loudly, the words and actions of human liberation in all its dimensions, including social, economic, and political dimensions.

It would be claiming too much to say that liberation theology introduced the Catholic missionary concern for people's temporal welfare. Indeed, the Church's missionary activity of the last five hundred years has always included the establishment of hospitals, clinics, orphanages, schools, and other social institutions. Many missionaries in Africa, Asia, India, and South America spent years of productive service in attending to local development projects. What seems to distinguish liberation theology (and its missionary component) is a new attention not only to aiding those who suffer poverty, but also to the factors—economic and political—which render them poor. For missionaries and theologians inspired by liberation theology, it is not enough for the Church to address the effects of poverty; the mission of the Church is to help eradicate the causes of poverty.[37] To this end, theologians speak of "social sin" as the situation which systematically renders a group of people to be poor, powerless, and enslaved. Drawing heavily upon the image of God as the liberator of those who are enslaved (as one finds Yahweh in the Exodus event), liberation theologians teach that the mission of the Church is the salvation or liberation of all people not only from personal sin, but also from social sin—political and economic structures which cause enslavement.

Furthermore, liberation theology, besides focusing on the consequences of social sin, calls into question the way theology itself has been practiced in the past, primarily as found in Europe and North America. There, they claim, theology has started with universally acknowledged principles (e.g., Scripture texts, patristic texts, etc.) and from them deduced particular applications. This method has often had the effect of maintaining the status quo economically, socially, religiously, and politically. Liberation theology, in contrast, begins with the experience of God's favored ones, the poor. From their experience, questions and strategies emerge which confront the Christian message. A "hermeneutical circle" is set up which starts from experience, proceeds to the Christian message, and returns to experience.

These three characteristics of liberation theology—a holistic view of redemption of humankind, attention to social sin, and "theologizing" out of the experience of the poor—profoundly affect the theory and practice of the Catholic missiological tradition. Indeed, the three most significant Roman Catholic documents on mission since 1968 reflect the deep penetration which liberation theology has made into mainstream Catholic thought.[38] These three documents are the Medellín Document (1968),[39] the Roman Synod's *Justice in the World* (1971),[40] and the same Synod's statement "On Human Rights and Reconciliation."[41] Myriad are other documents which echo the same concerns, but these three are both foundational and representative. We quote only from *Justice in the World:*

> God has revealed himself to us, and made known to us, as it is brought progressively to realization, his plan of liberation and salvation that is once and for all fulfilled in the Paschal mystery of Christ. Action on be-

> half of justice and participation in the transformation of the world fully appear to us as a constitutive dimension of the preaching of the Gospel, or, in other words, of the Church's mission for the redemption of the human race and its liberation from every oppressive situation.[42]

The fact that themes from liberation theology have been implanted in the heart of official Catholic teaching has not quieted the debate which such themes naturally engender. With regard to issues which we have already attended to, themes of liberation theology provide most interesting grist for the theological mill. Let me review some of them here.

If mission includes concern for the liberation of the whole person, does work for social justice then become a stepping-stone to the more specifically evangelical dimension of the Gospel? In other words, does the Church engage in so-called secular liberation movements in order to convert the other participants to Christianity? Richard Cote resents the question which asks whether evangelization or liberation takes precedence:

> We must reject the traditional attempt to correlate evangelization and development in terms of primary and secondary ends of the Church. All such attempts lead to a practical impasse and only protract the present missionary crisis in the Church. What is needed is a new definition of the mission of the Church, one which subsumes and integrates evangelization and development according to a higher principle. We strongly suggest that any new missionary synthesis will have to take universal grace seriously into account.[43]

Cote makes the above statement without really outlining how the doctrine of universal grace can be the new synthesizing principle, integrating evangelization and development. Perhaps what Cote intends is illustrated in the following testimony from a missionary priest in the field:

> The dispossessed masses must have something of the world as their own human space. All this and all further growth calls for their liberation. They need to be liberated above all from fear—fear of the landlord, fear of insecurity, of taking risks, of failure, of their own voices and of speaking up. . . . There is further need to liberate people from determinism, from belief in the inevitability of the *samsara* cycle of births and deaths, from helpless resignation to *karma* understood as fate, from undue dependence on horoscopes and the stars.[44]

We recall that this same missionary stated earlier that his mission was not to convert and baptize, but to liberate. This is not necessarily a representative statement, but when the missionary Church is seen primarily as a Church of witness and presence (sacrament), the urgency for converts is obviously going to be blunted.[45]

If liberation theology aspires to be a theology which emerges from the lived experience of the poor, then in many situations that "lived-experience" will be a non-Christian one. That is, if the missionary Church resides in a foreign country as a partner in dialogue, the mission of the Church might thereby become helping others to be faithful to the will of God as they hear it through their own (religious) traditions. As Gregory Baum has challenged:

> A rethinking of our theological tradition is necessary. Theologians must examine the possibility that the Church's missionary message exercises its salvational power where people in fact are, in their own cultural environment, enabling them to cling more faithfully to the best of their religious tradition and live the full personal and social implications of their religion more authentically.[46]

One of the more interesting dimensions of liberation theologians' reflection on the missionary task of the Church is the use of the Hebrew Scriptures as basic to their thought. Perhaps the fundamental reason one does not find a preoccupation with convert-making in liberation theologians' writings is their partial dependence for their primary symbols on images of God from the Hebrew Scriptures, which do not include a strong missionary tradition.

In pre-Vatican II missiology, use of the Hebrew Scriptures was often relegated to the vituperous condemnation of pagans and their religions. Missionaries looked to passages from Isaiah and the psalms which excoriated the idolatry of "the nations."[47] Occasionally, one found a countervailing direction in the Hebrew Scriptures (e.g., Jonah and Amos), but these trends never suggested that God could be reached through foreign religions; they only indicated that God's love for humankind extended beyond Israel's boundaries.[48] Frequently in New Testament writings, one finds the biblical authors taking over and reinterpreting notions of "election" and "chosen people of God" to foster Christian missionary zeal. We have already alluded to these exclusivistic trends in the Christian Scriptures.

Characteristic of liberation theology, in contrast, are the emphases on God as liberator and God's preference for the poor. Liberation theologians do not speak of the wickedness of the nations in their idolatry so much as they draw upon prophetic Judaism which castigates Israel's hollow religious practitioners who send up holocausts to God, but neglect the cries of the poor and the welfare of widows and orphans.[49] Understandably, in such a view, the Church's missionary goal becomes identified with the liberation of all peoples, and the judgment scene in Matthew 25 becomes central: What will distinguish Christians on Judgment Day will not be salvation, but that they will not be surprised that it was Christ whom they were feeding when they attended to the poor.[50] Crucial then to liberation theology is an understanding of the God of the Jews as one who frees from every kind of bondage and oppression. The liberating God of Exodus[51] becomes a primary symbol of the God to be served in a liberation missiology:

> In the Old Testament, God reveals himself to us as the liberator of the oppressed and the defender of the poor, demanding from man faith in him and justice towards man's neighbor. It is only in the observance of the duties of justice that God is truly recognized as the liberator of the oppressed.[52]

Whatever else one might say about the liberation theology movement and the missionary task of the Church, it is clear that no contemporary talk about missionizing is complete without a strong emphasis on the Church's commitment to support movements and aspirations that seek to transform society into structures and communities which foster true, complete, human opportunity for all. Justice has become a conscious, "constitutive dimension" of preaching the Gospel:

> The Church's proclamation is necessarily action. She does not civilize in order to evangelize. . . . She civilizes because that is an essential aspect of evangelizing. It is the most concrete and effective, indeed the indispensable, way of communicating to human beings their real worth—namely, the good news. For if the Church proclaims to people what they truly are here and now, and yet tolerates a variety of injustices visited upon them, she literally does not mean what she says.[53]

## V. ROMAN CATHOLICS AND A MISSION TO THE JEWS

If one observation seems to be emerging at this point, undoubtedly it would be that the mission of the Church, as discussed by modern Roman Catholic scholars, is marked less by a narrow preoccupation with convert-making and marked more by global concerns of liberation, an ecclesiology as sign among the nations, and dialogue with other world religions. It is no surprise, then, that the Church's mission vis-à-vis the Jews has come up for review and revision.

As we have already noted, the documents of Vatican II do not single out the Jews as particular targets of the Church's missionary venture. Rather they are presumed not to be excluded from conciliar documents which reiterate the universal dimensions of the Church's missionary task. Similarly lacking explicit inclusion of the Jews as objects of the Church's mission is Pope Paul's exhortation "On Evangelization in the Modern World." In 1975, the Roman Commission for Religious Relations with Jews issued "Guidelines and Suggestions for Implementing the Conciliar Declaration 'Nostra Aetate' (No. 4)." Here, while still affirming the universal scope of the Christian mission, the Commission did not mention convert-making as part of the Catholic attitude toward the Jews. And most recently, Tomasso Federici, Professor of Biblical Theology at the Pontifical Urban University in Rome, delivered an important paper on the "Mission and Witness of the Church" in which he noted that "the Church thus rejects in a clear way every form of undue proselytism."[54] This paper was delivered under the auspices of the International Catholic-Jewish Commission which is a consultative body to the Vatican's Commission on Catholic-Jewish Relations.

Some see this Roman Catholic reluctance to develop a mission to the Jews as simply a reaction to the Holocaust. That is, after what some Christians did (and did not do) during the Holocaust, Catholics should have the "courtesy" to leave the Jews alone. Others suggest, however, that Christian theology itself needs to be re-examined in the wake of the Holocaust. Is it possible, some Christians ponder, that the Christian belief that Judaism was outdated and superseded by Christianity after the first century contributed, in any way, to an atmosphere which supported centuries of Christian Jew-hatred, culminating in the Holocaust? What positive meaning can Christians find in the survival of the Jews despite centuries of Christian persecution and convert-making? Is it possible that God wills the survival of the Jews, God's first chosen, and that Christians must alter their practice of converting Jews to acknowledge God's will? How can Christians make any exceptions to the mandate to teach all nations?[55]

We have already noted that one's starting point is crucial to one's missiology. If one starts from Christ's mandate to preach universally, one cannot arbitrarily make exceptions. As we have seen, however, mission takes on a new cast when one begins with God's will to save all. Mission becomes sharing the realization of what Christ has done for us. Salvation precedes mission; it does not follow it. Salvation is God's work, not the missionary's. One witnesses to the work of Christ; one does not cause it.

Christians believe, with all their heart, that Jesus Christ stands as the forever valid sacrament and sign of God's saving action. That they are called as individuals to respond in community is the particular privilege of the Church, which stands as the sacrament of this belief. But as believers of both Testaments know and proclaim, God calls people not only as individuals, but also as communities. Yahweh's call in and through community is as irrevocable and unavailable-to-renegotiation as God's call to each heart is. Thus, this second part of Christian belief needs a sign and sacrament to be real to and for the world.

The Jewish people stand as the necessary sacrament and sign of this full message. God's election, given through Moses does not end, even with the definitive coming of salvation which Christians recognize in Jesus Christ. If Christians focus their energy on converting the Jews, they are systematically attempting to eliminate the sacrament and sign that Yahweh calls humans as community as well as individually. They may be undermining their very own belief. Furthermore, if by a convert-making enterprise Christians ever eliminate the Jews as a recognizable people in the world, as a nation faithful to the call it hears through the Torah, then they will obscure their own belief in God's faithfulness to election. That is, if the world sees an end to the Jewish nation, then the world may well conclude that God's election is "only for a time" until some other group obliterates it by conversion. What Christians witness to is that, by the gracious love of Yahweh, this election has been opened to the nations through Christ—a branch grafted on, as St. Paul puts it.

From a theological perspective such as outlined above, the Roman Catholic Church can make the Jews an exception in evangelization not because of any timidity or lack of faith, but because it believes passionately what has been revealed: that salvation is God's work, not ours, and that God chooses whom he wills for the kingdom. That Yahweh has chosen the Jews and not gone back on that word is a cornerstone of Christian faith; if the Church ever believed otherwise, then it might be cutting the very tree on whom its own branch finds life and nourishment. That is, if the Church ever comes to the belief that Yahweh has withdrawn his choice of the Jews, then the Church might have reason to despair that God's choice of them, in Christ, is an eternal one. The God of Abraham, Moses, and Jesus is a faithful God.

Admittedly, the preceding is not "official Catholic teaching," but I think that it articulates a *direction* which recent Catholic teaching is taking.[56] Dialogue with our Jewish brothers and sisters, deeper reflection on the nature of salvation as God's work, fundamental recognition of the Church as the sacrament of God's salvation through Christ, and a growing awareness of God's working through other religious traditions—all combine to bring the Roman Catholic Church, I believe, to a new understanding of the missionary posture vis-à-vis the Jews. It is a posture that comes not out of convenience, not out of embarrassment for the Holocaust, not out of a liberal Christianity which says that it does not matter what one believes; rather it flows from the passionate belief that a gracious and faithful God has called the Jewish people out of love for them and as a sign of an abiding, never-to-be-broken sacrament of election.

## NOTES

1. I am grateful for the suggestions and comments of William Kondrath and Mary McGarry-Walters in the preparation of this essay.

2. Cf., e.g., Roger D. Haight, "The 'Established' Church as Mission: The Relation of the Church to the Modern World," in *The Jurist* 39 (1979) pp. 4–39.

3. All quotations from the documents of Vatican II are taken from Walter M. Abbott, ed., *The Documents of Vatican II* (New York: Guild-America Press, 1966).

4. Cf., e.g., Herbert Vorgrimler, ed., *Commentary on the Documents of Vatican II,* 6 vols. (New York: Herder & Herder, 1967).

5. *Evangelii Nuntiandi,* Dec. 8, 1975 (Washington, D.C.: United States Catholic Conference, 1976).

6. Largely overlooked in papal documents is Pope Paul VI's first encyclical, *Ecclesiam Suam,* which puts forth a novel dialogical ecclesiology. There he proposed that "Church and mankind should meet each other and should come to know and love each other" (n. 3; cf. also nn. 73–83 and 87 for his understanding of the "dialogue of salvation").

7. *The Redeemer of Man,* encyclical of Pope John Paul II (Boston: Daughters of St. Paul, 1979).

8. For example, Karl Rahner, "Christianity and the Non-Christian Religions," in *Theological Investigations* (Baltimore: Helicon Press, 1966) V, pp. 121–132; "Anonymous Christians," in *Theological Investigations* (Baltimore: Helicon Press, 1969) VI, pp. 390–398; "Anonymous Christianity and the Missionary Task of the Church," in *IDOC International* (North American Edition), April 7, 1970, pp. 70–99; "Atheism and Implicit Christianity," in *Theological Investigations* (New York: Seabury Press, 1972) IX, pp. 145–165; "Church, Churches and Religions," in *Theological Investigations* (New York: Seabury Press, 1973) X, pp. 30–50; *Foun-*

*dations of Christian Faith* (New York: Seabury Press, 1977), pp. 311–321; *Encyclopedia of Theology: The Concise Sacramentum Mundi* (New York: Seabury Press, 1975), pp. 1499ff.

9. Richard G. Cote, *Universal Grace: Myth or Reality?* (Maryknoll, N.Y.: Orbis, 1977).

10. Karl Rahner, "Christianity and the Non-Christian Religions," *loc. cit.*, p. 123.

11. Cf. Anita Roeper, *Anonymous Christians* (New York: Herder & Herder, 1965).

12. Richard G. Cote, *op. cit.*

13. *Ibid.*, p. 133.

14. Karl Rahner, "Christianity and the Non-Christian Religions," *loc. cit.*, p. 125. In this same article, Rahner uses Judaism as a prototype of a non-Christian religion which is, at the same time, a lawful religion. Interestingly, Rahner does not repeat this when he covers essentially the same material in his *Foundations of Christian Faith.*

15. Richard McBrien, *Catholicism,* 2 vols. (Minneapolis: Winston Press, 1980), pp. 269f.

16. Richard Cote, *op. cit.*, pp. 86, 88, 133; cf. also Juan Luis Segundo, *The Community Called Church* (Maryknoll, N.Y.: Orbis, 1973) p. 11.

17. On this point, cf. Hans Küng, *On Being a Christian* (Garden City, N.Y.: Doubleday, 1976), p. 104.

18. Cf. Owen Thomas, ed. *Attitudes Toward Other Religions* (New York: Harper & Row, 1969), pp. 24f.

19. Obviously the relation between salvation, Christ, and the Church is rather intimate. I have noticed, however, that one's starting point—be it salvation, Christ, or Church—in large measure determines the urgency and nature of what mission in the Church is all about.

20. Gerald H. Anderson, Thomas F. Stransky, eds., *Mission Trends No. 5: Faith Meets Faith* (New York: Paulist Press, 1981); Gerald H. Anderson, Thomas F. Stransky, eds., *Christ's Lordship and Religious Pluralism* (Maryknoll, N.Y.: Orbis, 1981). Cf. also Donald Dawe and John Carman, eds., *Christian Faith in a Religiously Plural World* (Maryknoll, N.Y.: Orbis, 1978); Michael B. McGarry, *Christology after Auschwitz* (New York: Paulist Press, 1977); Lucien Richard, "Some Recent Development on the Question of Christology and World Religions," in *Eglise et Théologie* 8 (1977) 209–244; J. Peter Schineller, "Christ and Church: A Spectrum of Views," in *Theological Studies* 37 (1976) 545–566; Peter Schreiner, "Roman Catholic Theology and Non-Christian Religions," in *Journal of Ecumenical Studies* 6 (1969) 376–399.

21. Waldron Scott, " 'No other Name'—An Evangelical Conviction," in Gerald H. Anderson, Thomas F. Stransky, eds., *Christ's Lordship and Religious Pluralism, op. cit.*, pp. 58–74; quote on p. 61.

22. For a Roman Catholic expression of this view, cf. Paul F. Knitter, "A

Critique of Hans Kueng's *On Being a Christian,*" in *Horizons* 5, No. 2 (1978) 151–164.

23. Hans Küng, *op. cit.,* p. 112.

24. *Ibid.*

25. Mt 28:18–20; Mk 16:15f; in John Power, *Mission Theology Today* (Maryknoll, N.Y.: Orbis, 1971) p. 38, the author answers the question "Why is the Church essentially missionary?" with three "facts": "the desire of God, clearly expressed in Scriptures to save all men without exception; Christ's explicit command to carry the good news to every nation; the Church's obligation to give glory to God by leading all men to his knowledge and love." Cf. also Adrian Hastings "Mission," in Karl Rahner, ed. *Encyclopedia of Theology, op. cit.* p. 968.

26. For a history of this doctrine, cf. Hans Küng, *The Church* (New York: Sheed & Ward, 1967), pp. 313–319. Cf. also Gerald H. Anderson, Thomas F. Stransky, eds., *Mission Trends* (New York: Paulist Press, 1974) I, pp. 28f.

27. Adrian Hastings, *loc. cit.,* p. 968.

28. I am using this term as Avery Dulles has used it in his very helpful *Models of the Church* (Garden City, N.Y.: Doubleday, 1974).

29. Cf. John Power, *op. cit.,* pp. 14–58; also cf. the appropriate passages from the documents of Vatican II already cited.

30. William B. Frazier, "Guidelines for a New Theology of Mission," in Gerald H. Anderson, Thomas F. Stransky, eds., *Mission Trends* (New York: Paulist Press, 1974) I, p. 26.

31. Patrick Kalilombe, "The Salvific Value of African Religions," in Gerald H. Anderson, Thomas F. Stransky, eds., *Mission Trends* (New York: Paulist Press, 1981) V, pp. 50–68; quote on p. 64; cf. also Juan Luis Segundo, *op. cit.,* p. 72.

32. Karl Rahner, *The Church after the Council* (New York: Herder & Herder, 1966), p. 53.

33. Cf. Kenneth D. Eberhard, "Karl Rahner and the Supernatural Existential," in *Thought* 46 (1971) 537–561.

34. Samuel Rayan, "Evangelization and Development," in Gerald H. Anderson, Thomas F. Stransky, eds., *Mission Trends* (New York: Paulist Press, 1975) II, pp. 87–105, quote on p. 88.

35. William B. Frazier, *loc. cit.,* p. 27.

36. Representative of this movement would be such thinkers as Gustavo Gutierrez, Juan Luis Segundo, Rubem Alves, Jon Sobrino, and Leonardo Boff. For a partial bibliography, cf. Francis P. Fiorenza, "Latin American Liberation Theology," in *Interpretation* 28 (1974) 441–457.

37. Cf. the 1974 Roman Synod Statement on evangelization, in Joseph Gremillion, presenter, *The Gospel of Peace and Justice* (Maryknoll, N.Y.: Orbis, 1976) pp. 593–598.

38. Cf. *Evangelii Nuntiandi,* nn. 29–35, where Pope Paul VI outlines the intimate link between the Gospel of salvation and full human liberation.

39. Cf. Joseph Gremillion, *op. cit., ad loc.*

40. *Ibid.*

41. Cf. *Catholic Mind* 73 (1975) 50–52.

42. Quoted from excerpt in Gerald H. Anderson, Thomas F. Stransky, eds., *Mission Trends* (New York: Paulist Press, 1975) II, p. 255.

43. Richard Cote, *op. cit.,* p. 130.

44. Quoted by Samuel Rayan, *loc. cit.,* p. 89.

45. Cf., e.g., Juan Luis Segundo, *op. cit.,* pp. 78–86.

46. Gregory Baum, "Is There a Missionary Message?" in Gerald H. Anderson, Thomas F. Stransky, eds. (New York: Paulist Press, 1974) I, pp. 75–86; quote on p. 86. How Baum determines what is the "best" of another's religious tradition is unclear but, to be sure, making converts is not a primary activity in such a missionary perspective.

47. Cf. John Power, *op. cit.,* pp. 59–77.

48. Cf. Patrick Kalilombe, *loc. cit.,* pp. 56, 60.

49. Cf. Juan Luis Segundo, "A Biblical Tapestry," in *The Community Called Church,* pp. 150–160.

50. *Ibid.,* pp. 9f.

51. Cf. Gustavo Gutierrez, *A Theology of Liberation* (Maryknoll, N.Y.: Orbis, 1973), pp. 153–160. It would be difficult to exaggerate this theme in the various liberation theologies. Gutierrez was its first popularizer, but it recurs over and over in the writings of other liberation theologians.

52. Synod, 1971, *Justice in the World,* quoted from Gerald H. Anderson, Thomas F. Stransky, eds., *Mission Trends* (New York: Paulist Press, 1975) II, p. 255.

53. Richard A. McCormick, "Human Rights and the Mission of the Church," in Gerald H. Anderson, Thomas F. Stransky, eds., *Mission Trends* (New York: Paulist Press, 1979) IV, pp. 37–50; quote on p. 48.

54. *Origins* 8 (September 19, 1978) 273–283.

55. Much of what follows has been reworked from the author's "If You Start Making Exceptions: Jews and Evangelization," in *Process* (published by the Catholic Campus Ministry Association) (Summer 1977) 20–24.

56. For a similar expression of Catholic thought, cf. Gregory Baum, "The Doctrinal Basis for Jewish-Christian Dialogue," in *The Month* 224 (1967) 232–245.

# Contemporary Jewish Attitudes to Mission and Conversion

*Daniel F. Polish*

That Jews have in various ways through the centuries sought to bring other people to share their religious beliefs is, it would seem, beyond argument. No less deserving of assent is the observation that Jews have been considerably less energetic in this pursuit in modern times than either the Christian community or our own co-religionists of earlier days. What is a valid subject for discussion is the cause for this reversing of field. We may, perhaps, never be able to reconstruct the factor or convergence of factors that caused Judaism to assume the stance which is normative in our day. What can be known, and discussed objectively, are the attitudes now current within the Jewish community, and the actions which flow as consequence from them.

## I. THE CONCEPT OF MISSION IN RECENT JEWISH THOUGHT

The concept of "mission," so evolved in the thinking of the Christian community, and so evident, in a variety of forms, in the activities of that community, has, today, no correlative in Jewish life. Indeed, it is instructive that the term itself, when it was briefly employed in Jewish thought, had a meaning diametrically at odds with that conventionally understood to be its purport in Christianity. Reform Judaism, child of the emancipation, and conversant with Christian theological categories, appropriated the term mission for the Jewish people. Yet, as used by Reform Jewish thinkers early in this century, the idea of the "mission of Israel" did not carry any implication of the conversion of humanity, nor even of individual non-Jews to Reform in particular or to Judaism in general. Quite to the contrary, that notion designated a special role for the Jewish faithful. Jews were called to embody in their belief system an absolute, uncompromising and pure fidelity to the monotheistic vision, and in their actions a scrupulous devotion to the highest ethical standards—an ethical system corollary to that faith. The heart of the "mission of Israel" was the challenge that Jews be living embodiments of ethical monotheism.

This exemplification was not for the purpose of winning others to Judaism, but, rather, for calling others—and here it must be recognized that the "others" early Reform had in mind were principally the Christians among whom they lived—to the highest aspirations of their own respective religious traditions. When advocates of the mission of Israel admonished Jews to be a "light to the nations," that light was not a harbor light calling ships to one particular slip, but a floodlight illuminating the proper channels to the various ports.

If there is any sense of movement implied in the concept of mission as articulated by early Reform, it is clearly not from outside of Judaism into it, but rather outward from all particular embodiments of monotheistic faith to the broadest, most universalistic expression of that faith. When early Reform reiterated Isaiah 66, "My house shall be a house of prayer for all peoples," it did not intend that the nations would find their way to the doors of the synagogue, but that when all humanity came to the recognition of God's unity, the walls of all particular "houses" would fall and all people, standing together, would inhabit the greater mansion. In this spirit did the liturgists of this persuasion emend the *Shema*—the credal affirmation of Jewish faith in God's oneness—to declare: "Hear, O Israel, hear, O mankind, the Lord our God, the Lord is one."

Paradoxically, the concept of mission as employed in Reform Jewish theology of that period denoted not the particular enterprise of gathering others to one's own faith, but the most universalistic impulses inherent in that term. There is some indication that this transvaluation of the meaning of mission was not altogether un-self-conscious on the part of its proponents. Kaufman Kohler, the pre-eminent spokesman for early Reform theology, wrote:

> Noble as the heroic task accomplished by many a Christian missionary indisputably was, the task of the Jew during the dark medieval centuries

> of withstanding all the trials, the threats, the taunts, the auto-da-fés and the alluring baits of the Church was by all means far nobler and more heroic, and it was performed not by individuals, but by the entire people. It was a passive, not an active mission. Had they then gone forth among the nations to win the world for their teachings, they might have long ago been swallowed up by the surrounding multitude. Instead of this, the Jew proved to be the "Servant of the Lord" who "gave his back to the smiters," "the man of sorrows, despised and forsaken of men."[1]

The term "mission" is not a primary constituent of many modern Jewish theologies, but we might still conjecture the existence of activity predicated on the assumption of its premises. Here, it seems, we must construct an argument from the absence of data. What are we to infer from the fact that none of the denominational bodies of the Jewish community in this country has ever sponsored, however remotely, a program to "carry the faith" to non-Jews? Nor have any of the national bodies of Jewish life engaged in such activity. Sporadically, programs of Jewish outreach have been proposed and mounted on local levels. Yet a review of their histories indicates that invariably these efforts have failed to marshal appreciable, nor even sufficient, support within the Jewish community. Consistently, these programs have failed within a short period. There has, at no time, been sufficient strength in any of these programs to permit the creation of a national network among them.

Programs do exist in various national Jewish organizations to explain Jewish faith and the Jewish community to Christians. Significantly, such programs fall within the purview of what are called "defense agencies." The thrust of such activities is not the winning of Christians to Judaism, but the enabling of Christians, *as Christians,* to understand Judaism, so that it will not remain *terra incognita* for them. By dispelling misperceptions about Jewish faith and Jewish life, it is anticipated in the charter of these bodies, Christians will not feel threatened or frightened by the persistence of Judaism, or by the presence of a proximate Jewish community, and thus be less inclined to visit upon them the sort of antagonism and violence that were all-too-much a part of the interaction of these communities during other periods in history. Any effort at conversionary activities is clearly outside the province of these bodies, and even at odds with their fundamental purpose.

## II. MISSIONARY ACTIVITY IN MODERN JUDAISM

Among the programs carried out by some of these national organizations is the encouragement of interfaith "dialogue" on various levels between Christians and Jews. It is of interest to note the reaction of one Jewish body, the Rabbinical Council of America—the leading body of Orthodox Rabbis—to the proposal of dialogue. The Rabbinical Council asserted:

> Any suggestion that the historical and meta-historical worth of a faith community be viewed against the backdrop of another faith. . . and the mere hint that a revision of basic historic attitudes is anticipated are incongruous with the fundamentals of religious liberty and freedom of conscience and can only breed discord and suspicion.[2]

Implicit in such a rejection of conversion to Christianity as an outgrowth of interfaith contact is an eschewal of the converse agenda on the part of Jewish participants in dialogue. Representatives of the Jewish community engage in such exchanges not for the sake of making new Jews, but in the interest of helping Christians understand their own Christianity and be better able to live alongside their Jewish brothers and sisters.[3] An examination of the Jewish community reveals no programs with an explicit or implicit goal of winning Christians to Judaism.

The one program in Jewish life which most resembles the missionary programs of Christian groups in form has a decidedly different objective. The Lubavitch community of Hasidic Jews maintains a program of "mitzvah-mobiles." These vans can be seen on the streets of urban areas, manned by volunteers from that community. The volunteers stop passersby and ask, "Are you Jewish?" Unlike missionaries of other groups, however, if the answer is in the negative, they let the person continue on his way. Only if one is, indeed, already Jewish do the Hasidim pursue their objective, which is to encourage non-observant Jews to become practitioners of the *mitzvot.* Rather than a program of external prosyletism, Lubavitch is conducting a program of inward-directed "conversion."

In the recent past, however, there has been enunciated what appeared to be a call for the creation of a program of outreach to win non-Jews to Judaism. Rabbi Alexander Schindler, President of the Union of American Hebrew Congregations, addressing the leadership of his organization, made what was hailed as a dramatic proposal. Schindler called upon Jews to undertake a program of outreach to "unchurched" Americans.[4]

There is much to be learned about Jewish attitudes toward mission in the reaction of the Jewish community to Schindler's call for outreach. His proposal was vehemently attacked by Orthodox spokesmen and leaders of the so-called "secular" community alike. Some condemned the program for being at odds with historic Jewish practice and halakhic injunction. Others criticized it for being contrary to the spirit of pluralism and mutual respect that prevails in America.[5] These reactions caused Schindler to elaborate upon the intent of his suggestion. Interestingly, as Schindler clarified his statement, it seemed to recede further and further from being a program of active outreach to non-Jews.

As it now stands, Schindler's proposal has a far different thrust and texture than that which was first presented in the press. The program today includes concern that the Jewish community be more open and intentional in fully integrating those who have become converts to Judaism. Conversely, Rabbi Schindler calls upon rabbis to be less emphatic in discouraging those who express the desire to undertake such conversion, this especially in the case where an "unchurched"person is marrying a Jew. In these instances, Schindler asserts, we should be more welcoming of those who will be, or perhaps already are, spouses of Jews—though even here, he is careful to note, we should not tamper with those who profess another faith. The final point of Schindler's proposal has to do with the matter of patrilinear descent, a subject to which we shall shortly return.

It is interesting, in tracing the history of this particular episode, to note the trajectory of the conversation. The focus of the discussion, following that of the proposed program itself, shifted from the terrain of outreach—which seems akin to mission in Christianity—which was deemed uncongenial, to the subject of conversion, which was apparently considered less troublesome or threatening. At least it had the advantage of being less unfamiliar to the Jewish community. In the final outcome, the resistance of the community to programs of actively pursuing converts appears to have been sustained and even, if indirectly, reaffirmed.

## III. THE CONCEPT OF CONVERSION IN RECENT JEWISH THOUGHT AND PRACTICE

The redefinition of the Schindler proposal rests on a distinction between the active "outreach" to potential proselytes and the passive "reception" of such potential converts. Whatever the attitude of the community to the issue of outreach, it is clear that the contemporary Jewish community, like those of earlier periods, does accept converts. There are no universal rules governing the process of conversion. Nor has there been formal study about the process by which individual rabbis deal with the would-be converts. There seems to be near-universal agreement that a rabbi owes it to a potential convert to comply with the well-known halakhic injunction that mandates one to discourage conversion as vigorously as possible. Some rabbis pride themselves in their effectiveness at this and at the number of people they have dissuaded from converting. Others take pride in the number of converts who have been able to surmount the barriers they have put up and found their way into Jewish life.

Similarly widespread is the practice of a period of intensive study prior to conversion. The length and content of such programs of study vary from rabbi to rabbi. Some rabbis prefer to study personally with each potential convert. Others find it more productive for such potential converts to Judaism to take part in a class. In many communities in this country, the local board of rabbis or other group offers a community-wide course of study for those interested in conversion. These classes, as a rule, are not advertised to the general public and admission is usually only under the "sponsorship" of a referring rabbi. This policy is consonant with the attitude that is uncongenial to programs that might be construed as proselytizing in nature, but accepting of the more "passive" stance of receptivity to those motivated by a genuine personal desire to become Jewish.

Yet even the subject of "receiving" converts is greeted with less consensus within the community than might be expected. Halakha is explicit that a person seeking conversion must be motivated exclusively by religious devotion and be free of the influence of other, more mundane, considerations. Among those human concerns which might influence one to convert is an impending marriage to a Jewish partner. In holding to halakhic instruction, many Orthodox rabbis will categorically refuse to consider the request of anyone who wishes to convert for the sake of marriage or "family unity." Because the preponderant majority of conversions are motivated by marital considerations, many, notably Orthodox, rabbis simply do not perform conversions of any kind. Many rabbis or rabbinic institutions throw up virtually insuperable barriers to conversion, turning the process into a veritable obstacle course.[6] The policy of almost all Reform rabbis and most Conservative rabbis has been to discourage potential converts motivated by the desire to marry into the Jewish community, as one would discourage any convert. But if the desire to convert is deemed to be sincere and firmly held, liberal rabbis will accept as converts people whose initial motivation was matrimonial.[7]

The program initiated by Rabbi Schindler is predicated upon just this receptivity to converts prompted by familial concerns. Schindler calls for rabbis to be less resistant to such people than to other prospective converts, and even to be somewhat encouraging to the spouses, or prospective spouses, of Jews. Predictably, this stance was met with censure in the Orthodox community.

## IV. THE QUESTION OF "PATRILINEAR DESCENT"

Another area of contention between the various branches of Jewish life in America is the Jewishness of a child of a marriage between Jewish and non-Jewish partners. Halakha states that a child follows the religion of the mother, and is thus to be considered only if the mother is Jewish. The child of a Jewish father and a non-Jewish mother is halakhically a non-Jew. Orthodoxy maintains this distinction. Reform, on the other hand, has held that a child of a "mixed marriage" may be considered Jewish regardless of which parent is Jewish, if it is the intention of the parents that the child be raised as a Jew. In essence, this amounts to what may be regarded, in some cases, as a "conversion," by virtue of the environment in which the child is raised. The Rabbis' Manual, the guide for life-cycle liturgies of the Central Conference of American Rabbis, the Reform Rabbinical Group, states:

> Jewish law recognizes a person as Jewish if his mother was Jewish, even though the father was not a Jew. One born of such mixed parentage may be admitted to membership in the synagogue and enter into a marital relationship with a Jew, provided he has not been reared in or finally admitted into some other faith. The child of a Jewish father and a non-Jewish mother, according to traditional law, is a Gentile; such a person would have to be formally converted in order to marry a Jew or become a synagogue member.
>
> Reform Judaism, however, accepts such a child as Jewish without a formal conversion, if he attends a Jewish school and follows a course of studies leading to Confirmation. Such procedure is regarded as sufficient evidence that the parents and the child himself intend that he shall live as a Jew.[8]

Rabbi Schindler's proposal about "patrilinear descent" called for the formalization of this principle of Reform practice. Here, too, spokesmen for

Orthodoxy rejected Schindler's proposal. Rabbi Sol Roth, President of the Rabbinical Council of America, warned that such ideas "threaten the unity of the Jewish people," and predicted:

> This breach of Jewish Law by Reform leaders will create a sect which will erroneously regard itself as Jewish but whose Jewish identity will not be acknowledged by the mainstream of the Jewish people. Their marriages within the Jewish community will not be recognized by more traditional Jews, causing fragmentation and inevitable anguish amongst those who were guided by their Reform leaders.[9]

Various spokesmen for Conservative Judaism, on the other hand, have called for recognizing the Jewishness of the child of either a Jewish mother or father:

> Why, in light of the liberation and relaxation of the prohibitions against intermarriage, do we still insist that only the child of a Jewish mother be considered Jewish? Why do we not grant the same recognition to the child of a Jewish father, regardless of who the mother may be? . . . What I am suggesting is an extension of the halakhic rule to include the father. If one parent is Jewish, mother or father, and we have maintained the principle of *zera kodesh*, the offspring is to be regarded as Jewish.[10]

Even on the subject of passive acceptance of converts to Judaism, exclusive of the matter of proselytism, there exists, as we have seen, a wide spectrum of opinion. Liberal Judaism seems to be more open to the prospect of one becoming Jewish, and wider in its definition of who is to be considered eligible for such conversion, or to be considered originally "converted" by reason of descent. Orthodoxy, at the other end of this spectrum, is more restrained on the subject, and seems to suggest that conversion itself is less than desirable. Of course, it must be noted that the Orthodox resistance is not an implacable one, and that Orthodox rabbis do officiate at the conversion of those individuals who comport with their requirements and their expectations of what such conversion should entail. Regardless of the numerical distribution of the various sectors, the position of the Orthodox group should not be taken lightly. Orthodox Judaism exercises significant influence in Jewish life and articulates an attitude which is present in the "collective unconscious" of the community. Indeed, it seems fair to suggest that it does play a role in the thinking of even those whose actions run counter to the norms it enjoins.

## V. JEWISH RETICENCE ABOUT CONVERSION: BASED ON RACE OR EXCLUSIVITY?

What accounts for the resistance of Jews to programs of active pursuit of proselytes and makes them reticent even to accept converts who come out of their own volition? There are those who maintain that Judaism is a "racist philosophy." This accusation has gained greatest attention of late in the political arena. Yet, the equation of "Zionism is racism" has its roots, of course, in theological polemic on the concept of the "chosen people."

Leaving aside the particular odiousness of the Zionism/racism equation, it is clear that the notion of chosenness has been perceived, or more properly misperceived, as reflecting a kind of exclusivity. Can it be that Jews do not show enthusiasm for the missionary enterprise because they perceive themselves as standing in a relationship to God so special that it is to be preserved only for those in the "blood-line"? To begin with, there is nothing in Jewish teaching, either in the classic texts or subsequent literature, that enunciated this point of view. The complete absence of this sentiment must be accorded proper consideration in formulating a response to the question of whether Judaism is a racist doctrine.

Indeed, there is nothing in Jewish thought which views Jews as a blood group or a race. On the contrary, the notion of "seed of Abraham" has consistently been interpreted in the broadest sense as indicating a spiritual kinship to which those not of the blood-line can enter. Nor has race, as the term is understood by any school of thought, ever been put forward as a criterion for eligibility for conversion. The reality is that Jews form no genetically homogenous group, but embody within themselves all the physical characteristics of humanity in all its diversity.

Most significantly, there has never been any impetus to perceive the relationship with God, established by Abraham, as reserved for our own group. Instead, Jewish ideology has always maintained that God is the Father of all human beings, and that the role of the Jews in his economy of creation is to extend the knowledge of God and a sensitivity to relationship with God to all of his children. The end goal is the establishment of the kingship of God on earth. Jews are mandated to serve as God's partners in bringing about that time when, "the earth shall be full of the knowledge of the Lord as the waters cover the sea-bed" (Is 11:9), that is, the time when all people will stand in the same relationship to God that Jews have since their creation as a distinct group. Certainly, Jewish reticence on the subject of mission and conversion clearly cannot have its roots in any sense of exclusivity.

## VI. JEWISH RETICENCE ABOUT CONVERSION: BASED ON FEAR?

The explanation is often heard that Jewish attitudes to mission and to converts were shaped by the historical exigencies of the Jewish diaspora in Europe. The validity of this conjecture as an explanation of the actions of an earlier period is a subject properly for historians. Two caveats must, however, be taken. In the first instance, it does an injustice to the Jews of that community to suggest that they would not risk their lives in the pursuit of what they knew to be not merely right, but godly. The fact is that Jews of the European exile conducted themselves with great courage, not only in preserving their Jewish identity, but also in engaging in religious actions which had been prohibited by the laws of the states in which they lived. We might well assume that these Jews would have pursued proselytism, too, in the same sense of commitment with which they pursued other religious mandates, if they felt it, indeed, to be in the service of heaven.

Of significance for the contemporary setting is a second matter, that of the implication of changed circumstances. Even if Jews in an earlier time had curtailed activity in winning converts because of the consequences of such activities, how would these decisions affect Jews today, who do not live in an atmosphere which threatens reprisal? Jews in the West today are perfectly free to mount missionary programs, and yet they do not. How does the "argument from history" explain that?

Some might suggest that Jews are motivated not by fear of repression or punishment, but by some sort of "realistic calculus" which dictates that if the various religious communities were to engage in a "war of souls," Judaism would emerge the sure loser. There is a certain reflexive appeal to this hypothesis—a modern variant of the argument from historical exigencies. Yet it, too, seems, upon closer analysis, wanting. It is wanting, in the first place, because it seems to give too little credence to the spiritual validity or attractiveness of Judaism itself. Why should Judaism emerge a "sure loser"? Does it not offer sufficient nourishment to the spiritual hunger of its adherents? To every voice that is heard to answer, "If that is so, then it deserves to lose the contest," others should be raised to respond that Judaism does, indeed, offer spiritual nourishment. Jews know that Judaism does sustain us, does raise us to heights of exaltation, and insight and nearness to God. Ours is not a faith so meager, nor so beleaguered that it would not appear worthy when juxtaposed to other possible choices.

This hypothesis is wanting, too, in not fully appreciating the historical realities of this moment. The fact is that though Judaism does not engage in soul-skirmishes or reprisals, Jews are themselves subjected to an unrelenting battle for conversion. In its most passive and benign manifestation, it is evident in the fact that, by virtue of living in a Christian environment, Jews are constantly exposed to the blandishments—personal, social, cultural, and perhaps even spiritual—of the majority tradition. In its more dynamic mode, it manifests itself in the fact that various Christian groups maintain programs of active proselytization of Jews. We shall have more to say about this below. The fact is, however, that the very "war" about which the proponents of this hypothesis express concern is already being waged, albeit in a one-sided fashion. It seems unlikely that any such battle could be waged more aggressively or with more success (or lack of it) than this. Nor does it seem likely that a Jewish entry into the ranks of the combatants would exacerbate the situation of the Jews or prejudice the outcome of the exchange. Jewish attitudes, most likely, do not rest on the circumstances of the community at an earlier time, nor on an assessment of the communal consequences for the present time.

Perhaps some might attribute Jewish reticence about mission and conversion to the pervasive cultural relativism of Western society. It is almost mandatory, in the West, to maintain that all cultural expressions possess equal validity, that none can be deemed superior to others, and that one cannot and should not attempt to advance any one position at the expense of others. The very word "missionize" seems to have acquired a pejorative sense in polite society. Yet, at the same time that relativism is axiomatic, Jews are often derogated for their apparent sense of certainty. We do not believe that our own particular religious civilization is no better or no worse than others, nor do we imagine it to be interchangeable with others. Clearly, Jews, even in this society, believe Jewish religion to be "right," and preferable to other ways of life accessible to them. Why do we, then, not seek to extend its benefits to others?

## VII. JEWISH RETICENCE ABOUT CONVERSION: AN EXPRESSION OF MONOTHEISTIC VISION

A fair assessment of this question must take account of the religious realities of the current situation. Judaism, which emerged in a world sunk in the ignorance of the one God, and in thrall to idolatry, today finds its world to be one in which its message of monotheism has been accepted by countless other peoples. Doctrinal differences persist. Religious forms diverge. Communities of faith are divided. And yet, to Jewish eyes, the core truth is apperceived alike. The emergence of this situation has thrust a profound question upon the Jewish community: Should we seek to teach other monotheists the specific contours of Jewish faith, or are their own traditions and forms sufficient vehicles to convey the elemental teaching? Again we find ourselves in the realm of history. But it is, I believe, proper to assert that the Jewish impetus to preach the central vision of our faith expresses itself in inverse proportion to our proximity to other proponents of monotheism. While Jews were most active, even aggressive in preaching to idol worshipers, they have consistently been reticent about such preaching in the face of other monotheisms.

There is a history of discussion within Judaism on the question of this very issue. It expressed itself in exchanges about the application of the categories of Noahide law to all human beings—even non-monotheists: in philosophical exchanges about whether Christianity and Islam were to be considered monotheistic or idolatrous, in more recent writings about relations with Christians, and in the articulation of a "dual covenant" theory. Jews of today are heir to that whole history of discussion. Our attitude toward Christians—as toward Muslims—rests on the bedrock of their affirmation of God's unity. In recognizing that we share fundamental truths, any Jewish discussion of "outreach" and conversion today must, of necessity, consist of the issue of essence and accident.

In assessing our own tradition, we must assert that the essential element is the belief in the unity of God, and further establishment of a relationship, collective and individual, with that one God. The specific Jewish understanding of that one God, the manner of expressing that understanding, the various forms of religious life, indeed even membership in our particular community of faith, dedicated to service of that one God, can be considered as participating in the essence, or can be called accidents, incidental to that essential nature. The thrust of Jewish thought has consistently been to regard these as accidents. Without benefit of the philosophical apparatus, the common attitude of contemporary Jews has implicitly been to deem the particular features of our tradition to be accidents. While the accidents are constitutive of our particular faith group and tradition, they are clearly distinguished from the essence. If the accidents are understood to exist for the purpose of attesting to, and, in various ways, serving, the essence, the fundamental issue of this problem must be: Is it necessary to participate in the accidents in order to participate in the essence? Or is it possible to participate in the essence independent of the accidents?

In terms of mission and conversion, the issue devolves to participation in the essence. If the goal of faith has been understood to be participation in the essence, then it is not necessary to introduce others into the accidents in order for them to attain that goal. If the goal is faith in one God and relationship to that God, then participation in any of the monotheistic traditions, in whose midst Jews have found themselves, must be regarded as sufficient condition for meeting that goal. This is not to adopt a position of complete relativism which would hold that anything one could believe is of equal merit, nor even to maintain that any monotheism that one could conceive would be equally valid. We have stated simply that the particular monotheistic traditions which Judaism has historically encountered—Christianity and Islam—are deemed to afford access to participation in the essence of the faith to which we witness.

This being so, Judaism has felt no need to transmit to Christians or Muslims the accidents which contribute to the particular character of Judaism. Certainly, the accidents of Judaism enhance our ability to participate in the essence. And certainly the accidents point Jews toward the essence in a way other accidents could not. The accidents of Jewish faith are of profoundest significance for Jews, but Jews do not feel them to have similar importance for members of the Christian and Muslim communities. There is no compelling necessity to participate in the particular forms and modes and understandings of Jewish life when, by virtue of belonging to one of those traditions, the Christian or Muslim is afforded access to the essence.

Nor has Judaism felt compelled to address itself to the particular accidents of those other traditions which contribute to the shape of their respective identities. No doubt, the accidents of Judaism are troublesome to members of other monotheistic communities and may appear deficient or arcane. No doubt, they seem to detract somehow from the essential message. The accidental features of these other communities seem no less extraneous to Jews, and yet we have not felt it necessary to call on those traditions to purge themselves of their accidents, accidents which to our eyes must appear to be accretions to the essential faith.

## VIII. MISSIONARY ACTIVITY: RESPECT FOR OTHER FAITH COMMUNITIES

If mission and conversion denote the imposition of Jewish accidents upon those who already participate in the essence by virtue of other avenues of access, Jews have not felt those activities to be necessary. Jews have been content for Christians and Muslims to have the benefit of faith in the one God and relationship with the one God without having to do so in particular Jewish forms. Jewish reticence in these areas rests upon a respect for the authenticity of the monotheism of the peoples among whom we live. We feel that their faith, rather than demanding witness from us, itself testifies to the effectiveness with which we have carried the recognition of the oneness of God into the world.

The converse, it must be recognized, implies that Jews, too, be freed of the importunings to adopt the accidents of other traditions. Jews wish to be allowed to preserve their faith in the one God through the forms and in the manner peculiar to them. No doubt it may be harder for Christians—and perhaps, to a lesser extent, Muslims—to accept the possibility of faith without the particular accidents of their tradition. But an appreciation of the essential monotheism represented in Judaism may ultimately make such acceptance possible. This recognition would carry with it the corollary that no conversionary outreach to Jews was necessary, nor even warranted.

To regard the subject of this discussion from a slightly different angle of vision, the act of mounting a conversionary program against another faith group must imply a sense of the spiritual inadequacy of that tradition—that is, a fundamental attitude of contempt. It is fair to ask whether this is a proper way for a group to view another which shares the same essential monotheistic faith. Clearly, the Jewish community has made the fundamental decision that it is not. On the other hand, Christian campaigns of mission directed against Judaism must be seen as reflecting a real measure of contempt, acknowledged or not, for that faith tradition. It would do Christians well to recognize the extent to which such an attitude must underlie the various programs of proselytism that have historically been directed against Jews, and that continue to be put forth—and to ponder the source of that attitude. The goal of converting Jews betrays an antipathy to Judaism as real and profound as any action that Christianity collectively, or Christians individually, have taken against Jews in the two millennia of Christian-Jewish interaction.

## IX. JEWS AS THE SUBJECTS OF MISSION ACTIVITY

I suspect that few Christians recognize the pervasiveness of Christian missionary efforts to the Jews. Here I do not speak about generalized programs of witness or mission to all the "unconverted," but of specific programs of conversion targeted to the Jews *as Jews.* One aspect of being Jewish in the United States which goes strangely without public discussion is the constant evangelization directed at every individual Jew.

Here I must speak autobiographically. From my earliest childhood, I remember being importuned, evangelized, or witnessed to in one fashion or another by all kinds of people who professed to have my best interests at heart. I often felt as if the very fact of my Jewishness constituted me as a special challenge to these people. Invariably, their approach included an assurance that many of the people who had accepted their message were Jews.

I well recall the regularity with which my father, a rabbi, received missionary tracts, and personal appeals specifically directed to him as a rabbi. I can still picture vividly his reaction to such material. Often he became embarrassed, flustered, and even furtive about the literature he had received and treated the material as if seeking to shield his children from something distasteful, scurrilous or repugnant. At times, when I was older, he might, if I persisted in inquiring, share the material with me and express his dismay. I noted, as I recall it now, with consternation, or perhaps disgust, that some of the tracts were ascribed to former rabbis who had converted to Christianity.

I have myself been a rabbi for a little over a decade, my name being added to the various lists of rabbis. Scarcely a month has gone by since my ordination when I have not received one form or another of those conversionary solicitations. They have become, in my mind, one of the intrinsic features of the American rabbinate, though certainly not one of its more edifying aspects. It has, I confess, developed to the point where I can already tell from the envelope that "this" is "that" communication for the month. Invariably I find myself wondering what could have been going on in the mind of some poor confused souls as they prepared that mailing to win me and my colleagues over. I sometimes ponder if they ever give any thought to the countless hours devoted to the task of sowing the seeds which have yielded such an infinitesimal harvest over all these years. And still they persist, driven by I cannot even imagine what impulses. No doubt they believe themselves motivated by my best interests and some kind of "love" for me. How can they not understand that their act appears to me nothing less than an expression of the profoundest contempt for that which I hold most dear?

## X. JEWS FOR JESUS AND OTHER FORMS OF "CHRISTIAN" JUDAISM

Of late a new factor has been entered into the missionary equation, that which, if we are to be completely candid, must be called the element of deception. I speak of the phenomenon which goes by such names as "Jews for Jesus," messianic Jews, completed Jews, etc. For the past several years, numerous groups have put forward the claim that one can be Jewish and, at the same time, accept the messiahship of Jesus. Indeed, these groups have sought to convince individual Jews and Jewish opinion at large that the acceptance of Jesus as Messiah is not only congruent with Jewish faith, but is the fullest expression of that faith.

Groups of this orientation have been exceedingly active in appealing to Jewish individuals and Jewish groups. Their literature receives wide circulation, and the aggressive exponents of this position are increasingly to be encountered at all manner of public events of the Jewish community. What, it should be asked, prompts me to characterize such activities as deception? On the most basic level, groups of this persuasion often represent themselves as being what they are not, and as not being what they are. Jews for Jesus cells, for instance, will often depict themselves as being synagogues and advertise themselves as such. Yet the spiritual leaders of such "synagogues," people frequently identified as "rabbis," are in fact ordained graduates of Christian theological seminaries who maintain their membership in Christian ministerial groups. Programs of such groups widely advertised to the public as Passover Sedarim, or Shabbat services will culminate in the celebration of the Eucharist. In the most fundamental sense of the term, such practices must be acknowledged to be deceptive.

From the standpoint of ends and means these groups deserve, again, to be called deceptive. Objective investigation has revealed that the intent of these organizations is to serve not as a terminus, but as a conduit. People are to be attracted to these groups from the Jewish community, and moved through them to membership in main-line Christian bodies. They serve less as an expression of some sort of Jewish impulse than as an entry point into Christianity. Corroborating this perception, but not disclosed or discussed by these groups, is the reality that the funding necessary for their operation comes, significantly, from main-line Christian bodies and from groups within the Christian community whose specific purpose is to serve as missions to the Jews.

The description deceptive is, finally, warranted on grounds of pure logic. It is impossible for an entity to participate in two mutually exclusive categories. One cannot be both a Jew and a Christian. And yet precisely that claim constitutes the fundamental premise of these groups. We are here discussing, it must be remembered, not the question of Jesus' historicity—a matter which has itself generated heated discussion between Jews and Christians and within the Jewish community—but of his messiahship. Historically, Christianity split from Judaism and evolved as a separate faith group specifically because of the rejection by normative Judaism of the ascription of the messianic role to Jesus. The rejection of this assertion, as is well known, was not done out of caprice—nor because of sheer willful stubbornness or blindness—but because such claims were not consistent with the inherited teaching of Judaism of which they were supposed to be a part. Jesus' ministry did not precipitate the meta-historical events and conditions which, according to accepted Jewish teaching, could be expected to accompany (to some, constitute) the arrival of the Messiah. That is, the doctrine of Jesus as Messiah was—and is—at odds with the doctrine of the Messiah in Judaism. To claim that one can be Jewish and at the same time make certain basic theological assertions which run directly counter to Jewish theological teaching can only be the product of the most extreme kind of intellectual duplicity.

No doubt the various levels of deception involved in the Jews for Jesus movement have succeeded in confusing many Jews who are not sufficiently educated in their religious tradition or are not prepared for a more rigorous discussion of its theology. It may even have been successful in winning a certain number of such people to their cause and thence to Christianity. The greater number of Jews, however, view the activities of these groups with the profoundest skepticism, suspicion and dismay. In the final analysis, these programs are considered by most Jews to be nothing but another strategy for missionizing the Jews. The unhappiness which is felt toward the programs of these groups is frequently extended toward the general Christian community which is perceived as condoning, encouraging and underwriting this latest assault on the well-being and survival of Judaism.

## XI. THE CONSEQUENCES OF CHRISTIAN MISSIONARY ACTIVITIES TO THE JEWS

The existence of these various programs of Christian mission to the Jews must be recognized as having profound consequences for Jews and Christians alike. I speak not of the number of individuals who may move from one community to another, but of the effect, in each community, on its self-understanding and on its perception of the other.

Within the Jewish community, missionary activities contribute to a sense of being beleaguered and set upon by a "hostile world." They are perceived as yet another "assault" upon us by the various forces that would put an end to our existence. In terms of Christian faith in particular, they are understood to be yet another act of ill-will in a history of malice. They are felt, if you will, to be but the latest in a series of destructive designs. Such missionary activity serves to intensify our sense of disjunction from Christianity. It impels us to focus our attention on the "accidents" of Christian faith which distinguish Christianity from Judaism, and causes us to ascribe lesser significance to the "essence" which ultimately unites us. This devaluation of commonality must be recognized as a serious impediment to cooperation, indeed communication, between the two communities.

More pointedly, the promulgation of missionary activities must contribute to a sense of the starkest alienation from Christians and from Christianity. It cannot help but arouse some measure of suspicion on the part of Jews about the whole enterprise of dialogue. In the light of the prevalence of such activities, no Jew can help but maintain serious questions as to the ultimate intent of our Christian partners in interfaith exchange.

Indeed, the phenomenon of such witness may inject an undercurrent of tension into all relations between Christians and Jews. Certainly, it cannot help but cause Jews to harbor, on some level, a bitterness, even hostility, against the faith community which would subject us to such—let us call it by its starkest names—degradation and abuse. Mission and witness when directed against the Jews, as they are, play a destructive role in Christian-Jewish relations. The Christian community should have real concern about the way in which the activities of some of its number retard the advancement of better understanding—and fuller respect—between our two groups.

Serious Christians would do well to consider the effect upon Christianity itself of the pursuit of missionary goals. It must be sad, indeed, to have one's own faith turned into an object of opprobrium to others—particularly to one's "elder brother." No less tragic must be the consequences for Christian self-understanding of the various deceptive practices resorted to by some engaged in mission to the Jews. One wonders what effects the efforts to manipulate a faith to make it "attractive" to others can have on serious and sensitive people who profess that faith. Surely, such acts, done in all innocence or in cynicism, must have the effect of degrading that faith in the eyes of its perpetrators, and perhaps in the eyes of others of the faithful. Cannot such deception cause proponents of the faith to take the faith less seriously? Might not perpetrators and Christian onlookers alike be caused to wonder where lies the reality of Christianity beneath the variety of trappings in which it is caused to be arrayed, or the variety of forms into which it must be distorted for the sake of "export"? In the process of devising new "myths," in Bultmann's sense, to package the faith for others, it seems possible that the merchandisers, and those whose faith they are merchandising, might lose sight of the *kerygma.* If Christianity is, indeed, so flimsy a thing that it can be made to mean all things to all people, then perhaps it means nothing at all.

The specific act of directing mission to the Jews, deceptive or not, may have the unintended consequence of sustaining the virus of antisemitism in the bloodstream of Christian life. At the very least, such activity has the effect of preserving and encouraging some form of anti-Jewish feeling. Less benignly, the devaluation and contempt for Jewish faith too easily translate into feelings of antipathy for things Jewish—and thence for Jews. More specifically, such programs of proselytization of the Jews can, and most often do, take recourse to denigrating aspects of the way Jews live and of Jewish life. Too often they degenerate to caricatures of Jewishness which are reminiscent of nothing so much as classical anti-Jewish propaganda: Jews lead lives of empty materialism; they are soul-less and cut off from God; they are dangerously different from good (in this case Christian) people and should not be allowed to persist in that difference. These refrains occur interchangeably in current manuals for missionaries to the Jews and in diatribes calling for the destruction of the Jews. Christians ought to ponder why the expressions of "love and concern" sound so much like the preachments of hate. And they should contemplate the extent to which efforts to "save" the Jews contribute to the persistence of the rage to destroy them.

## XII. HOW CAN WE WITNESS?

What, then, are Jews and Christians to do? It is, I recognize, presumptuous for one to engage himself in the affairs of another faith community. And certainly no one should attempt to tamper with the self-definition of another. Yet I feel it not improper to note recent developments within Christian thought which point a way out of the dilemma. The various concerns we have noted, account, I believe, for the positive reception of the paper by Professor Tommaso Federici, discussed by Eugene Fisher in this volume. Federici's paper points the way for Christians to act and live in integrity without feeling called upon to engage in programs of converting the Jews. This has to be recognized as a significant and positive step.

## XIII. ACTIVE VS. PASSIVE WITNESS

It will be argued that witness is an integral part of Christian life. I believe that the same can be said, no less, of Judaism. And yet a way exists out of the dilemma in which we now find ourselves. Witness, I would suggest, has both an active and a passive connotation. Active witness consists of actions directed toward another. It is characterized as outer-directed, manifesting itself, in the context of this discussion, in activities undertaken to win someone else over to my faith. Passive witness is inner-directed. It consists of actions done for their own sake, or more immediately, of actions performed for my own sake. Passive witness in its highest sense is those things which I do *l'shem shamayim*—for the sake of heaven. These acts are done with no consideration for the effect they may have on some other who may—or may not—happen to observe me. Any effect of these actions upon such others is wholly incidental to its purpose.

There are real dangers inherent in active, as opposed to passive, witness. Active witness may subject one to the danger of arrogance. So sure must we be that our own perceptions are correct that we may lose the humility necessary to acknowledge the incompleteness of our own finite understanding, the impairments of our mortal vision. None of us is possessed of all of truth, less still of all the truth about the ways of God. Or, even in the hypothetical case that our understanding of God is perfectly whole and complete, we would, if we imagined that we, at any given time, were in perfect accord or complete harmony with God, be guilty of the most colossal arrogance. We must deafen ourselves to the imperatives of that modesty if we are to set out in pursuit of convincing others of the absolute correctness of our, necessarily partial, understanding.

Active witness demands, too, that we abandon humility—one could state more harshly, honesty—about our own motivations. Instincts of all kinds, base no less than admirable, play their part in all human activity. Pride, triumphalism, and greed have had their hand in even the most glorious of human endeavors and human attainments. Yet missionaries, engaged in active witness, behave in a way which suggests that they are blind to these components of their personality. Certainty of their righteousness has robbed them of that humility which is so properly a part of the truly godly individual.

Conversely, as we have noted, active witness may traduce us into the evil of contempt: contempt for the religious worth—perhaps the personal worth—of that other toward whom my actions are directed. That contempt itself, no less than the actions that may flow from it, should be regarded as a scandal by the religiously sensitive person.

Paradoxically, active witness poses, also, the danger of demeaning the value of the missionary's own religious life. The object of one's religious acts becomes not oneself, but the others. Winning them, saving them, become so important that the corollary may be drawn that there is not equivalent importance in the missionary's own self. His actions come to be performed not with an eye to himself, but fixed always on the other. The center of missionaries' religious attention becomes transferred from themselves to that other. Their religious lives become, in this way, distorted. The religious value of themselves becomes, it seems, lost in the process and its own importance is forgotten. So important becomes the other, the missionaries must believe, in the mind of God, that they themselves and their religious aspirations become obliterated. Who, then, will care as much about the "rescuer" as for the one they are "rescuing"?

Passive witness has the virtue of humility. It is done in its own name without the erroneous, or pretended, certainty that it possesses such absolute truth that it demands to be conferred upon another. It spares one, too, from the dangers of contempt or even unintended hurtfulness. It allows one to inhabit the center of one's own religious life, without relegating one to the role of being merely the instrument in the religious betterment of some other. We are in our relationship with God—as opposed to our relationship with other human beings—allowed to be the ends and not always means. Our own salvation, no less than that of the other, is of importance, and passive witness takes this into account.

In point of fact, my act of passive witness may have a profound effect upon the way other people understand me or understand themselves. But that effect is not the goal of the action. One might even conceive a situation in which the effect of an act of passive witness is indistinguishable from the effect of an act of active witness. The results may indeed be the same, but there is a difference, a difference of intent, a difference in the motivation of the act, and that difference is of cosmic dimension.

Jews and Christians should not be called upon to change the religious focus of their lives. Nor should they feel constrained from living out their religious convictions publicly. But in leading their lives by the tenets of their traditions, they should be guided by the impulses of passive, rather than active, witness, with a concern for the effects of their actions on themselves, not upon the other.

## XIV. THERE ARE THOSE WHO NEED OUR WITNESS

Perhaps at bottom we are speaking of honesty. Jews know that there are enough members of our own community whose religious lives are in need of enrichment. We need not scout land and sea to find them. Sorrowfully, they are in our very midst. Perhaps, at times, they are in our very hearts. The same situation, if truth be told, prevails in Christendom. Christians need not look to the Jewish community to find people in need of being put religiously aright. They can be found in Christian homes, indeed in Christian churches. Both communities can do God's work within themselves, without need of reaching into one another's perimeters.

And both live in a world still far from the vision of the kingdom which we have been called upon to build on earth. Enmity, famine, and war still plague our world. The threat of the utter annihilation of human civilization knells as clearly today as on the moment it became technologically feasible. The words of reconciliation and healing still need to be spoken and understood and put into practice. The imperative to teach the good and do the good to our fellowman and in the name of heaven—which is spoken from the essence of both of our traditions—still has claim upon us and upon our resources. In a world so unredeemed, we cannot escape the demand to feed the hungry, clothe the naked, care for the widow, the fatherless and the orphan, heal the sick and tend the wounded soul. For each of our communities, and both of them, hearkening to that challenge may be witness enough.

## NOTES

1. Kaufman Kohler, "The Mission of Israel and Its Application in Modern Times," in *Studies, Addresses and Personal Papers* (New York: Alumni Association of the Hebrew Union College, 1931), p. 189.

2. Rabbinical Council of America, Statement on Interfaith Relations, February 3–5, 1964.

3. For one assessment of the Christian and Jewish agendas in interfaith dialogue, see my article, "This Moment in Christian-Jewish Relations," in *The Ecumenical Bulletin* (November 1980).

4. Alexander Schindler, Presidential Address to the Union of American Hebrew Congregations Board of Trustees, December 2, 1978.

5. One wag suggested that adherents of Schindler's proposal should mount a program similar to that of the mitzvah-mobiles of Lubavitch. A cadre of volunteers is to be trained in a special technique. Having stopped passers-by with the question "Are you Jewish?" they should let people who answer "yes" continue on their way. If the person responds "no," they should say, "Now you are," and run away.

6. Theodore Friedman, "Jewish Proselytism: A New Look," in *Forum* 34 (Winter 1979) 31–32.

7. Yearbook of the Central Conference of American Rabbis, 1947.

8. Rabbis' Manual, Central Conference of American Rabbis, 1961, p. 112.

9. Rabbinical Assembly News Release.

10. Solomon D. Goldfarb, "Who Is a Jewish Child?" in *Conservative Judaism* XXX, 4 (Summer 1976) 70.

# An Asian View of Mission

*C. S. Song*

## I. PARABLES AND MISSIONS

Parables and Christian missions in Asia! At first sight they appear to have little to do with each other. No stretch of imagination seems able to get them related. A parable is a metaphor and a figure of speech. Surely Christian missions are not metaphors, even less figures of speech. Christian missions are a serious business, so serious that St. Paul did not hesitate to employ very militaristic language when he exhorted the Christian believers in Ephesus. "Take up God's armor," he wrote. "Fasten on the belt of truth. Take up the great shield of faith. Take salvation for helmet; for sword, take that which the Spirit gives you" (Eph 6:13–17). What an awesome portrayal of a Christian "soldier" engaged in a combat for the cause of the Gospel! In the course of its history the Church has often taken these words of St. Paul literally. It has shaped its image as a Church militant, putting infidels to the sword and burning its opponents at the stake. It is this militant Church that, protected by Western military powers, began a big operation in Asia in the nineteenth century to bring "pagan" Asians into the fold of "Christendom." If St. Paul had known that his words were to be put to such literal use, he perhaps would have refrained from using them.

But parables are not mere words; they are more than words. Parables are not mere metaphors; they are more than metaphors. And parables are not mere figures of speech; they are more than figures of speech. Parables that are mere words, metaphors, and figures of speech are weak parables.

They do not make you think deeply. They do not challenge you, and they are not capable of empowering you for certain actions. At most they belong to a convention of language that does not reveal a new truth or disclose a deep secret. Yet, a parable becomes powerful when it points to a secret. It even becomes formidable when it embodies that secret. The parables of Jesus in the Gospels are such powerful and formidable parables. They contain the secret of the reign of God that had not been made known before. They disclose the mystery of God's saving mission in the world. That is why Jesus' parables are much much more than just metaphors and figures of speech.

And what about Christian missions? Christian missions are a serious business, as I have said already. They are serious not because they come in full combat gear. They are serious not because of their frightening appearance with armor, helmet, sword and gunboat. They are a serious business because they point to a secret, are captive to a mystery, and embody an extraordinary message. Separated from that secret, that mystery and that extraordinary message, Christian missions are nothing; but linked with it, Christian missions are everything that a Church is and should be.

So, parables and Christian missions are not strangers to one another after all. In actual fact the secret they share keeps them together. The mystery they embody makes them interact one with the other. And the extraordinary message they testify to binds them in a common lot. They cannot betray each other without betraying that secret. They cannot undo each other without undoing that mystery. And divorced from that extraordinary message, they cannot keep their relationship intact. What then is this secret, this mystery, and this extraordinary message? It is the saving love of God for the world. It is, to adjust our focus a little, God's saving love for Asia.

Does this not enable us to say that Christian missions in Asia are in essence parables of God's saving love for Asia? Christian missions are parables. They cannot, and they should not, aspire to be more than parables. But these are no ordinary parables. They are extraordinary parables that carry and serve the marvel of the saving love of the suffering God for the teeming humanity of Asia. Can Christian missions in Asia be less than such parables? Of course not. Can they be more than such parables? Definitely not. To be no more and no less than parables of God's saving love—this should give us fresh insights into what Christian missions are about, not only in Asia but also in Europe, in Latin America, in Africa, and in North America. Here, through parables of the suffering God translated into Christian missions, we may gain a new entry into the world of religion, cultures and histories that have always existed outside the Christian Church.

## II. JESUS SPOKE IN PARABLES, NOT IN PRINCIPLES

Mission in parables—this is Jesus' mission. Jesus goes about his mission in parables tirelessly and persistently. At one point Mark is compelled to make a remark that Jesus "never spoke to the people except in parables" (Mk 4:23). Jesus must have had an inexhaustible resource of parables. There is nothing strange about it. For what he has to do with is God's saving love, and parables expressing it must be limitless. Fundamentally, love is parabolical and not theoretical. Life is the parable of love. Love gives birth to life and bestows meaning to it. Love suffers with life and kindles it with a vision of an eternal hope. Life is a rich spring from which one can draw endless parables of God's saving love.

The Christian churches have often spoken more in religious principles than in parables of the loving God. This is especially true when it comes to missions. Principles have overshadowed parables. Cold logic has triumphed over the warm heart. Theoretical rigidity has discredited the common sense. But, for all astuteness and preciseness characteristic of the Western mind, Christian missions have made people in Asia become confused about ways of Western culture and ways of God. And theorists of Christian missions continue fighting among themselves as if God's saving work depends on their winning the arguments.

Perhaps one of the most typical mission principles still influential today in many quarters of the Christian Church is that advocated by a German theologian, Gustav Warneck, in the nineteenth century. In his view, since Christianity alone possesses the full truth and salvation, mission "as the herald of this message of salvation . . . is the naturally necessary consequence of the absolute character of Christianity."[1] This sounds familiar to most of us, both in the East and in the West. It has served as the foundation stone for the expansion of the Christian Church beyond its Western base. The argument is clear and forceful. The mission outreach of the Church is based on a conviction that "Christianity alone possesses the full truth and salvation." The conviction has had powerful ideological impacts. It has impelled the churches in the West to send out missionaries to evangelize the third world and to convert its "pagans" to the Christian faith.

Like most ideologies, such mission ideology sounds more rhetorical than real, and as the historical horizon of Christians widens and their cultural contacts with the third world become more extensive, they have to take a second look at the theological presuppositions of Christian missions. According to recent statistics on the distribution of religious population in Asia, there are 515,449,500 Hindus, 433,001,000 Muslims, and 260,117,000 Buddhists, whereas Christians, including Protestants and Roman Catholics, number only 89,909,000.[2] These numbers tell us the simple fact that the great majority of people in Asia live outside Christianity "which alone has the full truth and salvation." These are not just numbers and statistics without faces and names, possessing no real life. As you walk on the streets in Hong Kong, these numbers turn into a sea of men and women that engulfs you. When you take your seat at a nightstall in downtown Jakarta, these statistics are transformed into people who overwhelm you with shouts and laughter. Are these millions of people left without truth and salvation until you come with "a full truth and a full salvation"? It does not require great imagination to see that Christian missions based on the principle of "Christianity alone" need a fundamental revision.

There is another mission principle that has gained some support in recent years. It is the Church-growth mission principle. It teaches in essence that "while mission biblically is a broad enterprise, winning men and women to Christ, multiplying sound churches, and discipling nations is always a chief and irreplaceable purpose of mission. Growth is the test of the Church's faithfulness."[3] Growth is a great catchword—growth in Church membership and Church buildings. Growth is of course a sign of vitality of an organic body. When growth slows down, its power weakens. When growth stops, it dies. Christian missions, compared to an organic body, must show vitality through increase in numbers of converts. And "the test of faithfulness" for a Christian community consists in the rate of increase in the number of churches. But unlike other organic bodies, Christian missions, whose vitality and faithfulness are measured almost solely in terms of growth in numbers, easily turn into conflicts of interests among Churches and their missions. Such Christian missions perpetuate disunity among Christians and isolate Christians from their neighbors of other faiths.

Jesus' mission, to the great surprise and embarrassment of many people now as well as then, is an unorthodox mission. It violates religious principles and defies mission theories. It relativizes moral absolutes. It disturbs the balance of religious values. And it introduces a startlingly new experience of God into the depths of the suffering human heart. How otherwise are we to understand that great parable of the father's love in Luke 15? God's unbounded love—this and this alone is everything. It is the most decisive thing. It does not weigh a person's worth on a scale. It does not expose a sinner's past, demanding a fair trial of it. But for such love, that son who had squandered all his money in a foreign country would not have been received back into his father's household. If we read the parable carefully, we will notice that what prompted him to return to his father was not a penitent heart, or a religious reawakening, as most evangelists want to have us believe. It was in fact his self-pity, and above all his empty stomach, that forced him to take the road home. In that dire situation that made him even envious of the pigs put in his charge, he said to himself: "How many of my father's paid servants have more food than they can eat, and here am I, starving to death" (Lk 15:17). This is not a very commendable reason for conversion, is it? Still, the father welcomed him back with open arms. Was the father so indulgent to his wayward son that he did not care why his son finally returned home? Was he so blind to his son's failures that without even a second thought he received him back with a great fanfare? No, God's love is neither indulgent nor blind. God knows that true conversion to him comes only after his love embraces people and touches their hearts. His love prompts conversion and not the other way around.

The elder son does not share his father's unbounded love, of course. He is a man of principle. He lets himself be guided by religious principles and moral codes firmly established within his own religious community. As he sees it, it is utterly scandalous for his father to welcome back his younger brother with such a great joy and such a big feast. "But now that this son of yours turns up," he snaps at his father, "after running through your money with his women, you kill the fatted calf for him" (15:30). There is a deep-seated anger in his protest. But who is this elder brother? He represents those who insist that conversion to God cannot be regarded as genuine until conformation to the rules and laws of the Church is proved, those who cannot accept others as children of God unless they become registered members of a particular brand of Christianity. But what the elder son has done through his religious and moral principles is to make God's love conditional, to put limitations on it. This kind of mission cannot go very far. It gives a distorted image of God and his love. In this kind of mission, God's love suffers from the glory of missionary achievements. God appears to be more like the deity of the Christian clan than the God of all humanity. His love seems more liable to be conditioned by Church membership than moved by the plight of suffering people in Asia and elsewhere. The mission of the elder son cannot take us to the bosom of the suffering God. But Christian Churches have conducted their missions more in the manner of the elder son than in the way of the loving father.

## III. MISSIONS WITH NEIGHBORS

The mission of the elder son type tends to become a monopoly type of mission. To let people know about the will of God is the specific task reserved for a group of people committed to the Christian faith. It belongs to Christianity and to it alone to turn a society to the faith in one true God. It is the supreme commission entrusted to Christians and to them only to bring about the kingdom of God on earth. That is why people easily become objects of Christian missions and targets of Christian crusades. In our days when the myth of Christendom has largely evaporated, this kind of Christian mission loses ground.

God's mission in the world cannot be monopolized by Christians. It is too big for Christians to tackle singlehandedly. It is too rich for the Christian Churches alone to measure its depth and breadth. It is too mysterious for Christian theologians to get hold of with a few theological theses. Christians in Asia are beginning to realize this today. They are learning to stand with their neighbors with whom they share centuries of cultures. They eat the same food as their neighbors. They breathe the same air and even have similar dreams, both individual and collective. Can there be Christian missions without these neighbors? Can we know God's love for the world much more deeply unless we come to know them much more intimately?

For many Christians this amounts to a radical change in their orientation—a change from Christianity-centered missions to the missions centered on God's unbounded love. A priest in the Kurungala diocese of the Church of Lanka in Sri Lanka tells us how he had to face this kind of change in his mission. He engineered a community development project in the dry zone, a village which depends mainly on monsoon rains for water supply. He wanted the project to be a typically Christian one—a project designed by Christians for Christians. Is this God's mission in this village peopled principally by Buddhists? Can such a Christian mission be a parable of God's saving love for the world? His fellow Christians did not put such questions to him. But one of his young Buddhist friends politely asked him if he was going to share his dream of a new community with Christians only. That query shook him. He confessed later: "It was due to such forthright questioning . . . that I was able to reassess my vocation as a Christian." His project then took a different turn. "These three young chaps, Gnanapala and Wijeratnek (Buddhists) and Gamini (Christian), brought to the many discussions we had on this subject their innate knowledge of their own people, habits and customs—a knowledge of which I am woefully lacking—and so helped the venture begin on a more realistic basis."[4]

A Christian mission program that includes Buddhists! Is this not very strange? What do Buddhists have to tell Christians? Is it not Christians who must tell Buddhists what they ought to know about God's love and what they should do about it? We have had missions to Buddhists, missions to Hindus, and missions to ancestor worshipers. But we have scarcely had a mission with Buddhists, a mission with Hindus, or a mission with Confucianists. This is because we have put God's love into the straitjacket of a "Christianity alone" syndrome. We believe that people of other faiths have no positive wisdom to share about God's love for the world. We are so preoccupied with ourselves that we cannot see God-meaning in what others believe, teach and do. It seldom occurs to us that God's love can become a parable, too, in the lives and faiths of our neighbors.

In the Lotus Flower of the Wonderful Law, a Buddhist *sutra* which contains a series of sermons delivered by the Buddha toward the end of his ministry, we come across a parable that bears a striking resemblance to the parable of the father's love we discussed earlier. The settings of the Buddhist parable are of course different. Its plot is less compact and dramatic. Its tone is more subdued and hesitant. But it superbly portrays the father's love for his lost son and his irrepressible although controlled joy at the reunion. The parable speaks of a young man

> Who leaves his father and runs away
> To other lands far distant,
> Wandering about in many countries
> For over fifty years.
> His father, with anxious care,
> Searches in all directions.

Although the father is surrounded with riches and comforts, his heart aches for his son. As to the son, he faces a plight that is very much like that of the prodigal son in the biblical parable.

> At that time the poor son
> Seeks food and clothing

From city to city. . . .
Famished, weak, and gaunt,
Covered with scabs and sores,
Gradually he passes along
To the city where his father dwells.

The son had no idea he had entered his father's city. The father at once recognized the emaciated man in rags as his son, but did not reveal himself to the latter. Instead, he had him hired as a servant and well taken care of in his own household. When at last the time arrived for him to reinstate his son before the assembled guests, he said:

This is my son,
Who left me and went elsewhere
Fifty years ago. . . .
All that I have,
Houses and people,
I entirely give to him;
He is free to use them as he will.[5]

This parable directs the listeners to the buddhas and not to the Father of Jesus Christ. It teaches them about the Nirvana and not about the kingdom of God. But is it purely accidental that the father's love for the runaway son also becomes parabolic in Buddhist search for meaning and salvation?

God's love for humankind is not lost even though the world has gone in different religious directions and taken diverse cultural paths. This must be a part of the basic assumption of faith as Christians engage in mission. It enables us to be free from the theological position that there is only judgment for those who remain outside the Christian Church. It helps us to be rid of the assertion that even God's salvation cannot dispense with the truth as we Christians understand it. After all, the chief business of Christian mission is not to straighten out truths about God, the world, and humanity. You may have all the correct understandings about the nature of God, and yet God may be helplessly remote from you. You may know what the world should be like in light of your faith, and yet you may be supporting its status quo. You may preach salvation for all humanity, and yet you may have little room in your faith and theology for those who do not quite share your convictions. Truths short of God's compassionate love cannot be the basis of Christian missions.

What a marvelous freedom Christians will gain when they begin to look upon their neighbors as partners, to be parables of God's love in this bleak world of strife and conflict! In fact Jesus has shown us such freedom, but, entrenched in our doctrines and daunted by the traditions of the Church, we have lost that splendid freedom. We have become very much like that lawyer who came to Jesus with all the truth, knowledge and principles about gaining eternal life. As a learned man and expert in the wisdom of his religion, he was able to give an impeccable reply to Jesus, quoting from the book of the law: "Love the Lord your God with all your heart, with all your soul, with all your strength, and with all your mind; and your neighbor as yourself" (Lk 10:27). Yes, he has grasped the fundamentals of his religion. He has passed his theological tests. He is licensed to teach and preach to his fellow believers.

And he has also mentioned loving neighbor as well as loving God. Not being an astute theologian capable of hairsplitting the letters of the law, Jesus must have looked at this lawyer with a mixture of admiration and compassion, as he did once before look upon that rich young man preoccupied also with eternal life. But Jesus must have decided to be more careful with this lawyer, for that rich young man let him down. Like this lawyer, the rich young man had all the correct answers from the book of the law. But when Jesus suggested that he sell his possessions and then follow him, the young man was crestfallen. As Mark tells us, "At these words his face fell and he went away with a heavy heart; for he was a man of great wealth" (10:22; par. Mt. 19:22; Lk 18:23).

Jesus' caution was justified. As expected, the lawyer who "wanted to vindicate himself . . . said to Jesus, 'And who is my neighbor?' " (Lk 10:29). Jesus must have suspected that the lawyer had an answer to his own question: his neighbor is his fellow believer, someone of the same color and creed. Jesus decided not to let him pass the test easily this time. He set him a test not from the familiar book of the law or from theological manuals, but from the actual life of people in danger. That is where the lawyer should find out who his neighbor was. This, of course, is the famous parable of the good Samaritan.

Once again Jesus drives home to his audience that God's mission of love and compassion does not recognize religious and racial boundaries. And he does it with such a powerful irony that no one can fail to understand his point. Does not Jesus know that "the Pharisees were inclined to exclude non-Pharisees"? The Essenes required that a man "should hate all the sons of darkness"; a rabbinical saying ruled that heretics, informers, and renegades "should be pushed (into the ditch) and not pulled out."[6] Even though a lay person, Jesus knows all these principles inside out, of course. But in Jesus' view, this is precisely what God's mission of love is not.

Seen against such formidable claims of his own religion, the parable of the good Samaritan is a bold and dangerous venture of faith. It makes the hated Samaritan, and not the religious leaders in power, a parable of God's love. Those who should be about God's business have failed God. To avoid a wounded person abandoned on the roadside on any ground, even on religious grounds, is to avoid God. But when others do it, binding the wounds of the victim of a highway robbery and seeing to his needs, even though they are hated Samaritans, hopeless pagans, or stubborn believers of other faiths, they are in God's mission. Do they not show us how God is at work in the world? Are they not living parables of God's saving love? Jesus told the lawyer: "Go and do as he did" (Lk 10:37).

Missions with the Samaritans! What an outrageous idea! The religious authorities of Jesus' time could not accept it. Indeed, Jesus was a radical missiologist. He was an unorthodox missionary. If he were to come to Asia today, he would certainly tell a parable of a good Hindu, a story of a compassionate Buddhist, or an example of a filial ancestor worshiper. He further would ask us and say: "Go and do as he did." Probably many of us Christians would take Jesus' bidding with a grain of salt. To do as that Hindu did? Would this not amount to admitting God's truth outside the Christian Church? To act as that Buddhist did? Would not this mean to confuse Christianity with religions of salvation through merits and good works? This is syncretism! This is betrayal of the uniqueness of Christianity! Jesus received even more vehement accusations than these in his day. He was accused of blaspheming God! But his command was then and still is today: Go and do as that Samaritan did!

Asia is a part of God's creation and comes within the perimeter of God's redemption. That is why some ninety million Asian Christians are concerned about the destiny of people in Asia. But why should not the spiritual and physical welfare of Asia be equally the concern of 520 million Hindus, 430 million Muslims, and 260 million Buddhists? Long before Christianity entered Asia, Buddhism had been there, preaching and doing the message of compassion and salvation to millions and millions of souls crying out for help from the depths of despair and suffering. Hinduism did the same, and also the other religions. What they have taught and done canot have been all correct, but it cannot have been all wrong either. We do not know why in God's plans it happened that way. But we can say that in God's providence it did happen that way. Why then should Christianity carry out its missions on the basis of outright negation of its predecessors?

The life and destiny of Asian people are the business of Buddhists, Hindus, or Muslims, as well as of Christians. It is their own life and destiny as well as the life and destiny of Asian Christians. Above all, it is the life and destiny in God's hand. To build a community on God's love and compassion—this is the mission that Christians should do in the company of their Buddhist neighbors, Hindu friends, and Muslim citizens. Such mission with neighbors will give new clues to Christian missions, shape them with different approaches, and provide them with a much wider goal.

## IV. THE SUPREME PARABLE OF GOD'S LOVE

So, parables move from words to deeds. They become transposed from stories to events. He who tells parables becomes the doer of parables. And as Jesus presses on with his mission of God's love, the contour of his parables becomes increasingly clear until it takes the form of the cross. On the cross we encounter the supreme parable of God's saving love—Jesus Christ crucified. The cross discloses the secret of God's mission strategy—overcoming pain through pain, conquering suffering through suffering, kindling hope through hopelessness, and giving life through death. Christian missions have no other strategy than this strategy of the cross. Imperial strategy resulted in Constantinian Christianity and created an illusion of empires and royal courts ruled by Christian kings and princes. Gunboat strategy pushed the sphere of Christian influence into the interiors of many Asian lands, but it also roused hostility in the people that Christian missions sought to convert to the God of love. St. Paul was right when he said: "I would think of nothing but Jesus Christ—Christ nailed to the cross" (1 Cor 2:2). He knew that only the cross-strategy would work. Nowhere else is so much concentration of suffering—suffering that seems the end of all hope. But nowhere else is again so much concentration of hope—hope that comes from God's own involvement in it. If God too suffers there on the cross, the cross cannot be the end of hope; it can in fact be the beginning of a new hope. This is the profound spiritual experience of Dietrich Bonhoeffer in his prison cell. For him only the suffering God can help.

The world that takes the suffering God to help—it is in this kind of world that Christians must be engaged in missions. Human beings who need the suffering God to rescue them—these are Christians themselves and also the people with whom they must have their missions. We do not need to go back all the way to the savage old days to know that history is in a real sense the arena of the struggle between the suffering God and suffering humanity. In our "civilized" world today, the struggle seems to become even bloodier and more gruesome. We have seen, if not actually gone through, the horrors of the Holocaust, on our television screen. We have heard the cries of the boat people on the high seas in Southeast Asia, falling prey to marauding pirates and an unmerciful fate. When the crime of genocide in Cambodia is brought to our knowledge, our hearts ache in pain and disgust. And as the repressive government in one country after another in Asia muzzles the mouths of political dissidents with martial law, bridles the conscience of those who stand for freedom and democracy with the charge of sedition, and invades prayer meetings and worship services of religious communities with intimidation and arrest, we know that this is no ordinary time for ordinary Christian missions. "Believe in Jesus, join the Church and receive the promise to heaven"—there is no place for such evangelism in Asia today or anywhere. Should such evangelism have been there at all, to begin with?

The suffering God in the suffering world calls for extraordinary Christian missions. He seems to tell us that the targets of Christian missions are no longer idols of world religions and fetishes of primitive beliefs. These idols have distorted God's true nature. That is true. But for that matter, has not Christianity, too, distorted it? Moreover, Christian missions have not been most effective in getting rid of idols and superstitions. Science and technology that have secularized the mysterious universe have done a better job. As the dominion of science and technology expands, the dominion of idols and spirits diminishes. But certain political ideologies such as communism have done an even better job. As it has happened in China, as the nation turned completely to socialism, believing in the power of people to defeat the tyranny of fate and build a socialist nation, superstitions lost their grip on the people. In a secularized socialist society, idols and superstitions have had their day.

No, the real threat to God does not come from those idols of religions and folk beliefs; it comes from the idols made by political and military powers. To the grief of the suffering God and to the misfortune of the suffering people, such idols are on the rise in Asia today. In comparison with the idols that used to be the objects of preachers' ridicules and evangelists' attacks, these other idols are utterly sinister and destructive. They are armed with martial law—you cannot ridicule them with impunity. They are protected by bayonets and guns—you cannot attack them without risking your own safety. They proclaim oracles of truth and nothing but truth—you cannot question them unless you are prepared to forego your freedom. They create laws and change the constitution in the name of national security and economic development—you cannot challenge them without bringing down their wrath on your head. These idols are really diabolical. Compared with the idols housed in temples and superstitions practiced by innocent villagers and fishing folk, they are fully alive, powerful and fearful. They despise the people who believe in the freedom of conscience, disdain those who favor democracy, and have no patience with Christians who insist that they cannot worship them in place of God.

Many more Christians in Asia are being awakened to the fact that they are called to a mission not built on conventional Christian wisdom and discretion but on fresh commitment to the cross of Jesus. Previously, Christian missions performed exorcism on idols and spirits that could not hit back. Spirits were driven out and idols were burned. New converts were added to the Church and there were celebrations of victory over powers of evil and darkness. But Christian missions cannot be such a tame affair anymore. Many Christians realize that they are confronted with new idols that can and will hit back. Instead of making a bonfire of these idols, the latter threaten to make a bonfire of them. In the place of victory celebrations, sober and earnest prayer meetings are held for those taken away to be tried at a military court. Christian missions have become a dangerous matter. And leading such dangerous missions is no longer the "sweet and comely" Jesus sung at evangelical rallies but Jesus with a crown of thorns staggering under the heavy cross. By force of circumstances, Christians find themselves having to cross swords with "the principalities and powers" of this world. They themselves become parables of the suffering God.

Christian missions are parables of God's suffering love. Here is a story about Noli, born Arnulfo Resus, a little over twenty years ago, in a typical middle-class Protestant family in South Luzon in the Philippines. He did not allow himself to lead a sheltered and easy life, for he realized that "all the injustice and suffering were but the inevitable and logical consequence of a social structure that is basically unjust." This was a dangerous awakening for Noli. He soon found himself "participating in programs designed to raise people's consciousness, in community development, and mass demonstrations of protests." His activities finally led to "his death at the hands of the military." In a tribute to him, his friends had this to say about him.

> He belongs to that rare, unique breed
> who is willing to live and take the risk,
> to die a death that lives on
> in the struggle, sacrifice and victory of the people.[7]

What a tribute a Christian can get from his comrades-in-arms fighting for a society that may have just a little more justice and love!

A fundamental change of direction has taken place in a Christian mission such as carried out by Noli. When the main forces of Christian missions were deployed to evangelize the "pagans," Christian converts demonstrated their commitment to the Christian faith by ridding themselves of idols and keeping a distance from their own cultural and historical heritages. To become a Christian is to emigrate[8] from the society shaped by cultures and ethos of other religions. This was confession of Christian faith by dissociation. But for Noli and for many other Christians in Asia today, confession of faith entails not dissociation but association. They have rediscovered their own culture as part of God's culture—the culture created, cultivated and owned by God. They have recognized their people—their neighbors—as people of God as much as they themselves are God's people. "We are not like you people out there!" This was a proud declaration of faith by Christians in previous times. But now Christian missions prove authentic when people out there say to Christians: "You belong to us out here!" They said this to Noli in their tribute to him. And they are saying this to more and more Christians in Asia today. Christians are no longer squatters with no right to the land on which they build their churches and cathedrals. Not anymore! They have ceased to be strangers to the history which, they thought, had little relation with the history of God's engagement in the world. They have earned their right to their own land. They have become subjects of the history of their own nation. Christian missions in Asia have begun in real earnest. Theirs are missions parabolic of the suffering God. Theirs are also missions with their own people who yearn and suffer for a community of love and justice.

Perhaps no one in Asia has more powerfully and with greater agony given witness to the suffering God who takes sides with the suffering people than Kim Chi Ha, a young Roman Catholic poet in South Korea. He has been tortured and imprisoned for life for his struggle with his own people for human rights and democracy under the totalitarian regime of President Park Chung Hee. His "Prayer," offered in the dead of the night from the profoundly silent and empty depth of his solitary cell, moves our hearts, if not the heart of a dictator:

> Let me pray alone:
> to be with the masses, at the bottom,
> to be beaten with them,
> to decay with them,

and finally to rise up gallantly from the earth with them
in the bright morning sunshine,
with our heads held high.[9]

What a prayer! What a parable! What a Christian mission!

"To be with the masses"—this is the heart of Christian missions. As a matter of fact, this was the heart of Jesus' mission. He was with the masses. The masses came to him, and he went to the masses. He knew their language—that is why he taught and spoke to them in the parables of the lost sheep, the hidden treasure in the earth, the dough and the leaven, or the mustard seed. He knew what kind of burden they had to bear—that is why he promised them a light burden and an easy yoke of the loving God instead of a heavy burden and a difficult yoke imposed on them by their religious authorities. He gave laughter to those who shed tears and never begrudged forgiveness to those petrified by the strict guardians of the law. His heart went out to the victims of the unjust sociopolitical and religious powers. He himself proved to be something radically new in the eyes of the masses. A bridge of deep understanding and common spirituality was built between him and them. Jesus became a liberating presence in the midst of them. It was a contagious kind of presence. People were drawn to him, feeling secure and hopeful in front of him. Touched by him, they felt they were freed from their fear and weakness. Listening to him, they realized that their hearts grew warm with a renewed faith in the God who was with them through thick and thin. Even the irony and bitterness of the cross did not destroy such experience and such faith. It was in fact this faith, shaken by the trauma of the cross but strengthened by the risen Christ, that inspired the demoralized followers of Jesus to take up the mission of becoming parables of God's suffering love.

## V. A CHRISTIAN ROLE IN ASIA

The role that Jesus' disciples and followers played in that post-cross-and-resurrection Mediterranean world seems the role many Christians in Asia are playing there at this time of history. Most people in Asia find it increasingly difficult to cope with tremendous social tensions caused by human greed and economic injustice. They feel helpless as the moral bases of their lives become more and more eroded. The political forecast is equally distressing. Conflicts between the politico-military elites who hold power and the masses who are awakened to their human dignity and sociopolitical rights will become intensified. Sadly, there are precious few signs that power elites are going to yield to people's demands for democracy and freedom. There will be more government repressions and people's demonstrations. We shall see more violence and counter-violence. There will be more arrests of political dissidents and trials of those whose only crime is to be the voice of the voiceless masses. As if this is not bad enough, military confrontations caused by ideological and racial conflicts will continue to produce dislocated people, broken homes and disrupted societies. Human suffering, both individual and collective, will sap people's already meager spiritual energy and becloud their vision of a future. In Asia, despite its enormous human and natural resources, people may come more and more under the grip of the fate that deprives them of their hope and future.

This is the time of great spiritual crisis in Asia. What is at stake is the question of how human beings can remain human. It is also a question of how their frightened, tired and withered bodies, minds and hearts can rise from resignation to determination, from despair to hope, and from death to life. In this kind of world Christians in mission must move. To this kind of people Christian Churches are called to minister. Christian missions must be a part of the efforts to mobilize Asian spirituality for a human community in which the forces of love, justice and peace may prevail over the powers of hate, oppression and inhumanity. And how else can Christians and Churches carry out missions of human restoration than by becoming parables of the suffering God?

There was Finn, so a story written by a Christian in Sri Lanka goes, who was a prisoner of war in a camp in the middle of a desert. In that immense emptiness of desert space, prisoners were reduced to sheer desperation and hopelessness, just waiting for decay and death.

The story goes on to tell how a bird came to the prisoner's window and dropped a seed there. This he planted in the dregs left in the teapot the prisoners were given. And the seed sprouted and grew and became a sunflower. It became for him a symbol for new life:

> The hope after suffering,
> The hope out of suffering,
> The renewal of one's own faith,
> The renewal of one's bond with God.[10]

To be a seed of hope and life—this is what many socially and politically awakened people in Asia seek to be in their struggles for democracy and justice. This is also what enlightened believers of other religions try to be.

Together with these people, Christians can help make hope emerge out of the dregs of social and political turmoils in today's Asia and help renew faith in God, the Creator and Redeemer, in the midst of spiritual wilderness in many Asian nations. They go about this task of human restoration in Asia not because they are different from and superior to their neighbors. But as Christians, in doing so they become engaged in missions to be parables of the suffering God. How else could they give witness to Jesus Christ, the supreme parable of God's saving love?

## NOTES

1. Cf. J. Verkuyl, *Contemporary Missiology: An Introduction,* tr. and ed. Dale Cooper (Grand Rapids, Mich.: William B. Eerdmans, 1978), p. 27. In the third chapter of this book, Verkuyl succinctly discusses "The History of Missiology during the Nineteenth and Twentieth Centuries."

2. The statistics are taken from *1978 Britannica Book of the Year* (Chicago: Encyclopaedia Britannica, 1978), p. 616.

3. Donald A. McGavran and Alan R. Tippett, "Theory of Missions," in *Concise Dictionary of the Christian World Mission,* eds. Stephen Neill, Gerald H. Anderson, John Goodwin (Nashville/New York: Abingdon Press, 1971) p. 596.

4. Cf. Nicolaas Rose, "Communities in Mission (Sri Lanka)," in *Witnessing to the Kingdom,* eds. D. Preman Niles and T. K. Thomas (Singapore: Christian Conference of Asia, 1979), pp. 60–63.

5. See *The Three Lotus Sutra* (New York/Tokyo: Weatherhill/Kosei, 1975), pp. 116–120.

6. Joachim Jeremias, *The Parables of Jesus,* tr. S. H. Hooke (London: SCM Press, 1963), pp. 202–203.

7. The story is told by Nimalka Fernand in her address, "The Reality of Asian Suffering," one of the Four Niles Memorial Lectures given at the Sixth Assembly of the Christian Conference of Asia in Penang, 31 May—9 June, 1977. See *Testimony Amid Asian Suffering,* ed. T. K. Thomas (Singapore: Christian Conference of Asia, 1977), pp. 9–16.

8. To borrow Hans Küng's terminology in his *On Being a Christian,* tr. Edward Quinn (Glasgow: William Collins, 1978), pp. 192–201.

9. Kim Chi Ha, *The Gold-Crowned Jesus and Other Writings,* eds. Chong Sun Kim and Shelly Killen (Maryknoll, New York: Orbis Books, 1978), p. 2.

10. See *CCA* (Christian Conference of Asia) *News,* XII, No. 7, July 15, 1977. The author of the play, in which the story of Finn is to be found, is Nalini Jayasariya of Sri Lanka.

# Mission in African Countries

*Kwesi Abotsia Dickson*

## I. INTRODUCTION

> The Bible is not a book for us. God at the beginning gave the Bible to the white people, another book to the Cramos, the fetishes to us.

These words form part of a statement made in 1876, some forty years after Methodist missionary work was started in Ghana, by a Ghanaian ruler in response to a request from an English Methodist missionary. This was when the missionary, Thomas R. Picot, arrived in Kumasi, the principal town of Asante in central Ghana, to try to urge the Asante king to do all he could to facilitate the work of his mission in the kingdom.[1] Kumasi had known English Methodist missionaries before 1876, but the missionaries had had no cause to rejoice because there was a decided reluctance among the people to lend support to the work being initiated in their midst. What had been learned by the king of the nature of the missionaries' work and concerns had suggested to him that the Bible was not the book for his people. He could not have spoken from first-hand knowledge of the contents of the Bible; he was going by what was reportedly the message proclaimed by the missionaries, a message that evidently had not enthused him, for he draws an interesting and instructive distinction between Christianity and the traditional religion of his people, which he obviously preferred, when he goes on to say to Picot: "Our fetishes . . . tell us too where the gold is with which we trade."

What the Asante king was saying, in effect, was that unlike the religion proclaimed by the white missionaries, African traditional religion had to do with the African's life in all its circumstances; the Christian religion seemed to him to have a limited concern: the God who was proclaimed did not appear to be interested in the totality of the life-circumstances of the African.

Some evidence could be adduced to show that in the early days of missions in Africa there was much missionary preaching that failed to relate the new faith to life as the African understood it, except in a negative sense that considered African life and thought to be incompatible with the new faith. However, this does not make any less erroneous the Asante king's understanding of the nature and contents of the Bible and of the new faith's significance.

Among the concerns of this chapter will be the exploration of the reasons for this misrepresentation: More positively, suggestions will be made regarding the way for the Church in Africa, as it responds to the realities of the African situation.

## II. THE HEBREW SCRIPTURES AND MISSIONS

In the circumstances of life in Africa which the early Western missionaries, given the cultural context in which they had been nurtured, could not appreciate there was quite early in the modern era of missions in Africa a certain amount of misunderstanding with regard to what mode of life was to be expected of African converts to Christianity in demonstration of their new status as Christians. It is an issue which had arisen in the early Church where it occasioned not a little controversy, the various reactions depending primarily on what the Hebrew Scriptures were heard to be saying by the different protagonists on the subject of the relation between God's chosen people and the other nations. It is not accidental that in championing a relaxed attitude, Stephen drew so much upon the Old Testament (Acts 7:1ff); likewise, the intrepid Judaizers undoubtedly found much support for their views in the Old Testament (Acts 15:1). Thus the Hebrew Scriptures become a crucial witness in this matter, and if we may here anticipate subsequent discussion, it is possible to argue that much of the controversy attendant upon the drive into the Gentile areas in the early Church was the result of a less than imaginative reading of the Old Testament.

Another dimension of the importance of the Old Testament for our inquiry is the oft-noted fact that Africans frequently demonstrate a predilection for the Old Testament, a fact which occasioned much disquiet among some missionaries working in Africa and which has not been sufficiently evaluated as to its significance for the Church in Africa. In the light of these matters it is necessary to investigate the Old Testament, even though this can be done only in a limited way, given the constraints of space.

It is a commonplace that the Old Testament does not present a uniform attitude to non-Israelite peoples and their traditions. It is possible, in fact, to discern three attitudes: there is a negative one of rejection; then, there is a "neutral" attitude which serves as a link between the negative attitude and a decidedly positive attitude. There are clear indications of a marked intolerance toward other peoples and their traditions; and, indeed, it would be surprising, given the fact of Israel's continuous hostile encounters with the nations of the time, if there were not on display in the Old Testament, a residual hostility toward other peoples (e.g., Is 14:3ff). As a matter of fact, it is primarily the conviction of having been chosen by God that explains Israel's sense of being set apart from those who did not worship Yahweh. Through all the periods of Israel's history as covered in the Old Testament, there is evidence of her exclusivist attitude. Thus Israel's sense of the humane is flawed by the injunction to decimate the peoples living in the land which God had given her (Dt 7:1f); the gods of the other peoples are spoken of in derisive terms (1 Kgs 18:27) and are even deemed to be non-existent (Is 44:6). In the circumstances of the exile, Jeremiah found it necessary to write to the exiled encouraging them to practice their religion even in a foreign land (Jer 29:1–28), and it is with a sense of controlled outrage that Ezekiel describes the un-Israelite religious activities that were going on in the Jerusalem temple (Ez 8).

The attitude described above as "neutral" is really a critical assessment of the significance of Israel's position as a chosen people. Israel is not to consider herself to be automatically deserving of God's attention in a special way by reason simply of her having been chosen. It is this critical assessment of Israel's chosenness which issues in the Deuteronomic conviction that Israel cannot expect to escape the fate of the peoples to be destroyed if she fails to keep God's commandments (Dt 8:11–20). Indeed, Amos goes beyond rejecting the view held by his contemporaries that the day of the Lord would be one of triumph for Israel and darkness for others (Am 5:20) to suggest that God is concerned more with righteousness than with Israel (3:2). Thus the strongly critical attitude in relation to non-Israelite peoples embraces Israel herself, suggesting that, in the final analysis, it hinges upon the people's relation to, or lack of awareness of, the sovereignty of Yahweh; and the Old Testament shows that Israel could be no less lacking than the nations in a sense of that awareness.

The "neutral" attitude merges into the positive, which is as prominent in the Old Testament as is the negative, namely: God is close to all peoples in the particularities of their life-circumstances. This positive attitude is expressed in various ways. Thus in Genesis the oneness of humanity is underlined: not only does God create mankind, but also the nations of the world are to be blessed through Abraham. Post-exilic prophecies contain clear statements of a new understanding of humanity; thus Isaiah paints the picture of a new world in which all the nations would come to Jerusalem in recognition of Yahweh's overlordship (Is 2:1–3), while Malachi asserts that, the worship of his contemporaries being hypocritical and out of step with Israelite tradition, God rejects it in preference to the worship of non-Israelite peoples: the sincerity of the latter makes it preferable before God (Mal 1:11). Indeed, there is much evidence in the Old Testament of Israelite religion having been enriched through contact with the Canaanites and the appropriation of certain Canaanite religious concepts.[2] The importance of this stance is beyond question; not only is it significant that it exists at all, side by side with the strongly condemnatory attitude, but it also plays a significant role in the New Testament, especially in the teaching of Jesus: in more than one parable Jesus presents the non-Jew as more acceptable to God than the Jew. And it was this more accommodating attitude that provided the motive for the drive into Gentile territory in the early Church, even though the evidence shows that its protagonists, such as Paul, were not able to adopt a sufficiently positive attitude to the traditions of non-Jews.

It is evident from the above that the Hebrew Bible provides justification for a missionary outreach, for it suggests a theological continuity with peoples of other traditions. This imposes a great responsibility upon the propagator and the recipient of the Gospel message alike; recognizing this continuity, they must allow the mode of presentation of the message to be shaped by it while the recipient must be faithful to God in and through the distinctiveness of his life-circumstances. To refer specifically to Africa, the Christian missions inherited a tradition, which has its springs in the Hebrew Bible, of a positive attitude to the peoples of Africa; whether or not the missionaries allowed this to shape their approach is another matter. Moreover, many missionaries evidently doubted that Africans could be faithful to God in and through their traditional life and thought. To this we shall return in the next section.

In the African context the Hebrew Scriptures are a particularly intriguing set of documents, for there is a demonstrable cultural continuity between them and African life and thought.[3] Since this matter will be brought up again, it will suffice to observe at this point that where the African convert has come to be familiar with the contents of the Bible, he has found much in the life and thought of Israel which seems to be recalled in his own. The realization of this fact made some of the missionaries uneasy about making the Old Testament available in translation to the African convert. It was at least one reason why the translation of the Old Testament into some African languages was done only after the New Testament or sections of it had been translated. In any case, the African is in a very good position to appreciate the human interest aspects in the Hebrew Scriptures. The Israelites were flesh and blood, though sometimes one gets the impression that among scholars there is little interest in this fact. Scholarly attention has often centered on the message of the Hebrew Scriptures, and the variety of formulations of that message is an indication of the conviction that the Old Testament contains an overriding message.[4] It is like a palimpsest, the message of reforming zealots having been written over that of the religio-cultural struggles which resulted from the Israelites' encounter and interaction with a variety of peoples in and outside Palestine (especially Egypt and Babylon). The message, whichever characterization of it is preferred, is important, but it should not be allowed to blot out the cross-currents of ideas met with in the Old Testament; for it is an appreciation of these that makes the message even more striking. The Israelite tradition was enriched in interaction with other peoples and traditions and, given the fact of the cultural continuity between the Hebrew Scriptures and African life and thought, African Christians can appreciate both the human interest aspect and the message written over it, as it were.

Thus the Hebrew Scriptures provide a strong basis for an approach to mission which takes into account the life circumstances of those being evangelized.

## III. WESTERN MISSIONS: PRESUPPOSITIONS AND REACTIONS

It is hardly possible to give in this article a detailed résumé of the story of missions in Africa, considering the size of the continent and the variety of mission bodies which claimed Africa as a mission field. Starting from the eighteenth century in particular, a profusion of missionary societies recruited and sent to Africa dedicated young men and women to evangelize its peoples and win them for Christ. There is no question but that the missionaries, to a considerable extent, succeeded in setting up churches whose members were so full of zeal for Christ that many were prepared to die with the missionaries when non-Christian Africans turned hostile to the Church and everything that it seemed to stand for. Many a missionary would have described his converts with the same kind of passion with which Paul describes the Christian conviction of his Galatian converts, as it was before the Judaizers succeeded in getting at them (Gal 1:6–10). Yet, so many African converts, as many missionaries testified in a variety of African countries and denominational settings, were still found to be attached to the African religio-cultural traditions to an extent which the missionaries considered unacceptable. After all, the missionary, like the European administrator in colonial Africa, often considered that his mission should also have a "civilizing" effect, which meant the "release" of the African convert from the shackles of the "weak and beggarly elemental spirits" (Gal 4:9), to echo Paul's somewhat contemptuous description of the traditional religion of the Galatians.

Given the frequent—and often justifiable—criticism in our time of missionary activity, it comes as a pleasant surprise to discover the extent of imaginative thinking that often went into the formulation of missionary policies. Many a modern missionary society adopted a policy of operation—at least on paper—such as Pope Gregory approved for application by Augustine in sixth century England.[5] The story of missions in Africa features many European missionaries who showed great understanding of African life and thought and demonstrated a willingness to have their strategy influenced accordingly. That there were many more European missionaries, however, who were unprepared to see anything of value in African life and thought is not to be doubted; there was a general feeling that the proclamation of the Gospel should have as a corollary the uprooting of African life and thought.

To account for this latter—and generally more predominant—*modus operandi,* one only has to realize that the Christianity brought to Africa by the European missionaries had been shaped in a Western milieu; it had received its character from the Western life-style. Given the prevailing Western attitude that Christianity is the most developed religion, the linking of Christianity and Western civilization was to be expected. Thus, the German scholar Ernst Troeltsch wrote some sixty years ago that Christianity and Western culture were so inextricably intertwined that it was doubtful whether non-Westerners could understand this faith;[6] inherent in this view was the belief that Western culture was superior to that of "primitive" peoples. That certain missionary attitudes were nurtured in such a theological milieu may be taken for granted. Some missionaries to Africa lived and worked in order to demonstrate such linking of Christianity and Western culture, and the fact that this had the potential for undercutting the very basis of missions went largely unnoticed. Evidence abounds in missionary records showing that in the initial stages of missionary activity in Africa every attempt was made to give the African convert such reorientation as would make him appreciate more readily the patterns of life and thought which the missionary was seeking to establish. Not only did the missionary encourage adoption by African converts of the colonial ruler's language, the Church ethos inculcated was also that known in the missionary's home church.

There are other dimensions of the story of missions which may be brought out here in order to achieve a more inclusive assessment of missionary activity in Africa, and to be in a position to give a more meaningful evaluation of the Church in Africa.

Earlier on, reference was made to the fact that the African convert is in a good position to appreciate the life and thought of ancient Israel. In contrast to this African predilection for the Old Testament, the history of Western scholarship shows that in certain theological circles, with German scholars among the key figures, the Old Testament was found to be a collection of documents whose atmosphere was uncongenial to Western man. When it was insisted, quite rightly, that the Old Testament should be approached primarily as a distinctively Hebrew phenomenon, Western scholars came face to face with a world which was unfamiliar and "primitive." It is a fact that such renowned German scholars as Friedrich Schleiermacher and Adolf von Harnack, to name just these two, could not identify with the Old Testament and tried to depose it from canonical rank.[7] In the context of Africa, it seemed to some missionaries that there was an even greater justification for suppressing the Old Testament; for it was observed quite early in mission activities that to African converts the Old Testament seemed very familiar. And, indeed, there is much in the Hebrew Scriptures, in the life and thought of ancient Israel, that seems to be recalled in African life and thought; this has been documented by a number of writers.[8] It was partly in consequence of this realization that some missionaries felt it might be prudent not to make the Old Testament available to converts in the initial stages of their Church membership. The missionaries feared that the converts might not feel inclined to go on to the New Testament. Since African religio-cultural traditions were considered inferior systems and since, given the cultural continuity between the Old Testament and African life and thought, this assessment served to reinforce the Western missionary's uneasiness with the Hebrew Scriptures, it was only to be expected that every attempt should be made to suppress the traditions of Africa's peoples.

One of the most fascinating characteristics of the Old Testament is its far-from-muted avowal of the fact that religion is inseparable from the rest of life. Reality is not compartmentalized into sacred and secular spheres, a distinction that would be meaningless in the context of the Old Testament because the ancient Israelite understood that life is lived before God. A wrong appraisal of certain characteristics of the Old Testament would seem to give this the lie. For example, the transcendence of God is enunciated in it; prophet after prophet pictures God as one who is over and above everything. It is made amply clear, however, that at the same time God is actively involved in the life of man in all its aspects. These two views of God are considered to represent one reality. In contrast to this, there is some evidence to suggest that missionary preaching, at least in the early days of missions in Africa, tended to emphasize God's transcendence, to the exclusion of his being involved with the "mundane" existence of man. It was in keeping with the European missionary's negative opinion of the African religio-cultural traditions that he should have emphasized the transcendence of God; for the missionary's concern was to impress it upon the African that God wanted him to turn away from the ordinary concerns of life. This, of course, contributed to the new faith being seen as somewhat unreal.

It has been made clear in the foregoing that Christianity in Africa came to a people with distinctive religio-cultural traditions. The African spirit-world is peopled by a host of spirits, but this is not to suggest a world without order, for, indeed, not only do these spirit powers have their spheres of operation, but there also is a clear awareness of a Supreme Being who, even though he may not be regularly worshiped, is nevertheless considered to be a vital element in the belief-system. Together with African religion goes a way of life; religion informs life in general, to the extent that it would be unreal to speak of religion and life as separate entities. Thus, when Christianity was presented as a faith that sought to take the African away from what he understood to be legitimate concerns of life, two predictable reactions were possible. On the one hand, some converts, in the belief that the missionary was right, would want to adopt this Western-oriented faith and reject African life and thought in its totality. Some of the early converts and African Christian leaders adopted this attitude, acting on the conviction that their traditional ways of life deserved to be obliterated, their zeal in this connection being sometimes greater than that displayed by the missionaries! Yet, this was by no means the predominant reaction. The position most commonly taken was for the converts to adopt as much of the new faith as was possible, without letting go of the traditional religio-cultural presuppositions. Many African Christians, whether consciously or unconsciously, held on with varying degrees of attachment to African life and thought, at the same time practicing the new faith as it had been handed down by the European missionary.

This latter reaction poses a real danger, even though it also has the potential of being very useful. On the one hand, it could perpetuate the dichotomizing of religious reality whereby Christianity and African religion are assigned to different spheres of life, such as to suggest that Christianity could have no vital connection with what is reality to the African. On the other hand, there is in this attitude the possible foreshadowing of a developing Christian faith that would take seriously the African religio-cultural traditions.

## IV. CHRISTIAN PRESENCE IN AFRICA —CONTEMPORARY SITUATION

### *1. Historic Churches*

This is the point at which to describe the contemporary situation. The Church enjoys considerable visibility in Africa. The historic Churches have largely become independent, relying on African leadership, and in most cases raising their funds locally, though at the same time maintaining connections—at varying degrees of intensity—with the parent Churches in Europe and America. But perhaps the most remarkable fact about these Churches is that, by and large, they remain fair copies of the parent Churches in the West. Thus Churches brought into being by, say, the United Methodist Church of America tend to have the ethos of the parent American Church. In other words, in most cases the modeling of the Churches in Africa after the European or American "original" has been very faithfully executed, initially by the Western founders and now by the African leadership who have apparently opted for maintaining the status quo. The historic Churches' theology is today just as it was originally received. Elsewhere we have remarked upon the unflattering ability of the ordained in these Churches to hold on to official theological positions even where they give rise to contradictions with some aspects of traditional life which cannot be said, by any stretch of the imagination, to constitute disloyalty to Christ.[9] This is not surprising for, by and large, the ordained members of the historic Churches were trained in seminaries in Africa modeled in course-content after those in Europe and America and were taught by Western as well as African theological educators. In short, the European creation emanating from the mission era has continued to be faithfully maintained, more or less.

Let it be understood that there are hundreds of thousands in the historic Churches who are in a position to testify to the Lordship of Christ and the change that faith has brought about in their lives. The European character of these Churches should not be understood as an indication of a lack of genuine personal Christian conviction. What we are seeking to suggest, in pointing to the historic Churches' lack of authenticity, is simply this: the Churches could serve their members better and be a greater force for good in society if they had a more authentically African character. In support of this contention, it may be noted that the record of these Churches with respect to social concern is decidedly suspect, and this can be explained by reference to their inauthentic character. The African continent has been passing through very turbulent years of oppressive rule, military coups, etc., since the 1950's, when Ghana became the first African country to achieve independence. It is a fact that the Churches have not said or done much, generally speaking, about these situations even though they adversely affect the lives of their members, and, indeed, the whole of society with which the Church claims to be concerned. The reason for the Churches' ineffectiveness in this regard seems to be that, just as at one time the mission Church was run by the European missionaries who more often than not worked closely with the European administrators in the African countries, and hence were more likely to see their role as complementing that of the administrators, so now the independent historic Churches, even though they have an African leadership, retain much of their colonial character and, having a distinctly middle-class image, seem to be more at home with those in power than with the ruled. It is difficult otherwise to explain the silence, or at best the extremely muted critical comments, of the historic Churches in Amin's Uganda and Nkrumah's Ghana, to name just these two countries which saw a great deal of brutality and fear.

Increasing awareness of the deficiencies so far noted has given rise to certain developments. For some time now, certain African Christians in the historic Churches have been pressing for the Churches to shed their colonial character by discovering what they can learn from African life and thought. In consequence of this, some concessions have been made to the fact that the Churches in Africa exist amid religio-cultural traditions different from those out of which European Christianity was shaped and brought to Africa. Thus, African music has been playing an increasingly significant role in the worship-life of these Churches and African cultural symbols are used more effectively. That these developments in Christian worship are important cannot be gainsaid, for they have resulted in more spontaneous and more meaningful worship than the use of entirely foreign idioms made possible. By and large, however, this development is more cosmetic than crucial because it still leaves the Churches' colonial character fairly intact. After all, music plays a limited role in a Church's life and thought, and it is possible to employ certain cultural elements while leaving the Church's received theology intact.

In the awareness of the limitations of these cultural changes, some African Christians are calling for the development of African theology and black theology, the latter mostly by black theologians in South Africa, the former largely by African Christians from outside South Africa. The protagonists of African theology are concerned that the Churches should not be satisfied with mere cosmetic cultural embellishments; hence they are calling for a complete reorientation of the Churches' theology, against the background of African life and thought. While insisting on the centrality of Christ, they insist also on the need for Africans to encounter Christ in an authentic way. For this development to take place, certain factors, it is recognized, should be taken into account. Since Africanness is God-given, it should be made to play a part in the evolution of relevant theology; the Bible is another of the essential "working materials," for it enshrines the story of God's dealings with man, a story which, though it has a particularity, should be the means of ever hearing anew God's approach to peoples in their various circumstances; the deposit of Christian thought over the centuries also is important, as long as it does not become a barrier to hearing God's call. In other words, Christian tradition should not become an impediment to the development of a meaningful theology in the context of a people's life-circumstances.

While those advocating the development of African theology have a distinctly cultural bias, black theology in South Africa has the flavor of black theology in America; it is aimed at expressing awareness of Christian responsibility in a situation of racism and socio-economic inequities. Hitherto, a sharp line of demarcation has existed between black theology and African theology, but it is our conviction that this is the result of a lack of awareness of the *full* implications of the two emphases. It is important that, whether in South Africa or elsewhere in black Africa, the situation to which theology addresses itself should be specified as fully as possible. It is a fact that the whole of black Africa, as a result of the coming of the Europeans, is riddled with cultural contradictions. On the one hand, Africanness does not show any signs of giving way before Europeanism; on the other, the presence of the latter, beneficial as it may be in certain of its aspects, gives rise to unresolved conflicts of identity. Similarly, oppression is not limited to South Africa. African countries often experience oppression at the hands of their African leaders. The people have sometimes been exploited and those in power enriched themselves, salting away in foreign banks much of their countries' meager financial resources. Military governments have not helped, for by and large these have become symbols of unbridled corruption. Most of black Africa, then, has to contend with these two problems as part of what we have described as life-circumstances. If theology is to be a force for the regeneration of society as a whole and if it is to speak meaningfully to the complex—in the religious sense and otherwise—societies which are developing in Africa, then it is essential that such theology be inclusive enough to address itself to the totality of a people's circumstances, rather than to some aspects of them only. In particular, the non-Christian world in Africa is one whose significance needs to be properly assessed by the Christian Church in Africa. To this point we shall return after we have completed our survey of the Christian presence in Africa.

*2. Independent Churches*

The historic Churches are only one element in the Christian presence in Africa. One of the most striking developments in recent decades is the proliferation of the independent Churches, a name given to those Churches which have developed outside the traditions of the historic Churches and have been largely founded by Africans. These Churches have been studied and written about a great deal, and from that research certain statements may be derived. In the first place, many Africans find themselves more at home in these Churches, not merely because they are founded by Africans but because their worship-life is found more appealing. In this connection it is interesting to observe that some members of the historic Churches are not beyond becoming members of the independent Churches while at the same time maintaining their original affiliation. The music and the free rein given to self-expression are among the characteristics attracting Africans to these Churches. Second, these Churches take the fears of their members seriously. Services may be held to cast out demons, to frustrate the machinations of witches and to bring physical and spiritual healing to members. What these two statements amount to is that there is a definite cultural orientation in these Churches, away from the Europeanism that still strongly characterizes the historic Churches. Third, there is in these Churches a more thoroughgoing integration of the various social classes that make up the membership. The excessive use of English in the historic Churches, founded from England and America, accentuates differences between the lettered and the unlettered. Whereas it is not unusual to see the latter remain silent during the singing of hymns in English in the historic Churches, in the independent Churches, by and large, indigenous languages are used, thus ensuring that *all* the members participate in worship services as fully as possible. Fourth, it has been established by a number of scholars that many of these Churches lean toward the Old Testament. The reasons for this are varied. In southern Africa, in particular, the exodus motif, indicative as it is of God's power to save the downtrodden and the oppressed, becomes the ground of a people's hope in a part of Africa where there is discrimination and oppression on the basis of color; it also is a fact that there exists a demonstrable affinity between the Old Testament and African life and thought regarding certain ideas, customs and various societal arrangements.[11]

That the independent Churches represent an important development in the history of Christianity in Africa is generally recognized, and one wishes that the historic Churches would feel challenged by their life-style and the great success they have achieved. This is not to suggest, however, that all that the independent Churches do and stand for represents the goal to which the Church in Africa should aspire. These Churches may have succeeded in creating awareness of certain aspects of Christian teaching, such as pneumatology and the Church as a closely-knit fellowship, among other insights which could with justification be said to be impressively exemplified in their life and worship. But in other respects they are seekers as much as the historic churches. Sometimes in their eagerness to model their life-style after the Old Testament, the independent Churches are not beyond misinterpreting the Scriptures, especially where the true reason for citing the Scriptures is to sanction a traditional custom which an independent Church is anxious to adopt or maintain. Furthermore, these Churches have yet to exploit fully the rich variety in African culture which might be used to good effect in worship services. In some of these Churches the music is hardly what might be described as authentically traditional; indeed, the cultural facets adopted may not always be of vital significance.

Thus, both the historic Churches (to a greater degree, perhaps) and the independent Churches (perhaps to a lesser degree) have yet to react meaningfully to the African life-circumstances in such a way as to develop a significant and authentic Christian faith that bears the unmistakable stamp of African thinking.

## V. FACTORS IN THE AFRICAN SITUATION

The Christian Churches, historic and independent, will have to come to terms with the African situation, which was partly characterized above by reference to the cultural, and socio-economic and political factors. As visible as Christianity is, even more visible is African traditional religion (African religion). The need to reckon with this has been clearly demonstrated by the increasing rate at which publications on the subject have been produced in the last two decades by African as well as European writers. Two facts are of interest here: the European assessment of African religion has changed dramatically from the early writings, which tended to put African religion at the other end of the scale from Christianity as a belief-system representative of the work of the devil, and the African scholars who have written on the subject are usually practicing Christians, mainly ordained members of the historic Churches, an indication of the change of the prevailing atmosphere as some Christians have tried to understand their faith in relation to African religion. As indicated earlier, there are African Christians who are firmly attached to the traditional forms of life and thought, even as they worship in church in accordance with the forms received from abroad. African religion is now seriously studied in university departments of religion and in seminaries; evidently it is considered indispensable for theological education in Africa.

In addition to Christianity and African religion, there is Islam which has been embraced by a considerable number of people in Africa (outside the Muslim countries in North Africa). The annual *Hajj* to Mecca sees many thousands of Africans expressing their devotion to Islamic beliefs. It is an indication of the extent of Islam's presence in Africa that, like African religion, this other religion is studied in many departments of religion and seminaries in Africa. Theological training in Africa has come a long way since the time when an English Anglican bishop in an African country threatened to withhold his Church's financial support for the department of religion in that country's university if it carried out its intention of adding a Muslim scholar to the staff and initiating courses in Islam.

Just as many African Christians demonstrate a willingness to follow "orthodoxy," the latter being defined as what has come from Europe and America, so African Muslims, perhaps to a more pronounced degree, tend to stick to Islamic "orthodoxy" as it has come down from the Arab world, to the extent that it is not unusual to encounter African Muslims dressed in Arabic garb and in other ways modeling their religious life after what obtains in the home of Islam. This is not to say that the practice of Islam in Africa has not been influenced in any way by African life and thought; there is evidence, for example, that the practice of Islam among the Yoruba in Nigeria was influenced by traditional Yoruba beliefs and practices.[11]

In addition to these widely-practiced religions, many Africans have shown a willingness to embrace such other religions as Buddhism; the patronizing of these Eastern religions, however, has not reached significant proportions.

In closing this section, it may be useful to recapitulate what should be seen as constituting the situation of which the Church in Africa must take account if it is to be established as a meaningful institution: a cultural reality which, however much it may have been hoped to give way before Christianity, has persisted and continues to shape African life; a socio-economic and political reality which has meant much oppression, mismanagement and not inconsiderable shortsightedness; and a religious pluralism which calls for a more imaginative assessment. In the face of these characteristics, what kind of Christianity would provide the best response? To a certain extent the answer has been indicated in the above discussion, but we shall now attempt an integrated statement.

## VI. CHRISTIANITY—AN AFRICAN DEVELOPMENT

### *1. Christianity in Africa should have such cultural characteristics as would make Africans see it as a faith that speaks to them in the particularity of their life-circumstances*

Many African Christian thinkers would readily endorse this. Those African Christians who have rejected this cultural emphasis have in some respects good reason to find this approach unrealistic. The black South African theologian, Manas Buthelezi,[12] rightly objects to that cultural emphasis which means nothing more than adopting the present Western-oriented theology as the basis for cultural modifications. Such a procedure, in fact, endorses the normative character of the imported theology, while the real concern should be a radical rethinking of what faith in Christ means in the

African context. To use a theological basis that has been shaped in one particular context is not the most helpful way of arriving at a meaningful theology in another. Of course, it would be foolish to write off the tradition of Christian thought, as it has accumulated over the centuries, as altogether unlikely to produce theological insights that might be of use in the development of thought in Africa. It is important, however, that the deposit of Christian thought should not become a barrier to encountering Christ in an authentic way.

To hope for the enrichment of Christianity by African culture is not being unrealistic, for indeed there is in the Church's Scriptures, specifically in the Hebrew Scriptures, an important illustration of how religion can be enriched by culture. One of the most interesting developments in the religion of ancient Israel was its enrichment by the adoption of various cultural expressions from non-Israelite sources and the adaptation of these in Hebrew religion. Thus, Egyptian ideas influenced the development of Wisdom literature in Israel. It was Canaanite culture which exercised the greatest influence. No more significant illustration can be found than the way in which the very concept of Yahweh was enriched through contact with the Canaanites: many of the more memorable images in the prophets (e.g., Israel as a bride or as a vineyard) are owed to contact with the Canaanites; and Hosea's prophecies show the broadening of the national faith through the presentation of Yahweh as having taken over the functions of Baal.

What all this means is that religion is not necessarily endangered when a cultural outlook is brought to bear upon it. There has been some uneasiness in Western circles about the call by African Christians, Protestant and Catholic alike, for the freedom to shape Christianity in the context of African life and thought. It was recently said in a preview (broadcast by the British Broadcasting Corporation) to Pope John Paul II's visit to Africa in May 1980 that this move by African Christians is giving the Vatican cause for concern. For many African Christians, however, the enrichment of the meaning of faith in Christ is based on the hope that African culture may play an important role. The Lordship of Christ could be enhanced thereby, much as the concept of Yahweh was enriched through Canaanite influence.

### 2. *It is essential that it should be carefully determined what constitutes African culture*

The present experiments in the Church with African music and other cultural elements suggest a rather narrow definition of what African culture consists in. Culture embraces a whole range of facets of a people's life and thought, so that political organization, religion, art, economics, etc., fall within the cultural heritage of a people; this is certainly true of African culture. Thus, African culture has a concern for a just society; a society in equilibrium is one in which there are such concerns as ensure that there is no oppression of the community by its rulers, and that there are no classes based upon economic factors, with some being disadvantaged and at the mercy of an affluent group. Julius Nyerere, the president of Tanzania, perhaps more than any African thinker, has in the last decade or so given a clear indication of this in his analysis of African socialism which, having a definite religious base, involves the establishment and perpetuation of a society in which the individual is as important as the community as a whole.[13] Thus, those desirous of giving a cultural orientation to faith in Christ have a much wider field of operation than the adoption of African music suggests; the totality of life is the arena in which Christ is to be encountered.

### 3. *There should be an endeavor by African Christians to gain a fresh understanding of the Scriptures*

The positive attitude to other peoples and their traditions found in the Hebrew Scriptures, to which much attention has been given above, is extremely significant, if for no other reason than that there is also, as already pointed out, a negative attitude. The reference to the contrasting attitudes is a reminder that in seeking to express faith in Christ in a more meaningful way it is essential that African Christians should engage upon a thorough study of the Scriptures in order to see more clearly the extent to which they provide a response to African longings in the Church. It is essential that the revelation of God to Israel should assume a clear meaning for the African Christian. In other words, for the Scriptures to be really meaningful, God must be heard speaking to the African today. Not to hear God afresh would mean for the Church in Africa to live on a borrowed faith; for it is of the essence of a living faith that it should issue out of a living encounter. Hence the importance of approaching the Scriptures with questions relevant to the expositor's circumstances.

### 4. *There should be a fuller appreciation of the implications of religious pluralism*

Western theological literature is replete with assessments of other peoples' religions. These assessments over the centuries have ranged from total rejection of other religions as the work of the devil to a more sympathetic appreciation of these as avenues of the revelation of God. In other words, instead of seeing God at work only in Christianity, many Western theologians are prepared to allow that there is one God of the whole earth whom the world's peoples, in their own distinctive ways, are seeking to worship. The truth of this is adumbrated in the Hebrew Scriptures, as we saw earlier, in those prophetic oracles which picture a time to come when all peoples would come to Yahweh, and especially in the prophet Malachi where he suggests that pagans are acceptable before Yahweh when they *faithfully* keep to their own religious traditions. African Christians have an excellent opportunity to gain a broader understanding of God's dealings with man, living as they do with kinsmen and others in the wider community who belong to other faiths, including African religion which is demonstrably ancient.[14] Gone are the days, in the era of Western missionary activity, when African Christians were sometimes physically separated from their non-Christian fellow countrymen into "mission compounds"; today, African Christians live in active and constant interaction with non-Christians and have gained an appreciation of their life and thought. Christianity in Africa will continue to be challenged by the other religions, and in this way a greater understanding may emerge of the meaning of God's coming to man.

One cannot help adding that there is a noticeable gap between what many in the Churches who live in close proximity with non-Christians feel about the latter, and what the Church's received theology says on the subject. For one of the frustrating facts about the Church in Africa is that its leadership tends to be preoccupied with preserving the Church's theological status quo. Indeed, rarely have the discussions taking place among theologians in Africa engendered serious deliberation in the highest councils of the Churches, a clear indication of the Churches' ambiguous character.

### *5. Theological education in Africa should begin to reflect the questioning of the last few decades*

Theological education takes place increasingly in Bible colleges, seminaries and university departments of religion in Africa itself. The seminaries have been making valiant efforts in recent years to broaden their curricula; in particular, many of them have introduced the study of African religion and Islam. The very fact that these subjects are taught is significant. Though their introduction may have been facilitated by publications on these subjects that were largely written by Christians, the main motivation was the realization of the need for theological institutions to better understand African societies. There is a great deal more to be done by these institutions in order to integrate theological students into their society and to make them more effective servants to their fellow men. A thorough re-examination of curricula must be undertaken, with a view to their being made to reflect the discussions on relevant theology, as they have been taking place in Africa. It should be unacceptable that a seminary teach the history of Christian thought without making room for the concerns regarding relevant African Christian theology.

With the blossoming of theological activism in Europe and America in our time, the Christian Church has been taking another look at traditional ecclesiastical postures regarding socio-economic and political realities. It seems to us that greater emphasis needs to be placed on so-called practical theology to exemplify the involvement of the Christian faith with the totality of the human experience. For African Christians this should be an inevitable development, not only because it would be in accordance with scriptural teaching which does not separate life from thought, but also because it would be in tune with the African experience which, as already observed, sees religion and life as one reality.

## VII. CONCLUSION

The situation of the Church in Africa today is analogous to the situation of African countries which have won their independence from their erstwhile colonial rulers. Independent African countries are saddled with problems attendant upon their inability to recognize the need for a radical rethinking of their goals and the means to achieve them. In April 1980, African heads of state, meeting in the Nigerian capital of Lagos, agreed to work toward the creation of an African common market. Laudable as this is, its realization may be thwarted by the apparent lack of a meaningful philosophy of development; there is in Africa a hankering after projects reminiscent of its ties with the former colonial rulers. Thus, many an African city glitters with symbols of "development"—oil refineries, imposing buildings and monuments, not to mention sizable armies which are a drain upon the resources of African countries. These symbols notwithstanding, real development has so far proved chimerical because the symbols have not been created in response to first-hand questions about what would best ensure the continued integrity of Africa's peoples.

Similarly, Christianity having been brought to Africa in the era of missions by Western missionaries, its African ecclesiastical leadership must yet rid itself of the notion that practice of the faith must be identical with that in Europe and America. Up to now, the trappings associated with Christianity in the West have by and large been maintained and with that goes the retention of theological ideas, some of which may for good reason have gone out of fashion in the West.

The Church in Africa will have to hear Christ and respond to him in authentic ways.

## NOTES

1. Kwesi Dickson, *Aspects of Religion and Life in Africa* (Accra: Ghana Academy of Arts and Sciences, 1977), p. 191.

2. See below.

3. Cf. Kwesi Dickson, "Continuity and Discontinuity between the Old Testament and African Life and Thought," in K. Appiah-Kubi and S. Torres, eds., *African Theology en Route* (Maryknoll: Orbis Books, 1979), pp. 95f.

4. Bernard W. Anderson, "The New Crisis in Biblical Theology," in Charles Courtney, Olin M. Ivey, Gordon E. Michalson, eds., *Hermeneutics and the Worldliness of Faith* 45 (1974/1975) pp. 159ff.

5. B. J. Kidd, ed., *Documents Illustrative of the History of the Church* (London: SPCK, 1941), III, 42f.

6. Ernst Troeltsch, *Christian Thought: Its History and Application* (London, 1923), pp. 21–35.

7. Cf. John Bright, *The Authority of the Old Testament* (London: SCM, 1967), pp. 60f.

8. E.g., Bengt Sundkler, *Bantu Prophets in South Africa* (Oxford: Oxford University Press, 1964), reprinted; G. C. Oosthuizen, *Post-Christianity in Africa* (London: C. Hurst, 1968), p. 163.

9. Kwesi Dickson, "The Minister—Then and Now," in J. S. Pobee, ed., *Religion in a Pluralistic Society* (Leiden: E. J. Brill, 1976), n. 34.

10. Cf. note 8 above.

11. Patrick J. Ryan, *Imale: Yoruba Participation in the Muslim Tradition* (Missoula: Scholars Press, 1978), Harvard Dissertations on Religion, 11.

12. Cf. Manas Buthelezi, "Towards Indigenous Theology in South Africa," in S. Torres and V. Fabella, eds., *The Emergent Gospel* (Maryknoll: Orbis Books, 1978), pp. 7ff.

13. J. Nyerere, *Ujamaa—Essays on Socialism* (Dar es Salaam: O.U.P., 1974), reprinted, p. 5.

14. M. Poznansky, "Archaeology, Ritual and Religion," in T. O. Ranger and I. N. Kimambo, eds., *The Historical Study of African Religion* (London: Heinemann, 1972).

# Notes on the Contributors

RABBI MARTIN A. COHEN is Professor of Jewish History at Hebrew Union College—Jewish Institute of Religion, New York. He has written extensively on biblical, rabbinic and early modern history. Dr. Cohen serves as chairman of the national committee on Jewish-Catholic relations of the Anti-Defamation League of B'nai B'rith.

RICHARD DE RIDDER is Professor in the Missiology Department and Chairman of the Church and Ministry Division, at Calvin Theological Seminary, Grand Rapids, Michigan. He served as collegiate minister of the Dutch Reformed Church of Sri Lanka and was Moderator of the Presbytery of Ceylon. His work included mission to the Buddhist, Hindu and some Muslim communities. De Ridder also held pastorates in Massachusetts and Silver Spring, Md., where he had close contact with Jewish communities.

KWESI ABOTSIA DICKSON is an ordained Methodist minister and Director of the Institute of African Studies at the University of Ghana. He has taught at Union Theological Seminary, New York as Henry W. Luce Visiting Professor of World Christianity. His publications include a series on the Old Testament for pre-university use, and three edited works on African religion and Christian theology in Africa.

DR. EUGENE J. FISHER is director of the Secretariat for Catholic-Jewish Relations of the National Conference of Catholic Bishops. He is author of *Faith Without Prejudice* (Paulist, 1977) and co-editor, with Rabbi Daniel F. Polish of the volume, *Formation of Social Policy in the Catholic and Jewish Traditions* (University of Notre Dame Press, 1980), as well as the author of over fifty articles for religious and educational journals. Recently, Dr. Fisher was named Consultor to the Vatican Commission for Religious Relations with the Jews. He chairs both the Israel Study Group and the Jewish/Christian/Muslim Trialogue Group sponsored by the Kennedy Institute of Ethics of Georgetown University, and is past president of the Chesapeake Bay region of the Society of Biblical Literature.

REV. MICHAEL B. McGARRY, C.S.P., director of Boston's Paulist Center, received his theological degrees from the University of St. Michael's College, University of Toronto. He is currently chairperson of the Catholic-Jewish Committee of the Archdiocese of Boston. He is the author of *Christology After Auschwitz* (Paulist Press, 1977).

RABBI DANIEL F. POLISH is rabbi of Temple Israel of Hollywood. He serves on the Executive Committee of Shalem, an institute for spiritual development, and on the board of the National Capitol Chapter of the American Jewish Congress. Dr. Polish has taught at Harvard and Tufts Universities and lectured at Boston University and Brandeis College. In addition to articles in numerous journals of Jewish and general interest, Rabbi Polish's book, *The Religious Bases for Social Policy,* was published recently by the Notre Dame Press.

C. S. SONG is the author (with Gayraud Wilmore) of *Asians and Blacks, Christian Mission in Reconstruction,* and *Third Eye Theology.* He was Professor of Systematic Theology at the Theological College in Taiwan and Visiting Professor of Theology at the Princeton Theological Seminary. At present, he is Associate Director of the Faith and Order Sub-Unit, at the World Council of Churches in Geneva.

DAVID M. STOWE is executive vice-president of the United Church Board for World Ministries, the overseas agency of the United Church of Christ. He served as missionary and university lecturer in China during the forties. Later, he was chaplain and chairman of the Department of Religion at Carleton College, Northfield, Minnesota. He has also taught in Beirut, Lebanon, and visited missions in Asia, Africa and the Middle East. He is the author of numerous magazine articles and of books, among them *When Faith Meets Faith,* on Christianity's relationship to other major faiths.

# Index of Authors and Subjects

*other volumes in this series*

*Stepping Stones to Further Jewish-Christian Relations: An Unabridged Collection of Christian Documents,* compiled by Helga Croner (A Stimulus Book, 1977).

Helga Croner and Leon Klenicki, editors, *Issues in the Jewish-Christian Dialogue: Jewish Perspectives on Covenant, Mission and Witness* (A Stimulus Book, 1979).

Clemens Thoma, *A Christian Theology of Judaism* (A Stimulus Book, 1980).

Helga Croner, Leon Klenicki and Lawrence Boadt, C.S.P., editors, *Biblical Studies: Meeting Ground of Jews and Christians* (A Stimulus Book, 1980).

Pawlikowski, John T. O.S.M., *Christ in the Light of the Christian-Jewish Dialogue* (A Stimulus Book, 1982).

STIMULUS BOOKS are developed by Stimulus Foundation, a not-for-profit organization, and are published by Paulist Press. The Foundation wishes to further the publication of scholarly books on Jewish and Christian topics that are of importance to Judaism and Christianity.

Stimulus Foundation was established by an erstwhile refugee from Nazi Germany who intends to contribute with these publications to the improvement of communication between Jews and Christians.

Books for publication in this Series will be selected by a committee of the Foundation, and offers of manuscripts and works in progress should be addressed to:

Stimulus Foundation
785 West End Ave.
New York, N.Y. 10025